THE DEBATE ON
THE ENGLISH REFORMATION

THE DEBATE ON
THE ENGLISH
REFORMATION

Rosemary O'Day

Methuen
London and New York

First published in 1986 by
Methuen & Co. Ltd
11 New Fetter Lane,
London EC4P 4EE

Published in the USA by
Methuen & Co.
in association with Methuen, Inc.
29 West 35th Street,
New York NY 10001

Typeset by
Scarborough Typesetting Services
and printed in Great Britain
at the University Press, Cambridge

British Library Cataloguing in
Publication Data

O'Day, Rosemary
The debate on the English Reformation.
1. Reformation – England – Historiography
I. Title
274.2' 06   BR377

ISBN 0–416–72670–4
ISBN 0–416–72680–1 Pbk

Library of Congress Cataloging in
Publication Data

O'Day, Rosemary.
The debate on the English Reformation.
Bibliography: p.
Includes index.
1. Reformation – England – Historiography.
2. England – Church history – 16th century
– Historiography.
I. Title.
BR377.033   1986   274.2' 06' 072
85–18861

ISBN 0–416–726–704
ISBN 0–416–726–801 (pbk.)

To David, with love

Contents

Preface

I have been thinking about writing this book for some time and my publishers have been extremely patient waiting for it. It has been written and re-written several times because I wanted to produce a book which would prove useful to undergraduates and their teachers as a companion to the historiography of the English Reformation. I owe especial thanks to Mr John Naylor, Ms Anna Feddon and Ms Merrilyn Julian of Methuen for their helpfulness and understanding. Mrs Sabine Phillips has patiently undertaken the typing of the manuscript and earned my heartfelt gratitude.

I wish to thank the Arts Faculty of the Open University for financial help which enabled me to read widely in pamphlet and secondary literature. I cannot thank enough my former supervisor, Patrick Collinson, for his kindness over the years and for arousing my interest in this present topic through his stimulating conversation. I wish to express my gratitude to Geoffrey Dickens, who has read the book in typescript and lent me the benefit of his wisdom in discussion. My thanks go also to Claire Cross, my first teacher in this area, who has offered considerable support.

Above all, I thank my family. My late father, whose library of Reformation works first acquainted me with the English Reformation. My mother and brother for their constant support.

David Englander for his love, encouragement, advice and critical appreciation. My son Andrew for practical help and my son Daniel for sleeping through the night for the first year of his life on earth!

Rosemary O'Day
The Open University
January 1985

Introduction

Process or event? If we have to define historical phenomena in such terms, then the English Reformation is more properly described as a process than as an event. So much so that it is often difficult to decide precisely who was and who was not a *contemporary* of the English Reformation. John Foxe? Of course. Thomas Cranmer? Yes. But what of John Whitgift, Richard Bancroft, William Laud, even John Strype? Just where do we draw the line? As will become apparent in the following pages, the idea of a continuing reformation – the completion of a half-finished job – remained with the English well into the nineteenth century. The issues raised between 1525 and 1662 continued to matter. Englishmen – Catholic, 'Anglican' and Nonconformist – felt deeply. This state of affairs was, in part, the result of the Elizabethan Settlement, which left the church 'but halfly-reformed' and which allowed so many interpretations of her nature and substance. For centuries, English people could argue, convincingly on all sides, that the Church of England was Catholic, Protestant or, indeed, neither. Historians are still rehearsing the pros and cons of the case – summoning as their witnesses the liturgies of Cranmer, the actions of monarchs, the declarations of reformers, the institutional apparatus of the church. Not only was there doubt about the precise nature of the church of England after its 'reformation', there was in some quarters a refusal to accept that the process was over and an insistence that more change was called for. Men who lived fifty or a hundred years after the Henrician break with the papacy regarded themselves as agents of reformation.

There is, of course, a strong case for arguing that the reformation of the English church was complete by 1662. The Restoration Settlement gave the Church of England as much definition as she would ever receive and, after it, nonconformity was given official recognition. Subsequently writers who commented upon the Reformation regarded it as a past happening – sometimes as a process which they wished to see continued or revived, but none the less as something which had already occurred. This was as true of Strype and Burnet as it was of Froude and Macaulay.

But an equally strong case can be made for the position that the English Reformation was a mid-sixteenth-century phenomenon. The Elizabethan Settlement confirmed the changes which had been made by Henry VIII and Edward VI. After this, churchmen and politicians debated the precise nature of these changes. They interpreted the Reformation. And the Reformation, which had at this juncture been accepted by only a small proportion of the population, now acted like yeast upon dough. The process of Protestantization was under way.

In the book which follows, I have elected to adopt the second position – that the Reformation was a mid-sixteenth-century occurrence, spanning the years from *c.* 1525 to *c.* 1570. The book examines in detail the contemporary and later debates about the nature of this sixteenth-century reformation. Who were its agents? What were their motives? What was the character of the reform? Was it 'official' or 'popular'? How did contemporaries see it? How have historians, men of affairs and others interpreted it since?

The book is organized to maximize its usefulness to students – particularly those studying historiography and/or the Reformation itself in universities, polytechnics and colleges. It is *not* an account of the Reformation: it is intended to act as the student's *companion* to other scholarly works on the Reformation. By using this volume, the reader should understand better the issues and debates which underlie histories of the Reformation period. These debates and issues are often implicit – here they are made explicit. The book places the debates in their context and offers a critique. By using the footnotes intelligently, the student should be able to follow up the debates and the criticism offered. On another level, the book is a study of Reformation historiography. Here are to be found treatments of the use of history in the Reformation itself; of the debate about the Reformation in the nineteenth century between Catholics and Protestants, and between Anglicans and Anglicans; of the historical position and methodologies employed by twentieth-century giants such as G. R. Elton, Patrick Collinson, A. G. Dickens and J. J. Scarisbrick. At a time when the study of history as a discipline is increasingly important for both sixth-formers and undergraduates, it is appropriate that there should be an easily accessible account of the contribution of Reformation historians to the discipline of history. It is necessary to understand how and why each generation has redefined and restructured the Reformation past.

The work is arranged in three parts. Chapter 1 is concerned with the historiography of the Reformation as seen through the eyes of men who were contemporaries of, and often actors in, the English Reformation – Tyndale, Frith, Barnes, Foxe and Bale. Chapters 2 to 4 examine the work of later writers who cared about the issues raised by the Reformation and saw them as deeply relevant to their own times. I have tried to explain *why* the debate mattered to them and not simply *what* the debate was. Their contribution to the development of history as a discipline as well as to Reformation historiography is underlined. Finally, Chapters 5 to 7 discuss the history of the sixteenth-century Reformation as written by professional historians of the later nineteenth and twentieth centuries who, whatever their personal religious or political commitment, have attempted to treat it objectively. They brought to bear upon the evidence the skills of the historian in order to describe, analyse and explain the Reformation in its context. These historians as individuals have none the less widely differing conceptions of the nature of the English Reformation; of the importance of individuals or movements in its initiation and spread; of the appropriateness of certain methodologies to its study. Above all, they have highly individualistic styles of approach. Here, in setting out the modern debates concerning the role of Henry VIII, or his ministers, the Reformation and the people of England, and the changes which occurred in the church as a result of the Reformation, I have sought to show how their work illustrates the preoccupations, trends and methodologies of twentieth-century history as a discipline and some of the criticisms which may be levelled against them.

Finally, I reiterate my wish that, through reading this book and keeping it at his or her side when reading other works listed in its footnotes, the student will find the pathway through English Reformation history easier to tread and be considerably enriched by the journey.

Chapter 1

Contemporary historiography of the English Reformation, 1525–70

On the face of it, it might seem that the Reformation of its nature rejected history. And so in a sense it did, or at least the force of recent precedent. After all, the new religion involved a break with that recent past – a denial of tradition as an authority for religious dogma, practice and doctrine; a denial of papal authority. But it is no less true that the English Reformation used history – an interpetation of the past – to justify its existence, its goals and its actions. It created its own historiography.[1]

In examining the way in which history was used by the re-formers it is important to distinguish between the attitudes of the 'religious' reformers (those who saw the Reformation as the fulfilment of the church's need for renewal) and the 'official' reformers (those who saw the Reformation as serving the needs of the monarchy or, at least, the English body politic). This distinc-tion is far from easy to make: the body politic was part of Chris-tendom and, no matter what the perspective of the reformer, a major issue was the relationship between the two. Reformers as a group looked to the past to justify the act of re-formation. But

---

[1] The best modern account of this process is to be found in Nicholson, G. D. (1977), 'The Nature and Functions of Historical Argument in the Henrician Reformation', upon which I have relied considerably.

their interpretation of that past varied sufficiently for us to admit that there was no *single* Reformation use of history. Reformers, after all, used the past to score differing debating points. The manner in which their varied interpretations informed their action and vice versa is of supreme interest to the historian. In large part the task before the modern commentator is that of discovering an individual's position with respect to the relationship between church and state.

The reformers had been reared in a tradition of historical literature which influenced them considerably. Their understanding of the process of history governed their interpretation of what had happened in Reformation England and what was about to happen. With what sort of history were educated Tudor men and women acquainted? The influence of the Italian humanist historians – Valla and Biondo – was certainly felt. There was some awareness of historical change, of the changing historical context of events. However, the emphasis upon biography found in Bruni and Polydore Vergil had a far more telling impact. English thinkers, whatever their position on relations between church and state, saw historical developments as the result of dynastic and personal activity. The prince was his people. Edward Hall's *The Union of the Two Noble and Illustre Famelies of Lancastre and York* (1548) is a good example of native writing which assumed that dynamic monarchs caused change. Shakespeare's history plays and his tragedies also provide good examples of this attitude. The inclination of contemporaries to dramatize their history – to put it on the stage – accentuated this tendency to display characters as more acting than acted upon. Contemporary literature also illustrates the nationalistic framework of English historical writing of the late fifteenth and sixteenth centuries.

Reformation writers were concerned to use history in support of their own cause. They, too, adopted a nationalistic and, often, a biographical approach. The obsession of lay historians with fifteenth-century history was transferred to a religious context. Monarchs, religious teachers and individuals of learning and pious life were portrayed as the moving forces of the English Reformation. The social, economic and geographic underpinnings went unrecognized.

Above all, the reformers urged that theirs was the historically accurate Christianity. William Tyndale (*c.* 1494–1536), pupil of John Colet, stood in the tradition of humanist textual criticism exemplified by Lorenzo Valla, Erasmus and Luther. His *New Testament* aimed to display a pure original text without accretions. In 1523 he spoke of his motivation:

> I perceived . . . how that it was impossible to establish the lay-people in any truth except the scripture were plainly laid before their eyes in their mother tongue, that they might see the process, order, and meaning of the text. For else, whatsoever truth is taught them, these enemies of all truth quench it again, partly with the smoke of their bottomless pit, that is, with apparent reasons of sophistry and traditions of their own making, founded without ground of scripture; and partly in juggling with the text, expounding it in such sense as is impossible to gather of the text, if thou see the process, order and meaning thereof. . . . This thing only moved me to translate the new testament.   (Walter 1848, xx)

Other Protestants shared his conviction that the Scriptures contained the key to the primitive church. Tyndale translated the Scriptures; some selected other means to prove the historical pedigree of reformed Christianity. The anonymous author of the preface to the Gospels in Anglo-Saxon urged: 'The religion presently taught and professed in the Church at thys present, is no new reformation of thinges laterly begonne, which were not before but rather a reduction of the Church to the pristine state of olde conformitie' (*The Gospels of the Fower Evangelistes*, 1571, sig. 92 r). Humanist scholarship, with its rigorous emphasis upon precise translation, became the handmaiden of early English Protestant argument.

In this chapter we shall examine the most important Protestant interpretations of the Reformation and its history penned in the sixteenth century, culminating with the works of John Foxe. Such an exercise is important not simply because the interpretations offered are intrinsically interesting, nor even because we should be aware of contemporaries' views of the Reformation in their midst, but also because the Protestant view of Reformation history which was produced provided, in large measure, the parameters of the debate about the English Reformation from that day to this.

Between 1525 and 1535 a number of English reformers were living in exile in Europe, unwelcome in Henrician England. Some of their works espoused a rather simple view of history. The writers – Simon Fish, Jerome Barlow and William Roye – took over, lock, stock and barrel, the doctrine of the English Lollards and, with it, their view of the iniquities of the fifteenth-century church. This was more than mere late Lollard propaganda. It was an attempt, and a successful one, to give the English Reformation a history – and a national one at that. Their interpretation of the past was Wyclifite: the wealth and power of the church on earth was but recently acquired and a fundamental denial of the essence of the primitive church, which had set no store on pomp and had maintained simple and pure doctrines based upon scripture alone. Wyclif had called for a return to the ways of the young, pristine and primitive church. Later Lollard congregations had continued this plea. The early Protestants made this argument part of the English Reformation tradition. This history was later presented to the nation by John Foxe in a much more detailed form, but it was there, in essence, in the writings of Frith, Roye, Barlow and, above all, Tyndale.

The Antwerp writers believed that there had once existed a golden age which had been subverted by the clergy. They added little, if anything, to the complaints of the Lollards against the clerical estate. Their view of the 'golden age' of England was no more subtle than their explanation of how it had been brought down:

> First when Englonde was in his floures
> ordered by the temporal governoures
> knowenge no spiritual iurisdiction
> Then was ther in eche state and degree
> Haboundance and plentuous prosperite
> Peaceable welthe without affliction.
> Noblenes of blood was had in price
> Vertuousnes avaunced, hated was vyce,
> Princes obeyed with due reverence.
>
> (Arber 1868, VIII, 138)

All this had been destroyed when the Crown of England fell under clerical influence. William Tyndale, in his *Obedience of a Christian Man* (1528), outlines the simple but long-drawn-out contest between the clergy and the Crown. King John, for example, is shown in dispute with the papal legate; Henry V is portrayed not as a national hero but as a monarch under the thumb of the clergy, who spills English blood in France to preserve clerical liberties. The church which held England's kings in its thrall was, moreover, heretical; it kept the Scriptures from the people in an effort to exalt itself.

So these early Antwerp Protestants cast the English monarch as the dupe of the clergy and, potentially, as the saviour of the church. In *A Supplicacyon for the Beggars* (1529) Simon Fish described the excesses of the clergy and showed them to be seditious. He prescribed a political remedy – a medicine to be administered by the Crown. In his chapter on Antichrist, William Tyndale made a similar appeal to Christian kings to save the church from the clergy. But by this time Tyndale was aware that kings might not view the Reformation in the same light – Henry VIII had refused to provide the people with the vernacular Scriptures. Tyndale sighed: reform would be possible 'if they [kings] were Christians, which is seldom seen, and is a hard thing verily, though not impossible' (Walter 1848, 239–40).

William Tyndale was, in fact, coming to appreciate that the Lollard interpretation of recent religious catastrophe as a result of clerical conflict with and triumph over English monarchs was a gross and unfortunate oversimplification. Here he owed much of his sophistication and awareness to his readings of Luther and Erasmus. Tyndale's *The Practyse of Prelates* of 1530 (Walter 1848) drew upon Erasmus's *Julius Exclusus* for its view of the Pope deliberately playing off princes one against the other. Kings were often not in opposition to the clergy – more often than not they were the willing dupes of the popes and bishops. When Tyndale edited the *Examinacion* of the Lollard John Oldcastle, he cast Henry IV as the villain of the trial, acting with Antichrist (the clergy) against Christ's true disciples (the Lollard knights). The translator's interpretation of what happened as a result of this oppression was more simplistic. The activities of Antichrist were repaid by the active vengeance of God – civil wars, social disorder, plague. Jonah's dire warnings applied to England in 1531 as well as to Israel (Walter 1848, 458–9).

William Tyndale set the whole of the Henrician 'official' reformation against this scenario of a king duped by and acting with the clergy to oppress the followers of Christ. The reformers were sceptical of Henry's intent when he did act to 'reform' the church. If he oppressed the adherents of the new religion, the sword of God would, in consequence, be turned against him and his government. The patterns of history repeated themselves. Henry – the oppressor – could not escape the wrath of God. For Tyndale, the study of history had demonstrated that kings could not reform the church. Instead, the church's hopes for renewal lay with individual Christians and their determination to divert her paths back to those of righteousness. In Tyndale we have an early example of the reluctance of Protestant historians to accept the 'official' reformation instigated by Henry VIII and his successors as a religious reformation at all. For Tyndale, the blood of the martyrs was indeed the seed of the church. Without it, no Reformation flowers would bloom.

For Tyndale, in exile, to declare the true reformation to be one from below was simple, to deny the validity of Henry's official reformation bold. But for those reformers who remained in England, and especially for those in Henry's service, the expression of such sentiments would have been nothing short of foolhardy. The issue of authority in the religious reformation presented a thorny problem for reformers in England from the Reformation Parliament onwards. The struggle to reconcile the duty of obedience to the monarch and obedience to God was the central preoccupation of many.

When thrust out from the state, religious writers were released – albeit temporarily – from the predicament. In a position of opposition to the state, William Tyndale was able to shake off the shackles of royal policy and interpret the origins and development of the English Reformation as he saw them – although at his peril, as it transpired. For Robert Barnes, taken into the king's service in 1531, the predicament was a pressing one. How did he solve it? The essence of his argument was the traditional view that the temporal and spiritual powers had entirely separate jurisdiction. In the past, the clergy had constantly overstepped their rightful jurisdiction. His *Supplication unto the Most Gracyous Prynce Henry VIII* in 1534 protested that the clergy, by violating this distinction and meddling in temporal matters, had always constituted a subversive element. Barnes then demonstrated in *Vitae Romanorum Pontificum* (1536) that the very decline of the Church of Rome was due in large part to the papacy's usurpation of temporal powers. But did all this mean that a monarch could or should rule the church? Not at all. The king's jurisdiction was also strictly limited. He might defend the faith – by banishing the clerical estate to its own sphere. But the form of religion must be settled by the clergy. The king might protect the church but he should not rule it. Barnes's conception of the role of the monarchy in church government was not, therefore, identical to that which Henry VIII held. The Protestant reformers were unprepared to replace one non-scriptural source of authority – the papacy – with another – the monarchy. As Tyndale put it trenchantly:

As God maketh the King head over his realm, even so giveth he him commandment to execute the laws upon all men indifferently. For the law is God's, and not the King's. The King is but a servant, to execute the law of God, and not to rule after his own imagination.   (Walter 1848, 334)

The sole authority for the doctrine and worship of the church must be Scripture (Cross 1977).

Barnes, like Tyndale, was prepared to concede that a godly prince might open the way for the reintroduction of the true religion to England. Further than this he could not go. For Henry and Thomas Cromwell, this in itself was an important concession at the time when Henry was making his first stand against the might of Rome and seeking shelter in any harbour. But Henry himself, doctrinally a Catholic and sharing little with the early Protestants other than a dislike of the power of Rome, was unlikely to remain content for long with such limited approbation. No doubt he hoped that English reformers would be won round, like Melancthon in Saxony, to acceptance of the visible church, as regulated by the temporal ruler, as the guardian of Christian truth. This hope was not fulfilled in his lifetime.

As it happened, it was chiefly Catholics like himself who provided Henry with the case that he required to bolster the royal supremacy. For Henry had no wish to replace the authority of a foreign pope with that of native Protestant churchmen. Who was it who rid him of these turbulent priests? Thomas Cromwell, Bishop Stephen Gardiner of Winchester and Edward Foxe, later Bishop of Hereford. All these men were involved in a campaign to use historical precedent to support Henry's claim to supremacy in the church. Henry and his advisers gradually became aware that the question of the divorce could not, as matters stood, be settled without papal approval. When this was not forthcoming, it became necessary to deny papal jurisdiction. The people of England, and specifically Parliament, were very ready to attack clerical privileges, but the papacy itself, which in fact impinged little upon the daily lives of Englishmen, was potentially a different matter. Such an attack involved an onslaught not upon abuses but upon accepted authority. Henry, with his lay and clerical advisers, became involved in a propaganda campaign on several fronts to make such an attack seem both acceptable and desirable to England's ruling élite. On the one hand this magnified the extent to which Rome had been parasitic upon English wealth, to arouse nationalistic feelings against the continuance of papal rule in England. On the other, it constructed cases based upon historical precedent in favour of Henry's claim. The need was to convince the political nation that the papacy must be ousted from England and to provide the ammunition for an attack. This was, quite simply, that the Pope of Rome had had no legal right to jurisdiction in England in the first place. Henry could and did use the arguments put forward by clerics of many religious opinions to support his case, but his concern was to convince his lay subjects, particularly in Parliament, and not the clerical reformers of the validity of his cause. Whether the clerical reformers agreed with him or not, Henry was casting himself as the defender of the true and ancient English church against the rule of the Great Pretender, Rome. Henry or his chief minister, Thomas Cromwell, constructed a historical backcloth for his play of the English Reformation.

> Where by divers sundry old authentic histories and chronicles it is manifestly declared and expressed that this realm of England is an empire, and so hath been accepted in the world, governed by one supreme head and king having the dignity and royal estate of the imperial crown of the same.
>
> (Elton 1960, 344–9, citing The Act of Appeals,
> 24 Henry VIII, *ch.* 12, 1533)

This alternative historiography of the Reformation was as potent for future generations in its way as was that of the 'religious' reformers. At the time, events suggested that it would win the day. Henry successfully imposed his interpretation of relations between church and state upon both church and Parliament. First of all Henry forced the reluctant clergy to admit that their allegiance to the Crown superseded their loyalty to the papacy. The 1529 Reformation Parliament saw the clergy come under attack from the laity. The Parliament sought to limit the powers of the ecclesiastical courts and to correct the abuses consequent upon pluralism and non-residence. In 1531 Henry himself accused the clergy of infringing the statutes of provisors, provisions and praemunire by seeking to set up an independent jurisdiction within England. In 1531 the clergy bought the king's pardon and confessed him to be supreme head of the church but only 'as far as the law of Christ allows'. Convocation still maintained that it could legislate for the church without royal assent when it met in 1532 and it was only after a battle, in which Archbishop Warham had the temerity to remind Henry of the struggle between Henry II and Thomas à Becket, that Henry secured the submission of the clergy to his sole authority. In 1534 an Act of Parliament recorded this submission of the clergy. The Act of Supremacy, passed in the second session of 1534, required that clergy and laity alike acknowledge the monarch to be 'the only supreme head in earth of the Church of England'. The Acts of the Reformation Parliament, the records of Convocation, the proclamations of the realm encapsulated the nature and history of the English Reformation as Henry wished it to be understood. In this scenario the king was not a revolutionary or an innovator. He was acting to oust a usurper from the realm – a usurper of his people's purses as well as of their affections. He acted with due historical precedent. He acted with the agreement of his people: even his clergy submitted to his will. In this account there is no mention of doctrine. In it there is no reference to the popular movements of Lollardy and early Lutheranism to which the Antwerp exiles had appealed.

The king's supporters never did things by halves. Henry's advisers inaugurated a search for texts which would uphold his high view of royal authority as derived from God. Edward Foxe and Stephen Gardiner appear to have directed a group of researchers during 1530. The product of their labours was the *Collectanea Satis Copiosa*, an index with over two hundred citations from the Scriptures, the early Fathers and medieval works addressing the questions of royal and ecclesiastical jurisdiction and power. In it appeared Old Testament precedents for priestly monarchy, instances from the early councils showing the trial of cases in the provinces where they originated, the Donation of Constantine and so on. The work supported the idea of a royal supremacy in spirituals (and this by the autumn of 1530) but also propounded the view that each province of the church had its own jurisdictional independence. There is evidence that Henry VIII carefully studied and annotated the *Collectanea* but, according to Geoffrey Elton, it was Foxe and Thomas Cromwell who sponsored the work, brought it to Henry's attention and showed him how it could be used to support a new policy, as conceived by Cromwell. Certainly, Foxe used it later as the basis for his *De Vera Differentia Regiae Potestatis et Ecclesiasticae* (1534, reprinted 1538) which was issued by the king's printer. Its arguments underpinned the legislation of the Reformation Parliament after 1530 (Elton 1977, 135–7) and Stephen Gardiner's influential *De Vera Obedientia* (1535) which saw church and commonwealth as a unitary body politic, comprehensive of all the people, and ruled over by a single person – head of the church, king of the commonwealth – to whom God ordered obedience.

Henry's clerical advisers argued that the king's jurisdiction in spiritual matters derived direct from God. Parliament only confirmed and declared this authority: it did not grant it. The clergy were given authority to govern the church by God but the power of coercion (*dominium*) to give this commission from God effect had to come from the prince (E. Foxe 1534, fols 22 a and b). The clergy continued to have a positive and distinct jurisdictional and legislative function under the king's protection. It is intriguing that they continued to accept the account of the Donation of Constantine despite the fact that this had been discredited by William Marshall in his translation, printed in 1534.

According to some authorities this view was not wholly shared by Cromwell. He appears to have been afraid that the clergy, under the king, would set up an authority independent of Parliament. Two memoranda on this issue were addressed to Cromwell in 1535 or 1536 and these gave rise to a number of treatises and papers. *A Dialogue Between a Doctor and a Student*, for example, urged that the entire church – laity and clergy – should define the nature of that church – that is, by determining what it was that the Scriptures laid down (Nicholson 1977, 225–7). The authority with which the king and ecclesiastics acted would be, therefore, an ascending authority. This ascendant theory was hinted at by Parliament in later legislation and Cromwell certainly sponsored work which argued along these lines. This included William Marshall's translation of Marsiglio of Padua, *Defensor Pacis*, in 1535. Support also came from independent quarters, namely Christopher St German's *A Treatyse concerninge the power of the clergye and the lawes of the realme* of 1535. There is some controversy about authorship (Elton 1973, 74–5; Nicholson 1977, 216 ff) but still support was forthcoming from other quarters.

It has been observed that, theory notwithstanding, the king and his ministers and advisers were in practice compelled to act with parliamentary support and confirmation. The Reformation Parliament gave credence to a view of the English constitution which became commonplace in the late sixteenth century but had scarcely been expressed before 1530 – that sovereignty rested with king-in-Parliament. A doctrine of parliamentary sovereignty emerged (Elton 1977, 199–200). Of course, there is much dispute as to whether this theory had any real bearing upon practice, especially in the reign of Henry.

So far we have identified two broad approaches to the Henrician Reformation: that which urged the separation between spiritual and temporal, and which traced a history of struggle between Antichrist and Christ in which kings might be cast either as help-mates or villains; and that which saw the king as the principal member of the church and the chief instrument of reformation. There was a half-way house, to be identified in the arguments put forward by Philip Melancthon. Melancthon conceded that re-forming kings might have a central role in the fulfilment of God's plan for his church on earth and a claim to being acknowledged as the chief members of the visible church.

But it is in the seminal work of John Foxe that the two ap-proaches are drawn together. The eschatological framework of contemporaries' thought about the Reformation is never more apparent than here, yet Foxe calls upon the monarchy to realize the providential designs. By the late seventeenth century, approximately ten thousand copies of his *Acts and Monuments* (often called his *Book of Martyrs*) had been bought. Its circu-lation was wider than that of any book except the Bible (Haller 1963, 13–14). Not only did individuals read it and groups listen to it being read – it was also preached in the pulpit (Aston 1977, O'Day 1982, 9–24). And the manner of its writing posi-tively invited 'humble folk' to participate vicariously in the historical epic of the English Reformation, as it recited the experiences and martyrdoms of craftsmen, traders, labourers and housewives, and indicated their role in the writing of this chap-ter of the history of the struggle against Antichrist (Eisenstein 1979, I, 423). History, argued Foxe, was being made by them. It follows that for at least 120 years it was Foxe's conception of the history of the Reformation which was shared by most Englishmen who thought about such matters, high and low, literate and illiterate. Before Foxe wrote there was no popular history of the Reformation; after him, there was no other. Foxe's perspective was so dominant that nineteenth-century his-torians who disagreed with him had their work cut out to de-throne him. And even today it sometimes seems that academic historians are doing little more than crossing the martyrologist's *t*s and dotting his *i*s.

Acts and Monuments fulfilled two functions: it provided a vivid account of events leading up to Elizabeth I's accession, concentrating upon the edifying lives and deaths of the martyrs of the Reformation; and it supplied a history of the Reformation within the context of providential history. Foxe's defence of the Reformation – both as an event and as a continuing process in the new reign – was conceived in historical terms, albeit not in the sense of history as we today conceive it. This historical defence was, at root, a counter-attack upon the claims of the Roman church to an authority handed down directly from God and St Peter. Foxe aimed to show that what had occurred was a reformation and not a revolution. The Church of England was 'not the beginning of any new church of our own' but 'the renewing of the old ancient church of Christ': the Church of Rome is developed and degenerate; the Church of England primitive and pure. This message is, as we suggested earlier, a-historical – for it suggests the plausibility of a return to the primitive church – but it is set within a historical framework of the 'rise and fall', and then the 'revival', of the Christian church on earth. His universal history covered five phases: 'the suffering time of the church' (*c.* 300 years after the Apostles); 'the flourishing time of the church' (*c.* 300 years); 'the declining time of the church' (*c.* 300 years down to 1000 AD); 'the time of Antichrist' (*c.* 400 years); 'the reformation' or the 'purging of the church of God'. Foxe, of course, concentrated upon the detailed history of the fifth phase, as it occurred in England, yet even so a large proportion of his book deals with the earlier history of the Christian church. If we ignore the wider context of Foxe's history of the martyrdoms, we miss the significance of his contribution to Reformation historiography and are unlikely to appreciate the impact which his interpretation of the Reformation was to have upon generations of Englishmen after him.

There were precedents. Medieval chronicles had been used for propagandist and persuasive purposes, and this tradition was built upon in the mid-sixteenth century. The legend of England as a people chosen by God appeared in the pages of John Stow's *Chronicles of England* (1580) and Raphael Holinshed's *The Chronicles of England, Scotland and Irelande* (Ellis 1807–8). The Antwerp writers stressed the Lollard tradition. And Matthew Parker's *De Antiquitate Britannicae Ecclesiae* similarly aimed to trace the apostolic origins of the English church (Parker 1572). It is the very popularity and accessibility of Foxe's account which makes it more important than all. He tells the story and makes his overall point with such consummate skill, ensuring the lasting impact of the history by including exciting and well-known detail. For instance, the *Book of Martyrs* displays the monarchs of the late eleventh century onwards struggling to defend both England and its church against Rome. Into this tale it weaves the popular stories of Henry II's struggle with Thomas à Becket and the Monk of Swinshead's poisoning of King John. The reign of Edward III heralds the beginning of persecution in the Church of England by the monarchy. Foxe gives a detailed account of Wyclif and his doctrines – of that time 'when the morning star of that glorious day arose in our hemisphere – John Wickcliffe'.

Why did John Foxe write in 1563 what was, in effect, a history of the Christian church? In order to answer this question we must know something of the martyrologist himself (Mozley 1940). Foxe was born in 1517 at Boston, Lincolnshire. In 1534 he began his education at Oxford, supported by his stepfather, who was a wealthy yeoman. While at Brasenose College, Foxe shared a chamber with Alexander Nowell, who was later Dean of St Paul's (under Elizabeth) and author of the most famous catechism. Foxe was granted his BA in 1537 and became a Fellow of the college in 1539. In the summer of 1543, he proceeded MA. By 1542 he was already a man of strong Protestant convictions and his views landed him in trouble with the college authorities, who on one occasion condemned him for heresy and planned to eject him, and on another removed him from the fellowship because of his deliberate refusal to take holy orders within one year of his regency: 'By the statute of our college I shall not be permitted to stay here beyond Michaelmas unless I am willing to castrate myself by rushing into the priestly order' (Mozley 1940, 24).

Foxe sought a schoolmaster's position either in a college school, a Protestant household or his own school. In the end, after a long search, he was forced to accept a position in the Lucy household at

Charlecote, despite the unpleasant living conditions – his predecessor had 'a chamber smelling so strongly of the sewer that its
occupant needs to have his nose cut off' (Mozley 1940, 26). After
two years Foxe took his new wife, Agnes, to London, where he
became tutor to the children of the Duchess of Richmond. While
in her employ he met and made friends with John Bale and was
ordained deacon. In 1553 he moved to Rygate and attempted to
convert the town to Protestantism. After Edward VI's death in
July 1553 Foxe's circumstances changed for the worse. The
release of the Duke of Norfolk from the tower meant that he
regained control of his two young sons, Foxe's pupils at Rygate,
and Foxe lost his job. In March 1554 both Foxe and his wife fled
to Antwerp and travelled on the Continent. By 1555 he was
living with other exiles at Basle. We know little of Foxe's activities in exile, other than his writing, except that John Aylmer
claimed that he had foretold in a sermon the return to England
after Mary's death (Mozley 1940, 59).

Even if the exiles did not anticipate a speedy return to England,
they were removed from her physically but not spiritually. In exile
as well as out, they saw themselves as evangelists – as John Jewel
had said in 1552 of preaching: 'This is our office, this we take upon
us, and this we profess; and except we do this, we do nothing, we
serve no use' (Haller 1963, 39). Foxe's absorption in penning his
martyrology has to be seen in this context. The exiles were
attempting to convert the English at home to a new faith. Two
long-distance strategies were adopted to achieve this, both of them
involving the use of the printing press. On the one hand there were
proposed martyrologies and histories; on the other, an English
version of the Bible, based upon Tyndale and Coverdale. The first
of these projects was sponsored by Edmund Grindal, John Foxe and
John Bale; the second by William Whittingham and other exiles at
Geneva. As early as 1555 Grindal had proposed a *Book of Martyrs* to
be published in both English and Latin. Foxe worked on both
versions but they were bedevilled by delays. Eventually, the Latin
edition was published in 1559 but the English version, in effect a
new book, had to wait until 1563. The Latin version – written
while Mary yet reigned – had a rather different purpose from the
English book – which was, above all, a call to action.

While he worked, Foxe came heavily under two major influences – the Bible, with its format of the history of a single, chosen
people with a sense of their identity as a nation set aside from all
others by their particular destiny, and its emphasis upon God's
grand design; and John Bale, who had influenced Foxe as early as
1548 and who was working alongside him in exile. Bale, too, saw
the English people as an elect nation, defending the true church,
and he strove to show his readers that the contemporary struggle
between the adherents of the new religion and their persecutors
was but part of the age-long struggle between Christ and Antichrist, described in the apocalyptic vision of St John. Bale was
more wont than Foxe to interweave scriptural lore with that of
the English chronicles but he, too, lent emphasis to the existence
of a tradition of 'reformation' in fifteenth-century England,
personified by the Lollards. His *Scriptorum Illustrium Maioris Britan-
niae Catalogus* (Bale 1557) was a gargantuan attempt to rewrite
the history of Britain within an eschatological framework, and
Foxe is known to have owned this book. And Bale, like Foxe,
tended to nationalism rather than to millennialism. In his vision,
the monarch was leading the nation in a crusade against Antichrist.

John Foxe, then, was important not so much for the reporting
of contemporary persecutions as for the point which he believed
this cumulative martyrology to make: that there was a struggle
between Christ and Antichrist, and that the second daughter of
Henry VIII was as a second Deborah to rescue the nation from
Antichrist and restore the rule of Christ. This motif was repeated
constantly in the pageantry and imagery of Elizabeth's early years
on the throne. The five pageants which accompanied her progress
from the Tower of London to her coronation at Westminster
Abbey told a similar story. Elizabeth united the warring factions
of York and Lancaster; God was giving her strength to fulfil his
grand design for England; she had played a waiting game to bring
the truth to her people and now she had God's Word in the
vernacular Bible to present; she was Deborah, consulting with her
estates, in order to govern Israel wisely and well. The ballad, 'A
Songe Betwene the Quenes Majestie and Englande', popularized
this vision:

England   Lady this long space/have I loved thy grace
           more than I durst well saye
           Hoping at the last/when all storms were past
           For to see this joyfull daye.

Elizabeth Yet my lover England/ye shall understand
           How fortune on me did lowre
           I was tombled and lost/from piller to post
           and prisoner in the Toure.

England   Dere Lady we do know/how that tirauntes not a
           fewe
           went about to seke thy bloude
           An contrarie to right/they did what they might
           That now bare two faces in one hood . . . .

England   Oh cruell tirauntes/and also monstrous giauntes
           That woulde such a swete blossome devour
           But the lorde of his might/defend the in right
           And shortened their arme and powre.

Elizabeth Yet my lover dere/mark me well here
           Though thei were men of the devill
           The scripture plainly saith/al thei that be of faith
           Must nedes do good against evill.

England   Oh swete virgin pure/longe may ye endure
           To reigne over us in this lande
           For your workes do accord/ye are the handmaid
           of the lord
           For he hath blessed you with his hand.
               (Sola Pinto and Rodway 1965, 60–3)

John Aylmer, later her Bishop of London, presented her in his *An Harborowe for Faithful and True Subjectes* (April 1559) as having been saved from martyrdom only by divine intervention (Mary's death), so that the English nation was committed to her preservation (Haller 1963, 87). So, when there were conspiracies against

Elizabeth, these were cast as conspiracies against the true church. For there was no doubt that God was English, nor that Elizabeth was identified with the cause of Protestantism in Protestant minds (if not her own). When John Jewel preached at the time of Norfolk's rebellion in 1569 on the anniversary of Elizabeth's accession (17 November), he merrily likened the situation to that of the Battle of Jericho. The adherents of the true faith were few in number and technically weak in military strength but they could defeat the enemy because God was with them – their cause was God's own. The accession-day jousts, bell-ringing and church services have more than an antiquarian interest – they mark Elizabeth's place in God's great plan of salvation (Neale 1966, 199–218).

Before he published his English *Book of Martyrs*, John Foxe had access to original sources which had not been available to him when in exile. What we know of his use of these sources suggests that Foxe was remarkably accurate and that charges of deliberate falsification of the evidence levelled at him appear to be unfounded. Where scholars have checked his use of sources they have been impressed. Even so, it may be that William Haller was right when he alleged that Foxe 'became possessed by the kind of excitement which overtakes the historical investigator when he uncovers untouched documentary evidence supporting a view of the past to which he is already emotionally and imaginatively committed' (Haller 1963, 158). This was the spirit in which he used documents relating to the life and works of Wyclif, accounts of the Lollard martyrdoms in episcopal act books and documentary evidence of contemporary persecutions. It was also the spirit in which he included in the book dramatic devices which lent force to his argument – Cranmer's hand thrust in the flames; evil omens; spiritual and physical travails.

J. F. Mozley painstakingly pieced together the making of Foxe's *Book of Martyrs* (Mozley 1940). His work shows how Foxe's book grew in response to events and the availability of new documentary material. Foxe had actually begun the book in England in 1552: his aim was to refute any idea that English Protestantism had begun with Luther and to sketch in some of its pre-Reformation origins. He had collected the materials for this and completed a rough draft by August 1554. *A Commentary on the*

History of the Church, and a description of the great persecutions through-
out Europe from the times of Wycliffe to this age was duly printed in
Latin (as *Commentarii rerum in ecclesia gestarum*) at Strassburg in
1554. Effectively this introduced both the English and foreign
scholars to the history of English Lollardy. (Jean Crépin's
martyrology, published in 1554, began with the martyrdom of
John Hus; after 1555 editions included important sections on
Wyclif and printed sections of Foxe's account.) During 1555
Foxe was diverted from his work on the martyrology by the exile
and by a suggested work on Cranmer. But Grindal continued to
send Foxe news of materials about the martyrs (e.g. the existence
of materials about Philpot), actual documents (the writings and
examination of Bradford), and caveats and suggestions about their
use. Foxe himself collected materials: he wrote to John Aylmer in
1557 for information about his erstwhile pupil, Lady Jane Grey.
Grindal and other exiles urged Foxe to continue his work and to
include the reign of Henry VIII while they located materials about
the reigns of Edward and Mary.

In 1559 Foxe published his Latin edition, divided into six
books. Book One was really a reprint of the book of 1554 with a
few additions; Book Two treated the reigns of Henry and
Edward; Books Three to Six dealt with the Marian persecutions,
ending with the execution of Cranmer, and including a list of
martyrdoms down to November 1558. This work suffered from
the defects of the sources which its author had been able to use.
For the reign of Henry VIII he had been reduced to consulting
mainly printed works. For the reign of Mary he had had to rely
upon accounts sent out from England. He had been unable to
search the registers or to check his authorities. This meant that
the narrative was littered with minor errors which he had to correct in later editions. It also meant that he gave far more space to
famous names than to the humble. In addition, because this Latin
version was directed at a foreign audience, considerable attention
was given to explaining matters to alien readers.

When Foxe returned to England he already had it in mind to
publish a better English version. He spent the winter of 1560 and
the whole of 1561 examining fresh documentary evidence. He
negotiated with John Day to reprint the work in 1563. Grindal

and Parker perhaps helped him to work on particular materials. The 1559 volume was translated into English. When the amended and enlarged work appeared, it extended to over 1800 folio pages, was bedecked with more than fifty woodcuts, and contained a calendar of martyrs and confessors which acted as an index.

This first English edition was considerably attacked in print by Catholic writers (for example, Nicholas Harpsfield, under the alias Alan Cope, wrote *Dialogi Sex* in 1566, and Thomas Harding a *Confutation* in 1565, which attacked both his account and his conclusions) and Foxe was spurred on by their criticisms to produce another, improved version. John Day, the printer, found new material for him, even interviewing Cranmer's chaplain, Ralph Morice, and Foxe himself hunted for new evidence of the persecutions. The 1570 edition, as a result, was even larger and more compendious than that of 1563. Notably, it enlarged on general church history to show that popery represented innovation and Protestantism the true, primitive church. More space was accorded the continental martyrs, to emphasize that the English struggle was part of a generalized struggle against Antichrist. Foxe stressed the use of a wide variety of ecclesiastical sources and used copyists to provide him with materials which he could not inspect in the original. The dramatic impact of the book was enhanced by the use of 1500 woodcuts. The calendar of martyrs was dropped and new prefaces made the message of the work patently clear. It was this edition which the bishops ordered to be placed in all cathedrals and which most parishes bought for their churches. Later editions, namely those of 1576 and 1583, were largely reprints in different formats, although they did introduce new evidence, including items discovered in the Tower of London.

How then did Foxe view the Reformation? If the book itself involved a rolling remake, Foxe certainly never revised the plot. The tradition in which he wrote was a biographical one, and one which emphasized the role of monarchs and other 'national' leaders. The English edition was first printed during the succession crisis of 1562–3: it could be seen as a timely reminder of what might happen again. The key part of the monarch in reformation was, therefore, perhaps doubly stressed. Yet Foxe could give only qualified commendation of Henry VIII. He unhorsed the Pope but left him with 'trappings and stirrups whereby the prelates went about to set him upon his horse again' (Foxe v, 697). It was Thomas Cromwell who really achieved reformation through his political acumen. Edward VI's reign foreshadowed the dawn of the new age which was heralded by Elizabeth's accession. Then almost half the work was devoted to reporting the martyrdoms of Mary's reign, the dramatic effect enhanced by the employment of woodcuts. It was clearly intended that no Englishman should ever forget this terrible persecution. The central importance of the devotion of humble men and women to Christ, from the time of the Lollards to the present, was highlighted. Yet the assemblage of stories of martyrdom had another purpose – the horror and carnage stood in stark contrast to the peace and tranquillity which Elizabeth's accession had brought. Elizabeth had almost fallen victim to the persecution; in her personal salvation lay the hope of the English people; under her, all would live under the olive tree's protective branches rather than in fear of death – all, that is, who adhered to the true faith.

The *Book of Martyrs* was, then, to our minds a strange history. It was 'the most elaborate expression of the apocalyptical expectancy with which the returned exiles and their party greeted Elizabeth at her accession' (Haller 1963, 124). In it the martyrologist set before the people the current Protestant realization of the traditional Christian conception of the meaning of history and how it should be applied in the English case. For history told not only of the past but of the future. It showed, to those who were alert to its message, what should be achieved in the present and future to ensure that the story could be told in accordance with the divine plan. It told Elizabeth what she must do. Historiography was, therefore, a science which the religious must master, not a luxury. Foxe's book was the most complete realization of this scheme but it belonged to the same tradition as the contemporaneous writings of John Bale and Matthew Parker. It was in a real sense 'history' (even if, to our eyes, an unscientific one) and not a catalogue of tales of martyrdom. If Foxe did not apply to the evidence which he examined the standards of modern historical scholarship, he none the less read it in the light of the 'truth' of the Protestant view of history. Falsification of the evidence would be a misleading charge: misreadings of the evidence would be the fault to which he and other Protestant 'historians' of the sixteenth and seventeenth centuries were most prone.

The importance of history and historiography to the Marian and Elizabethan Protestants can be demonstrated by the manner in which they marketed the *Book of Martyrs* and similar works. We have mentioned already that Edmund Grindal actively sponsored the production of Foxe's history. But perhaps even more important was the work of printer/publishers of strong Protestant views. As Foxe himself put it:

> The Lord began to work for his church not with sword and target to subdue his exalted adversary, but with printing, writing and reading. . . . How many printing presses there be in the world, so many block houses there be against the high castle of St Angelo Papal residence, so that either the pope must abolish knowledge and printing or printing at length will root him out.   (Foxe III, 718–22)

By far the most prominent Protestant printer was John Day (d. 1584), who under Mary printed the pamphlets of the exiles and was imprisoned for printing such offensive books, and who under Elizabeth printed high-quality editions of Protestant works. Matthew Parker, for example, used Day to print Ælfric's sermon – in *A Testament of Antiqitie*, 1567 – because it seemed to support the Protestant view of the sacrament; *The Gospels of the Fower Evangelistes translated in the olde Saxon Tyme*, 1571; and the *De Antiquitate Britannicae Ecclesiæ* of 1572, which argued the antiquity and purity of England's church. In 1560 Day published a mammoth edition of the writings of Thomas Becon, to be joined in 1562 by editions of the sermons of Hugh Latimer. Then in 1563 Day printed the first editions in English of Foxe's *Acts and Monuments of these last and Perillous Days*. Other books by Foxe rolled off his press: the 1570 edition of *Acts and Monuments*, Foxe's version of the Anglo-Saxon Chronicle, and the martyrologist's edition of the collected works of Tyndale, Barnes and Frith in one book with accompanying biographies and preface. Foxe had good reason to write:

> How praiseworthy are printers like John Daye, who at their own charges give to the world the stories of the martyrs and other ancient documents. Daye has diligently collected the scattered

writings, as many as he could find of these three learned fathers of blessed memory, chief ringleaders in these latter times of this Church of England. The book will be a light to all posterity. Men of every age can learn here, the young men from Frith, the middle-aged from Tyndale, the elder men from Barnes; and the simplicity and zeal of those former times is an example to the present generation.   (Foxe 1837, Preface)

Day did more than publish and print the books produced by leading Protestant luminaries: he collected the manuscript sources and commissioned editions of them or histories based on them. In a real sense he and others like him directed a propaganda campaign of significant proportions. His press brought before the English people the prevalent Protestant interpretation of Christian history and advice about future action. This was new and heady stuff to lay before a population nurtured on Catholicism. To wean the populace away from the Catholic view of history, it had to be dramatic stuff also. Interestingly enough, the Catholics do not appear to have employed the printing press to put forward their opposing view of Christian history, past, present and future. Instead, they printed liturgical and pious works, leaving propaganda to their opponents (P. M. Took 1979, *passim*).

The importance of the printer was not always viewed with approval by Protestant apologists, however. John Jewel was to write cryptically to Matthew Parker, 'I am afraid of printers: their tyranny is terrible' (Ayre 1850, IV, 1275).

The dominant themes of Foxe's Protestant history – that England was a nation elect of God to restore his church – continued to pervade Protestant literature. The occasion of the Gunpowder Plot, for example, occasioned considerable apprehension in the Protestant community. In 1610 a new edition of *Acts and Monuments*, with an attached account of the St Bartholomew's Day Massacre, was published. Laudian policies produced a like fear of popery. Further editions of the *Book of Martyrs* appeared in 1632 and 1642, duly brought up to date. The myth of Elizabeth as the second Deborah was fed by such works as William Camden's *Annales Rerum Anglicarum et Hibernicarum, Regnante Elizabetha* (1615), which was translated into English in 1627 (by Abraham Darcie) and in 1632 (by Robert Naunton). Thomas Heywood's *If you know not me you know nobody; or the troubles of Queen Elizabeth*, penned in 1603, was first printed in 1605 and appeared in a prose version, *England's Elizabeth: Her Life and Troubles during her minoritie from the cradle to the crown*, in 1631, and in a heroic verse form in 1639. Perhaps even more notably, Heywood's *Exemplary Lives and Memorable Acts of Nine of the Most Worthy Women of the World*, 1640, began with Deborah and closed with Elizabeth. Cornelius Burges preached a sermon to the House of Commons in 1640 on the anniversary of Elizabeth's accession which called upon the audience to 'Remember and consider that this very day . . . eighty two years sithence began a new resurrection of this kingdom from the dead . . . our second happy reformation of religion by the auspicious entrance of our late royal Deborah . . . into her blessed and glorious reign'. The analogy was much more than a literary conceit: it counselled the future behaviour of Elizabeth, her successors and the English people as a whole. The English were bound by covenant to complete Elizabeth's work of reformation. Even those who remained critical of the Queen's own role, such as John Milton, still saw England as an elect nation whose task it was to complete the Reformation. It is worth more than passing notice that there was no cult of Henry VIII, no celebration of his accession thirty-seven years after his death, no association in the popular mind between Bluff King Hal and Josiah which lingered to inspire other generations (Haller 1963, 228–39).

It would take much more than a few pages to suggest why it was that Protestant historiographical propaganda was so powerful, for powerful it certainly was: powerful, pervasive and long-lived. In the nineteenth century it was Foxe's account of the Reformation (as seen through his own and others' eyes) that was criticized, amended or accepted. Even in the twentieth century, historians use his book as a source and as an interpretation. Why? The book's popularity owed much to its sponsorship by the Protestant establishment. It was widespread in churches and in private libraries. It associated nationalism and religion, in a highly acceptable way. As time went on and it suffered attacks from within the church (from the Arminian wing), the book itself became a martyr to a cause: it was inextricably associated in the popular mind with English Protestantism. To attack Foxe's view of Christian history and, specifically, of the English Reformation was to attack the Protestant Reformation itself. Had the book seen only one printing and had it been suppressed in 1563 or 1570 it seems unlikely that many would have mourned it, but the book and the view of the Reformation which it presented had sufficient time to take a grip on the English imagination. England may not have been Protestant in 1563, but by the beginning of Charles I's reign it surely was.

But there is more to it than this. Foxe's *Book of Martyrs* was given official support and it was widely available, but was this the only secret of its success? Here we can only speculate. The book had endearing literary qualities. It told a dramatic story. It told a *contemporary* story. Where the Bible told of the exploits of a nomadic Middle Eastern people with strange, often inexplicable and always foreign customs, Foxe's *Book of Martyrs* spoke of near-contemporary England. Foxe had to explain matters to foreign readers: his book met with instant comprehension among an English readership. By using England as his measure, Foxe was able to open up the whole of Christian 'world' history to his audience.

Today's historian is interested in more than explaining whether and why the *Book of Martyrs* was popular. Far more important is the fact that it was itself an *agent* of reformation in England. Every schoolchild is taught that Foxe's *Martyrs* was both popular and important, but most are left wondering why. The book's popularity provides the latchkey to its importance. We tend to forget that England in 1563 was only *officially* Protestant – until the settlement most Englishmen had been conforming Catholics and after it most were but conforming Protestants. Foxe's *Book of Martyrs* laid before these people a book with a clearly defined Protestant view of history and of the place of the English Reformation in this history. To concentrate upon its martyrological components is to minimize its wider importance. The martyrology helped it to make its point – that England and Elizabeth were elected by God to complete the Reformation. The work, in an age when books of a popular appeal were few, was highly accessible – it told of the troubles both of humble men and

women, and high and mighty princes; it stressed the importance
of the monarch's leadership (of Deborah's good government), but
certainly did not diminish the importance of the people's service
(her troops in the battle); and it put in story-form events and
teachings with which the majority of the people were either
unfamiliar or poorly acquainted. For both teacher and taught it
provided a framework upon which could be hung otherwise
incomprehensible events, strange happenings and apparently
irreligious beliefs. Supported by other Protestant works, it gave
the Reformation 'form' and 'meaning' for contemporaries. To
appreciate its popularity and its importance we have to make a real
effort of the imagination to see ourselves in a world of few books,
poor communications and no public broadcasting, striving to
make sense of the jumble and turmoil of events in a society
normally stable and now turned upside-down. To the modern
reader the *Book of Martyrs* may seem as one book among many. To
the reader in 1563 it was the only book which told the story of
contemporary religious and political events in a comprehensible
manner.

Chapter 2

Interpretations of the Reformation from Fuller to Strype

During the period between the first English edition of Foxe's *Book of Martyrs* and the Restoration Settlement, not everyone accepted the martyrologist's account of the Reformation or his interpretation of the nature of the Elizabethan Settlement. In a real sense the religious controversy which absorbed so many in the sixteenth and seventeenth centuries concerned just this uncertainty – what was the nature of the Church of England? what were the practical implications of her reformation? Here it is not possible to examine the controversy in detail. In fact, the arguments were rarely couched in more than very general historical terms. On the one hand, the Reformation was seen as incomplete and in need of furtherance; on the other as something final – a blueprint for the future.

There was one notable attempt to rewrite the history of the Reformation and, in so doing, to weaken the hold of the *Book of Martyrs* on the minds of Englishmen and women. This occurred within the context of the Laudian attempt to redefine the relationship between church and monarchy. In essence, the Laudians rejected Foxe's belief that the nation would defeat Antichrist only with the leadership of the prince. But 'the Laudians dethroned the elect nation only to enthrone the elect church' (Lamont 1969, 67).

Laud and his supporters wished to restore the autonomy of the Church of England. This autonomy, ruled by bishops *jure divino*, would be used to bring about the defeat of Antichrist and the rule of Christ the King. In order to achieve this, the Laudians naturally had to convince the temporal powers by political argument that such a course was correct. Part of this political argument was a historical defence of such a position.

The best-known apologist of the Laudian position was Dr Peter Heylyn (1600–62). From early in his academic career at Oxford, Heylyn was convinced that the Foxian tradition was wrong: the Church of England stemmed not from the Wyclifite protest, as Foxe and others maintained, but from the primitive church. He argued this in 1627 against Dr Prideaux, Regius Professor of Divinity at Oxford:

> I fell upon a different way from that of Doctor Prideaux, the Professor, in his Lecture *De Visibilitate Ecclesiae . . .* in which the visibility of the Protestant Church . . . was no otherwise proved, than by looking for it in the scattered conventicles of the Berengarians in Italy, the Waldenses in France, the Wicklifists in England, and the Hussites in Bohemia. Which manner of proceeding not being liked by the respondent, as that which utterly discontinued that succession of the hierarchy which the Church of England claims from the very Apostles and their immediate successors.   (Robertson 1849, I, liv)

In this early disputation can be found the seeds of Heylyn's later argument in *Ecclesia Restaurata*: that Anglicanism was the purified Catholic church; that its bishops were in the direct apostolic succession, deriving their authority not from the Crown but from God through the laying on of hands; that the relationship between the temporal and spiritual powers was not as Foxe had conceived it.

William Laud recognized in this arch-enemy of John Williams, Dean of Westminster, an able protagonist and quickly enlisted his services. For instance, Heylyn delivered a sermon against the Feoffees for Impropriations in Oxford in 1630, and he prepared the case against the Feoffees and against Prynne's *Histriomastix* for Attorney General Noy. Most important of all, he began to collect materials for a history of the English Reformation and to prepare historical defences for the retention of episcopacy and for the English liturgy. But the Civil War intervened and Heylyn put the work to one side.

At the Restoration, Heylyn was restored to his prebendal stall at Westminster.

> Thus being settled in Westminster, he fell upon the old work of building again and repairing, which is the costly pleasure of clergymen, for the next generation, because building is like planting, the chief benefit of which accrues to their successors that live in another age.

The same might have been said for Heylyn's *Ecclesia Restaurata*, which did not appear until 1661, or the *History of Episcopacy* and the *History of Liturgies* which were published with other tracts under the title *Historical and Miscellaneous Tracts* in 1681. Yet the timing of publication was most apposite, given that the Restoration involved a definition of the nature of the reformed Church of England, the origins and character of its authority, and its relationship with the Crown and Parliament.

Heylyn's *History of the Reformation* recounted happenings from the reign of Edward down to 1566 after sketching in the contribution made by Henry VIII. There is a sense in which it presented no new facts of significance – even the documents it introduced were commonly already in print – but it certainly threw a new light upon the Reformation.

Heylyn was in no doubt that what we call the 'official' Reformation was not the real reformation of the church: rather it opened the way for a much deeper religious reformation. While acknowledging Henry VIII's importance, he yet maintained that the king had remained a Catholic until his death:

> The work first hinted by a Prince of an undaunted spirit, the master of as great a courage as the world had any; and to say truth, the work required it. He durst not else have grappled with that mighty adversary, who, claiming to be successor to St Peter in the see of Rome, and Vicar-general to Christ over all the church, had gained unto himself an absolute sovereignty

over all Christian Kings and princes in the Western Empire. But this King, being violently hurried with the transport of some private affections, and finding that the Pope appeared the greatest obstacle to his desire, he first divested him by degrees of that supremacy . . . and, finally, extinguished his authority in the realm of England, without noise or trouble, to the great admiration and astonishment of the rest of the Christian world. This opened the first way to the Reformation, and gave encouragement to those who inclined unto it: to which the King afforded no small countenance, out of political ends, by suffering them to have the Bible in the English tongue, and to enjoy the benefit of such godly tractates as openly discovered the corruptions of the Church of Rome. But, for his own part, he adhered to his old religion, severely persecuted those who dissented from it, and died (though excommunicated) in that faith and doctrine which he had sucked in, as it were, with his mother's milk. (Robertson 1849, I, v–vi)

During the reign of Edward VI, the Reformation proceeded. It was not, however, the minor on the throne, 'just, mild and gracious', who offered leadership. No: his 'name was made a property to serve turns withal, and his authority abused'. The furtherance of the Reformation was instead 'endeavoured by some godly bishops, and other learned and religious men, of the lower clergy, out of judgement and conscience; who managed the affair according to the Word of God, the practice of the primitive times, the general current and consent of the old catholic doctors, but not without an eye to such foreign churches as seemed to have most consonancy to the ancient forms'. But it was also promoted by great courtiers 'who, under colour of removing such corruptions as remained in the Church, had cast their eyes upon the spoil of shrines and images (though still preserved in the greatest part of the Lutheran Churches), and the improving of their own fortunes by the chantry lands'. Still, the Reformation proceeded apace and the publication of the *Book of Homilies* and the first prayer book was in accordance, Heylyn believed, with the Holy Spirit. It was John Calvin who spoilt it all: he criticized the liturgy and engineered the growth of a 'Zwinglian faction' which urged doctrinal and disciplinary innovations. The success of this tendency was encouraged when John à Lasco was permitted to set up a church, distinct in government and worship from the established church. It expressed itself with a concerted attack on vestments, on church furniture, and on the liturgy (Robertson 1849, i, vi, vi–vii).

When Mary came to the throne at Edward's death, she restored the country to Catholicism. She made the reformers pay dearly for their past activities, 'whose blood she caused to be poured forth like water, in most parts of the kingdom, but nowhere more abundantly than in Bonner's slaughter-house'. Meanwhile, in exile, the reformers fell out among themselves, there being a schism between the Genevans and others. 'Which woeful schism, so wretchedly begun in a foreign nation, they laboured to promote by all sinister practices in the Church of England, when they returned from exile in the following reign. The miserable effects, whereof we feel too sensibly and smartly, to this very day!' (Robertson 1849, i, x).

Elizabeth's reign saw the restoration of the pure Reformation. Elizabeth is portrayed as a committed Protestant, whose understanding of the wishes of her people and whose experience made her determined to 'satisfy the piety of their desire' once she had the power to do it. The liturgy, the creed and the government of the church were returned to their former condition. The apostolic succession was confirmed. The queen asserted her temporal and spiritual supremacy. She prevented the laity from encroaching upon the authority of the church. She held at bay the Puritan faction.

There are, in this history, many notable features. Heylyn, unlike Foxe and his adherents, does not present the princes of England as friends of the Church of England. 'All that was done in order to it under Henry the Eighth, seemed to be accidental only, and by the by, rather designed on private ends, than out of any settled purpose to restore the Church; and therefore intermitted, and resumed again, as those ends had variance'. Indeed, thought Heylyn, the Tudors were arch-despoilers of the church. Both Henry and Edward ravaged her wealth. Even Mary did not restore her lands. And Elizabeth – committed to the reformed Church of England as she was – appeared yet more culpable.

Deliberately, she kept sees vacant until she had profited from them and robbed them by advantageous exchanges. Here, Heylyn laid his finger on that plunder of the church as an institution, the extent of which has exercised historians of the twentieth century. And Heylyn showed himself equally aware of the implications of this weakened economic position for the church (Robertson 1849, I, ix; II, 308).

Heylyn's attitude to Elizabeth may appear confused. Yes, she despoiled the church. But she also was, in every sense, a daughter of the Reformation – political and religious. So, Heylyn portrays her mother, Anne Boleyn, as 'a great and gallant lady, – one of the most remarkable mockeries and disports of fortune which these last ages have produced: raised from the quality of a private lady to the bed of a king, crowned on the throne, and executed on the scaffold', to the last protesting her innocence (Robertson 1849, II, 251). So, he maintains that Elizabeth was a Protestant during her brother's reign. So, he urges that, for political reasons, Elizabeth appreciated that she must declare this Protestantism. 'She knew full well that her legitimation and the Pope's supremacy could not stand together, and that she could not possibly maintain the one without the discarding of the other' (Robertson 1849, II, 268). Her political acumen was such that 'it concerned her to walk very warily, and not to unmask herself too much at once, for fear of giving an alarm to the papal party before she had put herself into a posture of ability to make good her actions' (Robertson 1849, II, 268–9).

Heylyn was convinced that Elizabeth had intended a return to that model of the primitive church revealed in the liturgy, the Thirty-nine Articles and the established government of the church through bishops. Disorder and disunity resulted from a coincidence of circumstances. Briefly speaking, there was a faction which wanted further and more radical change in the church – in its doctrine, discipline and government. For a variety of reasons Elizabeth was forced to use members of this faction to govern her new church, with, according to Heylyn, disastrous consequences:

So it was, that, partly by the deprivation of these few persons, but principally by the death of so many in the last year's sickness [influenza] epidemic, there was not a sufficient number of learned men to supply the cures; which filled the Church with an ignorant and illiterate clergy, whose learning went no further than the Liturgy or the Book of Homilies, but otherwise conformable (which was no small felicity) to the rules of the Church. And on the other side, many were raised to great preferments who, having spent their time of exile in such foreign churches as followed the platform of Geneva, returned so disaffected to Episcopal Government, unto the rites and ceremonies here by law established, as not long after filled the Church with most sad disorders, not only to the breaking of the bond of peace but to the grieving and extinguishing of the spirit of unity.

(Robertson 1849, II, 296)

These men disagreed with the form of the Church of England and remained thorns in her side: Laurence Humphrey would 'pass amongst the nonconformists', Thomas Cartwright would 'prove an unextinguished firebrand to the Church of England' (Robertson 1849, II, 297).

Heylyn's narrative allowed him to solve several problems. He could demonstrate the enabling activity of Henry VIII and his successors while yet denying that they perpetrated the real reformation; he could defend the reputation of the early reformers – Cranmer, for example; he could condemn the despoiling of the church; he could defend Elizabeth's settlement as a return to Cranmer's church; he could show the returned exiles and leaders of Elizabeth's church as belonging to a distinct and foreign tradition; he could praise Elizabeth for keeping at bay the threat of that further reformation which Foxe and others had seen as her mission to promote.

One of the most important features of Heylyn's account was that it stressed the continuity of tradition between the Catholic church and the Church of England. The apostolic succession had been retained. The deprived Marian bishops, for example, were still bishops although their activities were suspended (Robertson 1849, II, 311–12), because Marian orders were recognized as valid. When Bishop Bonner refused to acknowledge the validity of Horn's Edwardine orders, Elizabeth confirmed the continuity of orders:

> all bishops as were consecrated by that Ordinal in the times precedent, or should be consecrated by it in the time to come, should be reputed to be lawfully ordained and consecrated, to all intents and purposes in the law whatsoever.
>
> (Robertson 1849, I, xiv)

Heylyn's history was, therefore, a Protestant history – he was no Roman – but it was a very different Protestant history from that penned by Foxe. It was a history which stressed the continuity between the English church and the Catholic church stripped of the accretions of the past centuries. It was a history which acknowledged such aid as the Crown had given the process of reformation but which demonstrated the mixed motives of the monarchy and maintained the autonomy of the Church of England. It urged the purity of the church's doctrine and discipline. It emphasized the strength of beauty and holiness. It abhorred attacks upon the authority of the bishops; the liturgy and forms of worship; the wealth of the church; the historical form of government.

Heylyn's book appeared in print just seven years after Thomas Fuller's *Church History* (1655) and must have seemed to be a response to it. Fuller's work bore witness to the continued strength of the Foxian apocalyptic vision. It also displayed its author's moderation and toleration. While Fuller was, like Heylyn, a cleric who served in Charles II's church, he held different views. For example, he believed that episcopacy was the form of church government which most nearly approximated that of the primitive church, but he maintained that it was not a *necessary* mark of a correct, reformed church. For this reason, Fuller had been able to serve the church under the Protectorate also. These views were anathema to a man of Heylyn's persuasion: for Heylyn the rule of the church by a properly constituted episcopate was axiomatic.

More influential than Fuller's *Church History* was Gilbert Burnet's *History of the Reformation of the Church of England* (1865). Burnet (1643–1715) was a Scot (the son of a prominent non-covenanting advocate and a Presbyterian mother of strong character), who began his career as a lawyer in Scotland but then entered the church. In 1664 he spent some time at the English court, joined the newly formed Royal Society, and took up the living of Saltoun in East Lothian, using the Anglican prayers. At about this time he produced a memorial against the abuses of the bishops: 'I laid my foundation on the constitution of the primitive church, and showed how they departed from it.' He persisted in attempts to bring about a diminution of the power of bishops, allying with Archbishop Leighton of Glasgow. Meanwhile he cemented his close relations with Charles II and James of York. He was promoted to the Chair of Divinity at Glasgow in 1660 and continued to further the cause of moderation. In 1671 he was called to London, where he occupied a position of great influence with Secretary Lauderdale. But he fell from favour when Lauderdale changed his policy and underwent considerable persecution. In the mid to late 1670s he spent his time writing and engaging in debate with Roman Catholics. In 1676 he produced his *Vindication of the Ordinations of the Church of England*. And he listened to the urgings of Sir William Jones, Attorney-General, that he write a history of the Reformation. Its publication during the uproar caused by the Popish Plot earned Burnet the praise of Parliament. Burnet's plain speaking to Charles II and the Duke of York lost him their favour, however, and the implication of his friends in the Rye House Plot put him under suspicion. When James ascended the throne, Burnet was forced into exile and became part of the Prince of Orange's circle at The Hague. He played a supportive role in the Revolution and was rewarded by the bishopric of Salisbury. In the House of Lords he stood up for the principles of moderation and toleration.

Why did Burnet write his *History of the Reformation*? In the preface to this work, Burnet explained. The Catholic Nicholas Sanders had attacked the English Reformation with great scurrility in his *De Origine et Progressu Schismatis Anglicani libri tres* first published in Cologne in 1585 and recently reprinted in English. But there was nothing of weight to counter his charges:

Fox [sic], for all his voluminous work, had but few things in his eye when he made his collection, and designed only to discover the corruptions and cruelties of the Roman clergy, and the

> sufferings and constancy of the reformers. But his work was
> written in hast, and there are so many defects in it, that it can
> by no means be called a complete history of these times.
>
> (Pocock 1865, I, 5)

and

> Doctor Heylin wrote smoothly and handsomely, his method
> and style are good, and his work was generally more read than
> anything that had appeared before him: but either he was very
> ill-informed or very much led by his passions; and he being
> wrought on by most violent prejudices against some that were
> concerned in that time, delivers many things in such a manner,
> and so strangely, that one could think he had been secretly set
> on to it by those of the Church of Rome, though I doubt not
> he was a sincere Protestant.

In the absence of a complete history, well authenticated, the bald
account told by the Catholics 'being that it was begun by the lusts
and passion of king Henry the Eighth, carried on by the ravenous-
ness of the Duke of Somerset under Edward the Sixth, and confirmed by the policy of Queen Elizabeth and her council to secure
her title' was given credence.

So Burnet, helped by Jones and by William Lloyd, produced his
answer to Sanders. His narrative attempted to explain the relationship between the policy of England's monarchs and the religious
reformation in a way which would preserve the achievement of
the reformers. He acknowledged that Henry VIII had sought a
break with Rome for personal reasons and had ravaged the
church. He was 'the postilion of the Reformation, made way for
it through a great deal of mire and filth'. 'I am not to defend him,
nor to lessen his faults' protested Burnet, but God used 'to
employ princes who had great mixtures of very gross faults to do
signal things for his service'. He confessed that the behaviour of
Cranmer and others had, on occasion, been less than heroic, but
he defended Cranmer against the charge of servility. With hind-
sight, members of the reformed church might know how Cranmer should have acted, but at the time the correct route was far
from clear. Cranmer and his associates were groping for truth and

'after all this, it must be confessed they were men'. And against the charge of inconstancy Burnet set that of Cranmer's real achievements and his proofs of penitence and humility at the end (Pocock 1865, I, 12, 14, 15, 17).

Burnet's *History* drew upon materials in the Cotton Library and upon sources contributed by John Evelyn and others. He was anxious to offer to the reader a well-documented account of the Reformation. In point of fact, the *History* is, for the most part, a collection of printed sources, but these are pushed into appendices in support of Burnet's interpretation. But Burnet reflected little on the problems of selection. That authentication of the 'facts' was perhaps the least of a historian's problems was not considered.

All the historians who have been mentioned in this chapter were concerned to show the correctness of their accounts. Thomas Fuller dwelt considerably upon the need for the historian to be impartial, well-documented, critical and sceptical, avoiding the contemporary and renouncing bias:

> I know Machiavel was wont to say that he who undertakes to write a history must be of no religion. If so, he, himself, was the best qualified of any in his age to be a good historian. But I believe his meaning was much better than his words; intending therein that a writer of histories must not discover his inclination in religion to the prejudice of truth. . . . This I have endeavoured to my utmost in this book; knowing that oil is adjudged the best which hath no taste at all, so that historian is preferred who hath the least tang of partial reflection.
>
> (Preston 1971, 207)

If Fuller's idea that by quoting his sources he divorced himself from the opinions expressed therein was a new one, it was certainly one which Burnet shared. Burnet, however, felt that more was needed. He criticized Heylyn for not giving references and pledged his own intention to provide full references and bibliography. He acknowledged his own bias against the Catholics, but maintained that he made a conscious effort to look dispassionately at the evidence and draw conclusions based upon it rather than his own prejudices. In fact, Burnet acknowledged that when he checked some of Foxe's references he found that Foxe was accurate. Craig Robertson, Heylyn's nineteenth-century editor, claimed that Burnet, a critic of Heylyn's methodology, had rarely had cause to correct Heylyn's detail in his own account. The point, however, was that full annotation gave the reader the opportunity to check up on the interpretation or facts offered, while in their absence the reader was helpless. Heylyn had used many sources, including the registers of Convocation and the Cotton Library, but because he neglected to give references he was unable to prove that he concealed 'nothing out of fear, nor [spoke] anythings for favour; [delivered] nothing for a truth without good authority; but so [delivered] that truth as to witness for me, that I am neither biassed by love or hatred, nor over-swayed by partiality and corrupt affections' (Pocock 1865, I, xi–xii; II, 667–8; I, xv).

John Strype shared Burnet's desire to write a true history of the Reformation, but with Strype, as with Burnet, the attempt to write such a history has to be set within the context of a contemporary debate.

The Reformation once again became the focus for heated debate in the early years of the eighteenth century. Its immediate occasion was the controversy over different types of churchmanship within the Church of England. On 5 October 1709, Dr Henry Sacheverell preached a sermon attacking Archbishop Tenison and other Whig divines who had maintained the Act of Toleration of 1689 and upheld liberty of conscience (Collinson 1979, 18–20). Sacheverell cloaked his real purpose by naming Edmund Grindal, Elizabethan Archbishop of Canterbury, as the object of his attack. Like most of his contemporaries he saw nothing strange or a-historical about drawing direct parallels between his own age and past times. In his work there was a simple equation: Grindal was Tenison; Elizabeth I the duped Queen Anne.

Sacheverell's attack on 'that false son of the Church Bishop Grindall' drew forth spirited defences of the bishop. One of these was the very strange *Strange News from the Dead*, which purported to be a letter written by Grindal from heaven in his own defence. Better known by far to posterity is *A Brief and True Character and Account of Edmund Grindall*, a laudatory tract by John Strype, vicar of Low Leyton, Essex. Strype followed this by a *History of the Life and Acts of Edmund Grindal*, which boasted a dedication to Archbishop Tenison himself.

It is tempting to see Strype's defence of Grindal as the work of a partisan in contemporary church politics. His action certainly earned him Tenison's attention and he received preferment from the archbishop in 1711. What looked like outright lobbying for place lost Strype many friends. Strype held definite views about the nature of the Church of England. He had long been active in support of these views. But to see the *Life of Grindal* as the product of a search for patronage or even of Strype's conception of the established church is to ignore the reality of Strype's absorption in the history of the Tudor period.

If we are to understand and evaluate the contribution which Strype made to the debate about the English Reformation, then we must understand the nature of his commitment to Tudor history (Morison 1976, Zinberg 1968).

John Strype was born in 1643 to parents of Dutch extraction who were living in London.[2] His father, a naturalized Briton, died some four years later at the age of thirty-nine, leaving his widow, Hester, and five children. On his death-bed the elder Strype, long consumed by the vision that 'these little fists shall thump the pulpit one day', made Hester promise to educate John up to the ministry. As a result, John went to Mistress Howard's day school when he was five, moving when he was seven to board at a private school in Eltham, Kent. After that both he and his brother Samuel were educated by Robert Skingle, MA. When John was fourteen he transferred to St Paul's, where he remained for four years. Because of his academic abilities, Strype was given the personal attention of the Highmaster, Samuel Cromesholme, learning Hebrew, Syriac, Latin and Greek. His favoured position in the school earned him the hatred of the Lowmaster – William Cox – who victimized him. When Strype was severely beaten for an offence which he had not committed, he fled the school 'without books or hat', and only returned on the guaranteee of the Highmaster that the Lowmaster 'would be warned never to

[2] This brief biography is based on Samuel Knight's contemporary Memoir of Strype contained in Cambridge University Library Add. MSS, vols 1–10 (Baumgartner MSS).

middle with him'. In accord with his late father's ambitions, John entered Jesus College Cambridge as a Pauline exhibitioner in 1661, transferring to St Catherine Hall in 1663 when the religious and political climate of Jesus became uncongenial.

Strype's position on conformity was intriguing. His family had supported the Parliamentary Presbyterians after 1649, and his sister and brother-in-law, Hester and John Johnson, had actually provided a haven for Nonconformist ministers in London during the early 1660s. Strype moved from Jesus on religious grounds. Yet, at St Catherine's, Strype was very much influenced by John Lightfoot, the Master, who was a Presbyterian during the interregnum but who conformed in 1662. John Strype was won over to a conformist Anglican position. In 1666 he was ordained both deacon and priest in the Church of England. Strype came to regard the refusal to conform as abhorrent. By 1674 he was categorizing Nonconformists as schismatic. A letter to his friend Richard Salter in December of that year bears witness to Strype's view that the children of Nonconformists should be compulsorily catechized with, if necessary, civil penalties (Letter to Richard Salter, CUL Add. MSS, Letter 12).

Strype's devotion to the English church and his conviction that it must not be undermined by schismatics of either the nonconformist Protestant or Romanist persuasions is clear. Why he should have become so involved with the history of the English Reformation is perhaps less obvious although his churchmanship, in fact, had much bearing upon this involvement. There were three main reasons. One was his inner conviction that the Church of England had been established by divine providence working through the Reformation. The way of the Church of England was the true way for the Christian. It was, therefore, a matter of extreme importance to show what the way of the Church of England was, particularly given the differing contemporary opinions on this very point. Accounts of the Reformation became crucial to this exercise. Another reason for Strype's interest in Reformation history was a combination of opportunity and scholarly inclination. Strype's patron at Low Leyton was Sir William Hicks, the descendant of that William Hicks who had been Lord Burghley's secretary. In 1680 Hicks discovered

Burghley's papers in his possession and he consulted Strype, already a scholar and an antiquary. Strype at first advised publication, but when he appreciated the size of the collection realized that this was scarcely feasible (John Strype's will, PRO, Prob. 11; 'Mr. Strype's Case 1714' CUL, Add. MSS, 40, fol. 7; Catalogue of the Hicks Collection in BL Stowe MSS 1056, fol. 44). Then, intrigued, he questioned John Laughton, Keeper of the Cambridge University Library, on the question of other materials which might supplement the Cecil MSS to provide the basis for a history of the Reformation and of lives of the Elizabethan archbishops. In 1689 he began a search for the papers of Matthew Parker. In 1690 he secured access to Lambeth Palace Library from Archbishop Sancroft and started to use Nicholas Batteley to do research at Lambeth. When he checked the text of Josselin's annotated life of Parker and Gilbert Burnet's *History of the Reformation* against the MSS registers, he began to realize that he would have to be a historian and not just an editor. Batteley addressed many letters to Strype making detailed and telling criticisms of Burnet's treatment, especially of Elizabeth's reign, between January 1691 and February 1693 (e.g. CUL Add. MSS, Letters 32, 36, 38). The idea formed in Strype's mind that he might produce a careful corrective to Burnet's history of Elizabeth's reign, using primary sources to tell the tale. By the spring of 1692 he was contemplating an even more ambitious project to cover the history of the entire Reformation period from Henry the Eighth onwards. Finally, and it was a relatively minor consideration, publication provided a means to attract the attention of eminent patrons. In 1684 he had used his edition of Lightfoot's works and biography to bring himself to Compton's notice (Strype 1684). Now he hoped to achieve national acclaim and patronage by writing a true history of the Reformation – a monumental work which would raise Strype's standing while at the same time lowering that of Gilbert Burnet. His project won him Tenison's regard and esteem, although Strype's unwillingness to compromise himself by toeing the party line was occasionally a source of grievance.

Strype, then, became involved in interpreting the English Reformation as a result of his complacent Anglicanism, his antiquarian and scholarly interests, and his ambition. These facts have a direct bearing on his answer to Sacheverell's diatribe. The defence of Grindal was not a defence of nonconformity or tolerance, but an indignant response to the suggestion that Grindal himself had been subversive. Strype wished to show that this was an evident misreading of the past. Although Whigs used the works on Grindal as a defence of Tenison, Strype had not written them as such. He was happy enough to see Tenison benefiting from his penmanship, but his own interest was in something very different – a defence of the past. Strype was *used* by Whig Parliamentarians and the Low Church party (Morison 1976, 153–88).

Strype's contribution to the historiography of the Reformation was unparalleled. The *Life* of Grindal formed part of a programme which covered the entire Reformation period (Morison 1976). Strype wanted to give a narrative account of the English Reformation to illuminate the manuscript collection in his possession: the Hicks and Foxe manuscripts. In other words, contemporaries would tell their own story. This programme was to an extent interrupted and to an extent complemented by a number of popular biographies designed to make money and to finance the greater works.

Strype's published historical writings commenced with a life of Cranmer, published in 1693. He then went on to write a life of Matthew Parker, Elizabeth's first Archbishop of Canterbury. This was completed by late 1695, but its publication was delayed while Strype worked on the reigns of Edward and Mary, and while the bishops considered the content of the manuscript. In the summer of 1696 Strype handed both books over to the publishers, but their publication was further delayed by the opposition of the bench of bishops and by a serious paper shortage. Shortly before this, however, the bookseller Thomas Cockerill suggested to Strype that he write a series of lives of eminent people aimed at a more popular audience. When Strype replied to him in June 1696 he was not overly enthusiastic, but he nevertheless took up the idea and began work on a life of Sir Thomas Smith. This was published in 1698 in a cheap octavo format and was a commercial success. Encouraged, Strype began to work on a similar life of Bishop Aylmer. Simultaneously he was trying to publish his work on Edward VI on a subscription basis. In 1699 Archbishop Tenison obtained access for him to the State Papers, which he used in connection with both works. In March 1701 he published his *Life* of Aylmer, while engaged upon the life of John Cheke. The *Life* of John Cheke was published in February 1705. By 1707 work on the *Life* of Grindal was already well under way and Strype was also seeking, unsuccessfully, Tenison's support for the publication of his monumental *Annals of the Reformation*. Publication by subscription seemed the only way: accordingly, during 1708, Strype secured sufficient subscribers and published the *Annals* in January 1709.

The works on Archbishop Grindal, published in 1710, preceded the publication of the *Life of Parker* (1711) and the *Life of Whitgift* (1717). The entire corpus of Strype's writings was completed with the publication of the multi-volume *Ecclesiastical Memorials* and *Annals of the Reformation* between 1721 and 1729.

Strype's works on the English Reformation are of supreme importance to scholars. More than any other historian he laid the foundations for the modern study of the Reformation in England and of English church history in general. There can be no question that he wished to write a *true* account of the sixteenth-century Reformation, based upon an exhaustive use of the original sources. He wanted to protect the past against abuse by contemporaries, who were willing to misinterpret historical events to suit their present propagandist purposes. Church historians even now rely on Strype's massive tomes. But how reliable is Strype's history? How scientific was his work? How sound was his interpretation? Let us hear the case for the defence.

Strype certainly approached his historical work in scholarly fashion. He was much influenced by his old mentor, John Lightfoot, whose standards of rigorous biblical criticism Strype applied to historical documents both primary and secondary. He shared Lightfoot's critical sense and his awareness of the superior value of original manuscript sources. Lightfoot had also held the view that biblical writings could not be detached from a historical understanding of the context in which they were penned. All this helps to explain why Strype's works consist of documentary sources with a supporting historical narrative. (Strype 1701, v; Strype 1693, xv, mentions debt to William Somner, author of *The Antiquities of Canterbury*, London 1640, who printed whole documents.)

In his work Strype strove to be impartial. He did not overlook material which cast an unpleasant shadow on the pure origins of his beloved established church. For instance, he noted Lord Burghley's alienation of church lands and revenues for his own personal profit (Strype 1711, 495).

Strype wanted to produce a true narrative account. He had criticized Burnet for misinterpreting the Reformation. He criticized Sacheverell similarly. True to his word, he showed himself more than willing to correct his own errors of fact and interpretation. There are many examples of this willingness, but perhaps the most notable is Strype's readiness to revise his opinion of Bishop Bonner after initial acceptance of John Foxe's account.

In Strype's defence as a historian of worth we cite above all his determination to unearth all the original sources necessary to construct his histories. He gained access to the Foxe MSS, to the official papers of the Province of Canterbury at Lambeth, to the Hicks papers, to the State Papers, to the Parker MSS and to the Wharton Papers. He employed researchers to search these records for him. He drew to the attention of contemporary and future historians the existence, whereabouts and importance of the major collections.

The defence rests. The case for the prosecution is, however, a strong one. Strype's works are defective as history, it maintains, not because his intentions were not laudable – they undoubtedly were – but because their execution faltered. How so?

Firstly, Strype set great store upon accuracy and the use of primary sources but, unfortunately, he did not always practise what he preached. He was horrified by the errors of interpretation which he encountered in Burnet, yet his own researcher, Nicholas Batteley, let him down grievously. The *Life of Cranmer*, published in December 1693, was not well received, at least in part because it was shown to contain many errors. This was due to Batteley's habit of using transcripts of the manuscripts rather than the originals. When Anthony Hamer published his *A Specimen of Some Errors and Defects in Bishop Burnet's History of the Reformation* (1693, *passim*), it became evident that Batteley had not even located the errors in Burnet for himself! Strype was not particularly fortunate in his next researcher, either: Thomas Harrison proved too old and worn for the task of rigorous source raiding. Strype's later researcher, Thomas Baker, was much more reliable.

Some of Strype's unreliability can be put down to his researchers, but not all. Strype boasted of his own care in transcribing original manuscripts but the modern scholar is often shocked by 'Strype's loose, inaccurate mode of copying, and his great liability to mistake'. There are several examples in the *Life of Cranmer* where Strype misread words; omitted phrases and passages without indication; and even conflated different documents without informing his reader of the fact. S. R. Maitland believed that this was because Strype often wrote his volumes on the basis of notes and transcripts made years before, by which time 'he had in great degree forgotten what they were about, and whether they were extracts, abstracts or full copies'. He was more reliable when quoting from papers in his continued possession – the Foxe or Burghley papers – than from notes and transcripts on other collections. Yet mistakes are distressingly frequent whatever the source. On points of detail, Strype was slipshod (Maitland 1849, 4, 5–10).

It is in most cases possible to check Strype's errors of transcription – the documents which he quoted and used are still available. The scholar does not find such a task onerous – no historian worth his or her salt would quote a document from a secondary source without checking its accuracy against the original. The student may not find the task so easy – if the detail in Strype and the interpretation in Strype are unreliable, then the generalist student and reader will be either blissfully unaware of this fact (or at least of the location of the mistakes) or will not have the equipment or time at his disposal to check the account.

Yet more serious by far are the defects in Strype's interpretation of events, often arising from such errors of detail and slipshod technique. For example, James Cargill Thompson showed that Strype was the first church historian to declare that Bancroft's Paul's Cross sermon represented the first statement by a post-Reformation Anglican divine of the *jure divino* theory of episcopacy. Thompson also demonstrated that Strype made this leap, which others like Peter Heylyn and Collier had not, because he 'carelessly misinterpreted a piece of documentary evidence . . . [H]e rashly assumed that a syllogism by Sir Francis Knollys, attacking an unnamed preacher for maintaining that bishops enjoyed their superior authority "jure divino" must refer to Bancroft's sermon, when, in fact – as he should have observed – it explicitly referred to a sermon preached on a different date'. Thompson drew attention to Strype's equally careless handling of the relationship between the committee of divines set up by Elizabeth as a result of the *Device for alteration of religion* in order to draw up a prayerbook and the committee of divines who in fact revised the 1559 Prayer Book. He leapt to the conclusion that they were one and the same, without one shred of solid, incontrovertible evidence to that effect (Thompson 1980, 200).

Another serious problem arises with regard to Strype's interpretation. Strype believed that the sources would speak for themselves and would always tell the truth. It was important, therefore, to quote archival sources.

> In this work I have pursued truth with all forthfullness and sincerity. My relations of things are not hearsays, not taken up at secondhand, or compiled out of other men's published writings; but I have gone as near the fountainhead as possible, that is, to archives, state papers, registers, records and original letters, or else to books of good credit, printed in those times, directing more surely to the knowledge of how affairs then stood.   (Strype 1824, I, vii)

and

> I have chosen commonly to set down things in the very words of the records and originals, and of the authors themselves, rather than in my own, without framing and dressing them into more modern language; thereby the sense is sure to remain entire as the writers meant it. Whereas by affecting too curiously to change and model words, the sense itself, I have observed, often to be marred and disguised.
>   (Strype 1824, I, i, 8)

Thus naively did Strype ignore the whole problem of source selection, of the possibility that the sources themselves told only one side of the story. His works, as a result, reflect the biases of the sources which he relied upon most heavily – the Foxe manuscripts, the state papers, the papers of the bishops and archbishops of the Church of England. Roman Catholics and Puritans alike are under-represented. He sees the English Reformation through the eyes of the establishment and not through the eyes of the critical historian. He did not read the sources, consider their virtues and defects, and then write his own informed account of what happened and why. Instead, he viewed the sources as 'Holy Writ', incapable of challenge.

If the charge be that Strype was unreliable in his handling of the evidence, then the prosecution case seems proven. If, however, the charge is that Strype did not approach his history in the fashion of a modern scientific historian then the case, if demonstrably true, seems unjust. For Strype did not pretend to be such. The works represent Strype's attempt to make the Hicks papers available. As he worked he found that he needed to provide more and more in the way of a narrative to render the documents themselves intelligible to a reader. He went to great lengths to produce just such a narrative and to make it informative. If he was a historian in the twentieth-century sense at all it was by accident rather than by design: probably, in the world of twentieth-century scholarship, he would be an editor.

Once we know that this was Strype's intention, it seems futile to criticize him for producing mere annals rather than history or to charge him with being a 'scissors and paste' merchant. Because he was editing documents, he naturally arranged the material chronologically and treated together episodes with little more in common than their coincidence of date. Because he was editing documents, he naturally sacrificed form and pattern in the interests of intelligibility. There could be no beginning, middle and end to his 'annals' because he was not indulging in history as a literary genre. He was not imposing his interpretation on the past. The manuscripts guided his pen. He stood in the tradition of the great annalists and chroniclers, yes; he heralded the beginning of a long line of great editors, yes; he marked a turning-point in the writing of history – no.

For too long historians have seen Strype as the forerunner of modern scientific historians with their emphasis on the use of archival materials. But Strype – in attempting to be faithful to what happened in the past – explicitly denied himself the role of historian in the modern sense of interpreter. For the modern historian plays a constructive, creative role: he or she imposes a pattern on the past while striving for complete accuracy. No such claims were made by Strype or indeed by any of his contemporaries. Until those who studied the past faced squarely the problems of bias – both in themselves and in their sources – men would continue to believe that it was possible to produce a nonpartisan account or to allow the sources to speak for themselves (Preston 1971).

Strype, then, was no scientific historian in the modern sense of that term. Unlike the modern breed, he did not write an interpretation of the past based on a careful analysis of the primary sources, using quotation to exemplify his points and enliven his prose. Instead, he printed documents verbatim or in paraphrase and inserted a linking narrative, devoid, as he fondly believed, of interpretation. Strype's main significance for the development of history is that he drew attention to the importance of the original sources and, in several cases, was the occasion of their direct and indirect preservation.

If it is the case that Strype's contribution to the development of history as a discipline was much more slight than has sometimes been thought, has he nevertheless made a contribution to the modern debate about the Reformation? After all, we have already noted that he did not want to *interpret* what had occurred, simply to give the truth an airing. Did he, in fact, say anything?

The answer, of course, is yes. Strype saw himself as mute but this does not mean that he was. Both consciously and unconsciously Strype *selected* the sources which he presented to the public. For the most part, the documentation conveyed the establishment's eyeview of the Reformation period. The views of Catholics and Puritans were neglected, as a result. Strype's main contribution to the debate about the English Reformation, therefore, was this. From henceforward the Reformation was seen as the official reformation – the reform of an institution by Crown and ecclesiastics. The development of the Church of England as an institution became all-important to historians. The significance of this point is perhaps best brought out by the prevalence of departments of church history and ecclesiastical history in British universities at the expense of departments of religious history. Strype's bias – picked up from the sources at his command – reinforced the tendency to explore institutional church history and the relationship between this institution and the state to the detriment of other aspects of religious life and experience in Britain.

Chapter 3

Historians and contemporary politics: 1780–1850

In the early nineteenth century, the history of the Reformation was written against the background of the debate about Roman Catholic emancipation which culminated in the passing of the Emancipation Act in 1829. Catholics constituted a tiny minority within England and Scotland – there were perhaps 60,000 in England and half that number in Scotland in 1780. This minority was led by a number of ancient and prominent Catholic peers. According to Cobbett, in October 1821 'to be sure the Roman Catholic religion may, in England, be considered as a gentleman's religion, it being the most ancient in the country'. At the beginning of the eighteenth century, severe penal laws had restricted the lives of these Catholics, but by the reign of George III the application of these laws was much more lenient. From 1771 onwards a number of relief acts were passed to modify the penal legislation. By the Relief Act of 1778, Catholics could henceforward acquire land by inheritance or purchase and open schools without fear of life imprisonment. Freedom of worship was granted by the Relief Act of 1791. In 1793 these concessions were extended to Scottish Catholics. These were tremendous steps forward, but Catholics still suffered from considerable religious and civil disabilities. In Scotland they could not open schools.

Neither Scottish nor English Catholics could celebrate marriages
or funerals in public. Catholics did not have the vote and they
could not hold any rank in the army or navy. A Catholic could not
sit in either House of Parliament. Whereas he could now become
a barrister he could not proceed to become a High Court Judge.
He could not attend either university, where the test acts were
still in force. Living with such restrictions must have been
irksome to Catholics, but even more offensive must have been the
general animosity towards them of the population at large – they
were regarded as a disloyal and alien minority in their native land.
England and Scotland were Protestant countries, imbued with
Protestant values and cultural forms even where active participation in religion was negligible. British Catholics had to accommodate themselves to a generally hostile environment. Civil and
religious emancipation would ease this process, but only a change
of heart in the British populace – aided by Catholic efforts at
effective public relations – could truly integrate the Catholic
community into British society. The Catholics who sought emancipation, therefore, were also concerned to display historical
Catholicism in a more favourable light to their Protestant neigh-
bours in order to improve the general attitude towards Catholicism.

Nineteenth-century historians had a multiplicity of traditions
of Reformation history upon which to draw. The Roman
Catholic tradition was represented both by the polemics of
Catholic writers such as Reginald Pole, Nicholas Sanders,
Nicholas Harpsfield, William Allen and Robert Parsons, and also
by the much quieter, more conciliatory tradition of late Elizabethan writers such as William Watson (1601) and the Appellant
priests. The non-Catholic tradition was yet more varied. Peter
Heylyn and Thomas Fuller, with their clear memories of the
Puritan revolution, and Jeremy Collier, affected by the non-juring
schism, wrote of the beauty of holiness, of the apostolic succession,
of the independence of the English church in convocation, and of
the ancient church. John Foxe was representative of a virulently
anti-Catholic and providential Protestant history – a tradition continued if modified by Gilbert Burnet and John Strype in the late
seventeenth and early eighteenth centuries. The *Chronicle* of

Edward Hall and the *Annals* of William Camden took a more nationalistic, political perspective. The providential and national traditions merged in the Whig histories of the late seventeenth, eighteenth and early nineteenth centuries, typified by those of Burnet and Rapin de Throyas.

Standing apart from the various Catholic and Protestant traditions stood the work of David Hume, *The History of England from the invasion of Julius Caesar to the abdication of King James II, 1688*. Yes, Hume did have an animus against Roman Catholics, but this was coupled with an objection to all religious establishments. For him the word 'religion' spelt 'fanaticism and superstition'. And he challenged the Whig view that the Reformation had been accompanied by an extension of political liberty. He agreed that social progress had accompanied religious change, but saw the Tudor monarchies as despotic and tyrannical, and thoroughly contemptuous of the Constitution. He claimed that the people of England had acquiesced in their subjugation through 'the submissive, not to say slavish, disposition of his parliaments' (Hume 1861, III, 456, 308–9).

> The party among us who have distinguished themselves by their adhering to liberty and popular government, have long indulged their prejudice against the succeeding race of princes, by bestowing unbounded panegyrics on the virtue and wisdom of Elizabeth. They have been so extremely ignorant of the transactions of this reign, as to extol her for a quality which, of all others, she was the least possessed of; a tender regard for the constitution, and a concern for the liberties of her people.
>
> (Hume 1861, III, 344)

All these various traditions were important resources for nineteenth-century British historians. But – a word of caution. Religion was a powerful influence upon nineteenth-century historical writing. Indeed, such writing was often undertaken in the context of contemporary religious controversy and, specifically, the cause of Catholic emancipation. But, while religion united the Roman Catholic controversialists in this fight, politics often divided them, so that Catholics had varied interpretations of the past and wanted different things for the future. The division within Catholicism is best explained in terms of the division between the liberal Catholics who had been affected by the enlightenment and who wanted a more tolerant Roman Catholicism, and the conservative Catholics who asserted the infallibility of the Pope and the divine authority of the bishops. The liberals, led by Charles Butler, a liberal layman, and Joseph Berrington, a Staffordshire priest, had Catholic emancipation as their goal. In 1782 they formed the first Catholic Committee to this end, and in 1787 the second Catholic Committee. In 1792 they founded the Cisalpine Club and became known as the Cisalpinists. The tactic of this branch of Catholicism was to play down the 'foreignness' of Roman Catholicism – to portray Catholics as loyal Britons with no superior allegiance overseas. In his *Appeal to the Catholics of England* (c. 1792), Berrington persisted, 'I am no Papist, neither is my religion Popery.' But the Transalpinists, headed by John Milner, Bishop of Castabala and Vicar-Apostolic of the Midland District, and Charles Plowden, defended papal infallibility and asserted clerical authority over the laity. In their eyes Cisalpinism appeared merely as a despicable Catholic form of Protestantism. So, while both the Cisalpinists and Transalpinists wanted Catholic emancipation, they disliked one another cordially and fought with very different weapons (Drabble 1975).[3]

The Catholic protagonists, of whatever complexion, drew upon a historical armoury for their weapons. In his *Reminiscences*, Charles Butler, Secretary to the Catholic Committee, cheerfully admitted that he had never missed an opportunity to use history to prove his polemical points (Butler 1822, 234). Similarly, John Milner's *The History, Civil and Ecclesiastical, and Survey of the Antiquities of Winchester* (1798–1901) was, in the words of the *Monthly Review* in April 1800, 'a deliberate design and laboured effort to vindicate the avowed patrons of this obnoxious system Roman Catholicism from deserved reproach, and to degrade the most distinguished advocates of that Reformation from popery, to which our country is principally indebted for the civil and

---

[3] For a more detailed account of the Catholic use of history see Drabble, J. (1975) 'The Historians of the English Reformation, 1780–1850' and for a study of the position of the Catholics in early nineteenth-century England see Ward, B. (1911–12) *The Eve of Catholic Emancipation*.

religious liberty by which it has been blessed'. A writer in the *Quarterly Review* in May 1810 urged:

> The History of Winchester is not to be regarded as a mere topo-graphical work. . . . It is a vehicle for 'Truth severe in faery fiction drest'. . . . The subject which Dr Milner has chosen, the periods on which he enlarges with the great alacrity, the nimbleness with which he is ever stepping out of his way to disparage some distinguished character of the Protestant Church, or . . . to rescue some infamy, some champion of his own; these and many other appearances on the face of the work, lead to a suspicion that . . . narrative is but the vehicle for conveying his own principles and doctrines.

The contemporary politico-religious concerns of the nine-teenth-century Catholic polemicists were served by history and shaped their interpretation of the historical past. The works of Joseph Berrington provide an interesting case in point. In 1793 Berrington published *The Memoirs of Gregorio Panzani*, with an introduction and historical supplement. His book contained a feature common to almost all early nineteenth-century Catholic writing: its emphasis upon the reign of Elizabeth, almost to the exclusion of the events of the early official Reformation. In Berrington's case, the reason for this lay in his belief that Elizabeth had no particular religious settlement in mind when she ascended the throne in 1558, notwithstanding her parentage (Berrington 1793, 4). Rather, the activities of the Pope (Paul IV) and his agents had served to convince Elizabeth that a Protestant settlement was essential: 'Paul IV soon took to fix her resolution; and to him, perhaps . . . may be imputed the defection of England from the communion of Rome' (Berrington 1793, 5). Berrington derived this opinion from Peter Heylyn's assessment in the *Ecclesia Restaurata* of 1660. Heylyn claimed that Paul IV had offered a direct insult to Elizabeth via her emissary, charging 'that the kingdom of England was held in fee of the apostolic see; that she could not succeed, being illegitimate' (Robertson 1849, II, 268). Berrington concluded from this that 'the admission of such a monstrous prerogative could not consist with the safety and independence of her throne. If in high and indignant resentment she then made her choice. . . . I may be sorry, but I cannot be surprised' (Berrington 1793, 4).

The departure of England from the Roman communion was to be explained by the Pope's haughty action. Joseph Berrington portrayed Elizabeth as rejecting the papacy in order to preserve her temporal sovereignty. The papacy had, in his opinion, laid claim to powers which were not acknowledged by the Catholic church. For the power of the papacy had always been undefined and restrained by councils and bishops. In a series of works, then, Berrington attacked the 'prerogative which arrogant ambition had usurped, and which, for a long time, the weakness or ignorance of mankind durst not infringe'.

In adopting this line Berrington was making a strong historical case for the tightening of restrictions upon the powers of the contemporary papacy. In 1790 the Pope had annoyed many of the Catholic laity by seeking to appoint to two vacant sees over the heads of the Catholic Committee. Democracy within the Catholic church and national control were crucial contemporary issues. Berrington was toeing the line of his patron, Sir John Throckmorton, who had in 1792 described His Holiness as a 'foreign prelate' who, by appointing English bishops himself, had usurped the ancient privileges of the clergy. Throckmorton had in that same year argued that English Catholics might take the Oath of Supremacy because Queen Elizabeth had taken only the temporal power of the Pope and had been loath to assume spiritual power. Rubbing salt into the wounds of the Transalpinists, Berrington supported his patron's argument by citing the work of Charles Plowden's brother, Francis, on the nature of the royal supremacy.

Praise was reserved by Berrington for those loyal Catholics who had 'in silent resignation bowed their heads conscious that to submit to the laws . . . was their Christian duty' and blame showered upon those who, consumed with missionary zeal, had travelled to Catholic seminaries abroad and imbibed the traitorous tenets taught therein. Berrington pointed out that persecution of English Catholics had not been severe until the 1570s and that it would not have grown severe 'if we had founded no foreign seminaries, we had provided no foreign laws'. Unfortunately for Catholics in England, the new priests courted and achieved persecution and martyrdom. All this, Berrington urged, was proven by the fact that the old priests were not persecuted nor even the new in so far as they condemned papal tyranny (Berrington 1793, 15–16, 24, 29).

In making this case, Berrington made Robert Parsons the arch-villain of the piece:

> a man with the sound of whose name are associated intrigue, device, stratagem, and all the crooked policy of the Machiavellian school . . . whose whole life was a series of machinations against the sovereignty of his country, the succession of its crown, and the interests of the secular clergy of his own faith. Devoted to the most extravagant pretensions of the Roman Court . . . pensioned by the Spanish monarch . . . his work has helped to perpetuate dissensions, and to make us, to this day, a divided people.   (Berrington 1793, 25–8)

This perspective, which so suited Berrington's and Throckmorton's present purpose, was not original but was derived directly from the writings of the Elizabethan appellant priests. In 1585 thirty priests had appealed to Rome against the appointment of George Blackwell by the Pope as archpriest, coupling this with a denunciation of the seditious Jesuits. Of the appellant writings, William Watson's *Important Considerations or a Vindication of Queen Elizabeth from the charge of unjust severity towards her Roman Catholic subjects* . . . is perhaps the best known to posterity and was certainly the most useful to Berrington's case. Watson's charge that the Jesuits were guilty of high treason and the appellant priests' signature of a declaration of allegiance, denouncing the bull deposing Elizabeth and affirming their loyalty to the Crown, were invaluable weapons in his arsenal.

This interpretation of royal policy – that of a queen anxious to create a church which would tolerate if not embrace Catholic subjects, provided that they were loyal – naturally did not find favour with the Transalpinist Catholic writers. Far from laying the blame for the persecution of Elizabethan recusants at the door of the Catholics, these writers returned it to the porticoes of Elizabeth's palace. '. . . the penal laws were the cause of the seminaries, not the seminaries of the penal laws', stormed John Milner in his

Ecclesiastical Democracy. Milner agreed that these laws were not rigorously enforced until after the founding of Douai in 1568, the Northern Rebellion and the Bull of Deposition, but Charles Plowden insisted that Elizabeth had never pursued a line of moderation towards her Catholic subjects. She had, he said, acted not only against Cardinal William Allen and Robert Parsons, but also against the adherents of the old religion. Plowden, moreover, vigorously defended Robert Parsons against the charges of treason. He alleged that Parsons's letters were evidence of his charitable and peaceful spirit and that the education of seminary priests did not concern itself with politics (Plowden 1794, 76, 84–6, 147–8).

> I, who have searched for the guilt of the first seminarists through volumes of MS records and letters written, have not yet discovered a trace, a symptom of any plot or contrivance to dethrone or to destroy Elizabeth, in which the founders of the seminaries, or any of their friends or dependents had the smallest concern.   (Plowden 1794, 147–8)

His conclusion was that, as there existed no evidence of treacherous activity, Parsons and his co-religionists died for their speculative beliefs and not because of Elizabeth's well-founded fear for her kingdom at their hands.

The question of Catholic loyalty to the English Crown was indeed a pressing issue. The first Catholic Relief Act had been passed in 1778. This imposed an oath of allegiance upon Catholics. Transalpinists such as Milner and Plowden objected strongly. By the 1790s the issue of loyalty was again uppermost. Within England, the Catholics were finally admitted into the legal profession, and English Roman Catholic churches and schools were freed from penal disabilities. But there was widespread fear of Jacobins and in Ireland there was political unrest. The latter resulted in rebellion in 1798. The English government proposed a veto on Irish episcopal appointments for political reasons. Such suggestions were rejected both before the Act of Union (1801) and after (1808), but were still under discussion in 1813. In 1813 a Bill for the Relief of English Catholics, which contained a clause for a royal veto and a clause allowing commissioners to examine papal bulls on non-spiritual matters, was entered. This was defeated, at least partly due to the determined opposition of John Milner. Future Catholic Relief Bills (1813, 1819, 1821) all contained guarantees of Catholic loyalty.

Pressing though the issue of loyalty was, the English Catholics trod circumspectly when it came to dealing with the question in their histories. In his *History of Winchester*, Milner expressed sympathy for English Catholics who had acknowledged the Pope's spiritual supremacy without 'ascribing to him one atom of temporal authority' and who had never had any charge of treason proved against them (Milner 1798–1801, 385–6). Milner was understandably wary of treating the question of the papal claim to a right to depose heretical princes. In 1800 he considered the issue in *Letters to a Prebendary*. Here he alleged that this right was a speculative doctrine rather than an article of the faith and, more-over, one that had never gone unchallenged by Roman Catholics. In so far as the Pope did have such a right, it pertained to him as first bishop, and therefore arbiter, of Christendom rather than as a temporal prince. And Elizabethan Catholics had never accepted the bull deposing Elizabeth: 'The fact is, only one person in their whole number, John Felton, a lay gentleman, who affixed it to the door of the bishop of London's house, is known to have approved of it, for which he died, condemned by the whole Cath-olic body no less than by the Protestant' (Milner 1800, Letter VI). Berrington, as has been noted, berated the papacy and the Jesuit priests of England for maintaining the papal right to depose the queen. He drew a picture of a Catholic community divided between the loyal and quiescent Marian priests and the disloyal missionaries. Charles Butler was more equivocal. In his *Historical Memoirs of English Catholics* he maintained that both Elizabeth and the Pope had acted imprudently, but he nevertheless felt that the Pope was more to be criticized than the Crown. The deposing bull of Pius V was, according to Butler, 'ever to be condemned and ever to be lamented' (Butler 1819, I, 347–8). When it came to assigning guilt among the missionary priests, Butler's discovery of a British Museum manuscript which dealt with the responses of missionary priests to six questions on the deposing power of the papacy forced him into a moderate position. Campion and two others were found guilty and executed; three were explicitly exonerated; many were evasive. Butler noted that the pardon of those priests who answered the questions to the satisfaction of the examiners indicated that a specific disclaimer of papal claims to deposing power would have ensured better treatment for English Catholics. At the same time, he had to acknowledge that, while a few missionary priests were disloyal, the great majority of English Catholics were loyal to the Crown. However, when it came to the crunch, Catholics were killed, not because they acknowledged the deposing power of the papacy, but because Elizabeth had made treasonable the denial of her *spiritual* supremacy (Butler 1819, I, 212, 343–4, 347–8, 426; II, 46). Another historian, John Lingard, completely exonerated the missionary priests of charges of disloyalty. He argued that Elizabeth should not have executed men whose answers were merely evasive – instead she should have offered liberty of conscience in exchange for adjuration of the temporal pretensions of the papacy. Lingard went on to minimize the extent to which the Catholics had encouraged plotting against Elizabeth and to criticize the quality of the evidence against English Catholic rebels at the trials of the Duke of Norfolk, Throckmorton and Babington (Lingard 1827, VIII, 112–14).

If loyalty was a crucial contemporary issue projected back on to a historical screen, then intolerance was no less so. The entire Protestant tradition rested on the belief that Catholics had persecuted adherents of the new religion both cruelly and needlessly. The impact of Foxe's *Acts and Monuments* had been profound and lasting. Roman Catholics in the nineteenth century, as before, recoiled at such charges, but the matter had a new urgency at a time when these same Roman Catholics were seeking practical toleration and emancipation from the penal laws under a Protestant government. Once again, Catholic writers unashamedly sought to vindicate sixteenth-century Catholicism in order to improve their contemporary lot. In *Letters to a Prebendary*, John Milner put it like this:

> If it be proved that Catholics are bound by their principles to persecute and extirpate persons of a different religion from themselves, it is absurd in them to look up to a Protestant legislature for any extension of their civic privileges. . . . But if this

charge can be refuted, there does not remain a pretext for the
continuance of these penal laws, which still exist against them.
(Milner 1800, 111)

For this reason, he accorded the Marian burnings a good deal of
attention – they had been used by Protestant writers to justify the
spirit of resentment and counter-persecution of Catholics.

'First, then, it is to be observed, that, if Mary was a persecutor,
it was not in virtue of any tenet of her religion that she became so'
urged Milner in *The History of Winchester* (Milner 1798–1801,
355). Rather her persecutions were a defensive response to Protestant acts of militancy – Wyatt's rebellion; seditious printed
propaganda; attempts on her life; prayers for her death. He
conceded that there were a few intolerant Catholics who urged
Mary to persecute, but alleged that their number was more than
balanced by Protestant fanatics and was, moreover, unrepresenta-
tive of the majority of Catholics. Cleverly, Milner looked to
earlier Protestant histories to indicate Mary's tolerance. He used
Heylyn, Dodd, Phillips and Collier most skilfully. Other writers
adopted a similar line – sometimes marshalling the evidence to
better effect than Milner. John Lingard, for example, provided
detailed evidence of Mary's tolerant attitude to Lady Jane Grey
and Elizabeth after Wyatt's Rebellion, of Elizabeth's implication
in Wyatt's Rebellion, and of Protestant provocation. Interestingly, he challenged the documentary foundation for Bishop
Burnet's picture of Gardiner as a persecutor: 'This charge is not
supported by any authentic document: it is weakened by the
general tenor of the chancellor's conduct', and of Bonner as
initiator of persecution (Lingard 1827, vii, 154, 158).

Both Milner and Lingard demonstrated at times an awareness
that attitudes and values had changed since the sixteenth century.
Lingard maintained, for instance, that, if Mary had been intolerant, then this was to a great extent because she was a product of
her own times and of her own education. He stressed the discrep-
ancy between her age and the more tolerant nineteenth century:

After every allowance it will be found that, in the space of four
years, almost two hundred persons perished in the flames for

religious opinion;[4] a number at the contemplation of which the mind is struck with horror, and learns to bless the legislation of a more tolerant age, in which dissent from established forms, though in some countries still punished with civil disabilities, is nowhere liable to the penalties.

(Lingard 1827, vii, 168–9)

Milner also sought to stress that intolerance had been a feature of sixteenth-century culture, not specific to Catholicism and, indeed, perhaps even more characteristic of Protestantism. Milner, Charles Butler and Lingard all expended a good deal of energy constructing a Catholic martyrology from a variety of sources and an analysis of penal legislation against the Catholics.

Once historians appreciated that historical context was all important, it became, of course, much more difficult to project contemporary controversies back into the past. Catholicism in Mary's reign had been shaped by sixteenth-century events, habits of mind and education. Nineteenth-century Catholicism could, in reality, justify its claims to full integration into British society by an appeal to nineteenth-century conditions and attitudes. But neither Lingard nor any other Catholic historian faced up to this implication and took the next step. Blithely they sought to vindicate contemporary Catholicism by an analysis of Catholic and Protestant behaviour under Mary despite their acknowledgement that this behaviour had been moulded by now extinct forces.

It was thought necessary to divert Protestant attention from the persecuting activities of Gardiner, Bonner and Pole under Mary I by vilification of Thomas Cranmer. Looking back upon writings of the period by Catholics and Protestants, Dean Hook explained:

> By party writers, on one side an attempt is made to represent Cranmer as a persecutor, and on the other, to explain away his share in the religious persecution under the reigns of Henry and Edward, and to make him appear as tolerant as . . . so far as the rack and the stake are concerned . . . men are compelled to be in the nineteenth century. (Hook 1868, vii, 62)

---

[4] In fact, three hundred died.

This vilification took an extreme form in the works of Milner and Butler, but it was Lingard's *History* which prompted the Protestants to answer in the form of a veritable flood of lives of and defences of Cranmer in the 1820s and 1830s. In these writings much turned upon whether or not Cranmer had opposed the deaths of John Frith, John Lambert and Joan Boucher. The writers concerned became involved in a detailed examination of the evidence in order to establish the truth of their cases. For example, there was much debate about the true meaning of the *Reformatio Legum Ecclesiasticarum* – the reformed code of the canon law begun under Henry VIII and continued under his son – which Cranmer had helped to prepare. Lingard argued that the code was an instrument designed specifically with mass murder of Catholics in mind. In so doing he reviewed previous interpretations of the code, denying Burnet's assertion that title three (which dealt with the punishment of heretics) abolished capital punishment for heresy and following Jeremy Collier, who had in his *Ecclesiastical History* maintained that thenceforth heretics were handed over to the secular power for punishment by the death penalty. Lingard argued that the word 'punishment' in the *Reformatio* meant nothing less than 'privation of life'.

> Fortunately for the professors of the ancient faith, Edward died before this code had obtained the sanction of the legislature: by the accession of Mary the power of the sword passed from the hand of one religious party to those of the other; and within a short time Cranmer and his associates perished in the flames which they had prepared to kindle for the destruction of their opponents.   (Lingard 1827, VII, 153–4)

Unsurprisingly, this sparked a Protestant outcry, particularly in the pages of Henry John Todd's *A Vindication of the Most Reverend Thomas Cranmer, Lord Archbishop of Canterbury and therewith of the Reformation of England against some of the allegations which have recently been made by the Reverend Dr Lingard, the Rev. Dr Milner and Charles Butler Esq.* (London, 1826). Todd argued that the British Museum manuscript of the code indicated, in a clarifying note, that no terror was intended by Cranmer, 'either that he may be driven into banishment for life, or thrust into the perpetual darkness of a prison . . . or punished at the discretion of the magistrate, in any other way which may seem to be most expedient towards his conversion' (Todd 1826, 333). But Lingard, using Strype, was able to show that the British Museum manuscript represented a draft and not the finished version of the code at all. In the final resort, Lingard, Milner and Butler were unable to make a watertight case against Cranmer, however, because of the inscrutability of the language used in the *Reformatio* and elsewhere. Careful textual criticism, appeals to past historians and the evidence of the persecutions themselves could yield just so much and no more. Ultimately, interpretation still had to be called into play (Lingard 1827).

Already, by their efforts to vindicate the past behaviour of Catholics in Britain and thereby to make Catholic emancipation more acceptable to the British public and, especially, her ruling class, the Catholic historians had challenged the traditional Protestant interpretation of the Reformation in several important respects. Catholicism, they urged, had never been a disloyal, seditious and 'foreign' force in Britain. The persecuting spirit had never been a characteristic peculiar to Catholicism. Catholics, like Protestants, had been products of their own age and had shared sixteenth-century attitudes to toleration of contrary beliefs. But they, unlike the Protestants, did not rejoice in the task of persecution.

It would be possible, on these grounds alone, to make a strong case that these Catholic historians had brought about a major revision of traditional interpretations of the Reformation, but their chief challenge to orthodox views of the Reformation lay elsewhere. Prior to this, Protestant historians had portrayed the English Reformation as a spiritual reformation – a cleansing operation, a purging of the corruption of the body of medieval Catholicism, a return to primitive purity. Even historians interested in the church as an institution, and even those concentrating upon the political and national ramifications of the process, nevertheless shared this overall view. Now Catholic writers of reputation forced a reassessment and a response from Protestant writers.

This is not to say, of course, that earlier writers had not acknowledged Henry VIII's baser motives. Catholic polemicists of the sixteenth century had not hesitated to expose that monarch's weakness: 'He gave up the Catholic faith for no other reason in the world than that which came from his lust and wickedness'. Protestant historians such as Gilbert Burnet were undeceived by Henry's claims to godliness, but preferred to marvel at the mysterious ways through which the Almighty worked and to draw attention to the sanctity of the reformers who carried out his work:

> He attacked popery in its strongholds in the monasteries, and thus he opened the way to all that came after, even down to our days. So, that while we see the folly and weakness of man in all his personal failings, which were many and very enormous, we at the same time see both the justice, the wisdom and the goodness of God, in making him, who was once the pride and glory of popery, become its scourge and destruction; and in directing his pride and passion so to bring about, under the dread of his unrelenting temper, a change that a milder reign could not have compassed without great convulsions in rescuing us by this means from idolatry and superstition; from the vain and pompous show in which the worship of God was dressed up, so as to vie with heathenism itself, into a simplicity of believing, and a purity of worship, conforming to the nature and attributes of God, and the doctrine and example of the Son of God.
>
> (Pocock 1865, III, 303)

Nevertheless, the Catholic writers of the early nineteenth century forced Protestants to face up to the charge that the Reformation had not been a spiritual cleansing at all, but a division of the spoils of the wealthy but pristine Catholic church by money-grubbing monarchs, courtiers and climbers. Not only Henry came under attack, but also accepted Protestant martyrs and heroes. And the Catholic historians, moreover, backed up their charges with a reliance upon original documentation which their Protestant counterparts found more uncomfortable and more difficult to compass than mere polemic.

The Catholic attack upon the godliness of the Protestant Reformation was many-pronged. Broadly speaking, it combined a

defence of Catholic sanctity with an assault upon Protestant spirituality. The balance struck between these two lines of attack in
the writings of Catholic authors varied: those who wanted reconciliation with the Protestants (the Cisalpinists) tended to spend
far less time vilifying the Protestants than did the hard-nosed
Catholic Transalpinists.

Here it is sufficient to look in some detail at the attacks made
upon the sixteenth-century Protestants in three areas – the dissolution of the monasteries; the Protestantism of Anne Boleyn; the
character of Archbishop Cranmer – and the responses which these
elicited among Protestants.

Most of the Catholic histories played down the corruption of
the monastic ideal in England and emphasized the base motives
for the Henrician dissolution. For Milner and Butler it was possible to sum up the motivation for the dissolution in one word –
avarice. The results of the closure of the monastic houses had been
felt in society as a whole immediately: charitable and educational
provision had been irreparably damaged. The effects of the
abolition of religious orders were, moreover, long-lasting. John
Milner also decried the cultural effects of the plunder of
England's monasteries and cathedrals. In his article on Gothic
Architecture in *The Cyclopaedia* (1800 edn) he lauded Gothic as
an achievement both sublime and beautiful, and regarded its
defacement by the Protestants as barbarous and soulless in the
extreme. To such writers the monastic ideal, in its medieval
flowering, characterized a Christian system in which the great
and powerful and wealthy cared for the poor and weak and needy
in such a way that God was praised. Alone among them stood
Joseph Berrington, who seriously doubted the value of the
monastic institutions as they stood in the early sixteenth century
(Milner 1798–1801, 102–30; 1800, 39–65; Berrington 1799,
654).

Milner's account left the reader in no doubt about his interpretation of Henry VIII's motivation in suppressing the monasteries
or his view of the value of the religious houses in English society.
Henry VIII was a hypocrite among hypocrites – even a
Protestant historian such as Jeremy Collier confessed that 'The
suppression of the monasteries was thought the easiest way of

furnishing the exchequer' – but Milner exposed the king's attempts to conceal this motivation:

> Nevertheless, to give colour to these proceedings, a visitation of all the convents, that were marked out for destruction, was set on foot, by the king's active vice-gerent, Thomas Cromwell, under pretence of reforming, by his ecclesiastical authority, the abuses that had crept into them. But the Commissioners . . . made use of such arts and violence, as did not fail of answering the intention of their employers, by furnishing a pretext, grounded on the feigned motive of religion, for an act of parliament, by which all monasteries, whose revenues did not amount to the sum of 200 l., were to be dissolved.
>
> (Milner 1798–1801, 329)

Henry's deceit might have been bearable had the charges levelled against the religious orders been true. But they were not. Milner looked at Stow's chronicles for evidence that the religious houses had been popular and that their closure was 'not generally acceptable to the people'.

> These complaints of course became much louder at the suppression of the greater abbeys. These, as they had it more in their power, so they were generally more beneficial to the public. By their doles and alms they entirely provided for the poor, insomuch that no poor-laws existed until soon after their dissolution. The monks let their farms at easy rents, and made allowances for unfavourable seasons, so that abundance and population increased around them. They received into their houses and entertained strangers of all conditions, according to their rank, *gratis*. They provided hospitals for the indigent sick, and seminaries for poor children. Their magnificent churches were the schools of the arts, both liberal and mechanical, and their scriptoria and libraries were the only asylum of the sciences and of classical literature.
>
> (Milner 1798–1801, 333)

Yet the whole infrastructure of social welfare in Tudor England was swept away simply 'to gratify the passions of one sensual king and to raise the families of a few wicked courtiers'.

This attack upon the traditional view of the monasteries and their position in English society before the Reformation is interesting to us chiefly because of the response it drew forth from non-Catholic contemporaries involved in nineteenth-century politics. It opened the floodgates for a Tory-radical critique of English society in the early nineteenth century, and particularly of the provision for the poor and needy within England.

The most significant work in this new tradition was undoubtedly William Cobbett's *A History of the Protestant Reformation in England and Ireland* (1824–7) which had as its subtitle the words 'showing how that event has impoverished the main body of the people in those countries'. Cobbett appears to have become interested in the subject as a result both of reading Lingard and of observing the plight of his many Catholic constituents in Preston, but he also related the matter to the contemporary debate over poor relief. At the same time his *Political Register* was actively espousing the cause of Catholic Emancipation in Ireland.

Cobbett's *Protestant Reformation* can scarcely be regarded as a work of history at all: it is a work of literary invective, of caricature, of political polemic. But it is extremely important because it is a prime example of the ease with which an interpretation of historical events can be popularized and seep almost unnoticed into national consciousness. Cobbett's book produced a new and powerful *social* interpretation of the Reformation which has had a profound influence upon both nineteenth- and twentieth-century perceptions of socio-economic developments.

For, to Cobbett, the Reformation signalled the introduction of oppression into English society. Prior to the dissolution of the monasteries, the religious had cared for the poor, sick and needy. As far as Cobbett was concerned, the punchline of Milner's account had been, 'insomuch that no poor laws existed until soon after their dissolution'. For the caring community had provided for the poor and there had been no need for oppressive legislation. After the Reformation all that had changed. Poverty and need were born. The rich rode roughshod over the rabble. Cobbett's *History of the Protestant Reformation* replaced the view of the Reformation as a blow fought for human freedom and intellectual honesty with a new and harsher indictment:

> The Reformation, as it is called, was engendered in beastly lust, brought forth in hypocrisy and perfidy, and cherished and fed by plunder, devastation, and by rivers of English and Irish blood, and that, as to its more remote consequences, they are, some of them, now before us in that misery, that beggary, that nakedness, that hunger, that everlasting wrangling and spite, which now stare us in the face and stun our ears at every turn, and which the 'Reformation' has given us in exchange for the ease and happiness and harmony and Christian charity enjoyed so abundantly, and for so many ages, by our Catholic fore-fathers.   (Cobbett 1824–7, 4)

The Reformation had destroyed the natural unity of the English and Irish peoples, and had set them at one another's throats. It had provided a justification, by devious and deplorable means, for the hatred of and oppression of Catholics within the community. Worse still, it had impoverished the people: 'It was not a refor-mation but a devastation of England, which was, at the time when this event took place, the happiest country, perhaps that the world had ever seen, and, it is my chief business to show that this devastation impoverished and degraded the main body of the people' (Cobbett 1824–7, 19).

In telling the story of the English Reformation, Cobbett was declaredly and unashamedly didactic for, to his mind, 'the great use of history is to teach us how law, usages and institutions arose, what were their effects on the people, how they promoted public happiness or otherwise; and these things are precisely what the greater part of historians, as they call themselves, seem to think of no consequence'. So he set out to show the ways in which the monasteries had benefited the community and 'especially how they operated on behalf of the labouring and poorer classes of the people', and to demonstrate the grievous consequences of their destruction. In particular, he attacked the system of tithe pay-ments to the clergy and the married priesthood: 'In short, do we not know that a married priesthood and pauperism and poor rates all came upon this country at one and the same moment?' (Cobbett 1824–7, 19, 26–7, 123–4).

To serve his didactic and partisan purpose Cobbett employed every trick in the book. Catherine of Aragon he portrayed almost as a saint, certainly as a paragon. Thomas Cranmer 'a name which deserves to be held in everlasting execration' and the justice of God was upheld only by 'our knowledge of the fact that the cold-blooded, most perfidious, most impious, most blasphemous caitiff expired, at last, amidst those flames which he himself had been the chief cause of kindling'. The *Acts and Monuments* was described as 'lying Fox's lying book of Protestant Martyrs!', Good Queen Bess became none other than a 'gross, libidinous, nasty shameless old woman'. The standard techniques of popular journalism – rhetorical questions, colourful language and heaped adjectival abuse – aided Cobbett's presentation: sarcasm and pillory abetted it. Speaking of the divorce from Aragon the Paragon, Cobbett wrote:

> Having provided himself with so famous a judge in ecclesiasti-cal matters, the king lost, of course, no time in bringing his hard case before him, and demanding justice at his hands! Hard case indeed; to be compelled to live with a wife of forty-three when he could have, for next to nothing and only for asking, a young one of eighteen or twenty! A really hard case; and he sought relief, now that he had got such an upright and impar-tial judge, with all imaginable dispatch.
>
> (Cobbett 1824–7, 32, 188)

If we must not look to Cobbett for a work of historical accuracy, of scholarship and caution, we must none the less look to him for the popularization of an interpretation of the Refor-mation which has had a profound effect upon the Reformation debate down to and including the present day – that the Refor-mation devastated social provision in the interests of a rapacious monarch and a hungry aristocracy.

As we can see, he also picked up on two of the other hallmarks of the Catholic school of writers in the early century – the role of Anne Boleyn and the character of Thomas Cranmer. The treat-ment of Cranmer by early nineteenth-century historians was in

fact but a much intensified version of their treatment of other Protestant heroes and martyrs. Milner, for example, associated Latimer,
Hooper and Ridley with every imaginable vice. Ridley and Hooper
were charged with pillaging the church; Hooper was accused of
violating his vows as a Cistercian by leaving the order and marrying
a former nun; Latimer and Ridley were both alleged to have dis-
sembled their own Protestant views under Henry VIII and to have
persecuted Protestants. Even Charles Butler, who wanted reconciliation with the Protestants, was tempted to describe Latimer as a
mere temporizer. But by far the most potent attack on a Reformation leader was John Lingard's attack on Cranmer.

In examining the impact of Lingard's treatment, it is as well to
be aware of the prevailing attitude to Cranmer's role in the
English Reformation prior to Lingard's intervention. Although
there had been criticisms of Cranmer from both Protestants and
Catholics in the sixteenth and early seventeenth centuries, Cranmer had been eulogized by mainstream Protestant writers since
the Civil War. Gilbert Burnet dubbed him 'a man raised by God
for great services, and well fitted for them' and went on to set the
record straight.

> He was naturally of a mild and gentle temper . . . and yet his
> gentleness did not lead him into such a weakness of spirit, as to
> consent to everything that was uppermost . . . . He was a man
> of great candour; he never dissembled his opinion, nor dis-
> owned a friend. He laid out all his wealth on the poor and pious
> uses . . . . His last fall was the only blemish on his life; but he
> expiated it with such a sincere repentance and a patient mar-
> tyrdom.   (Pocock 1865, II, 537–8)

And Strype was the Archbishop's most ardent admirer:

> The name of this most reverend prelate deserves to stand upon
> eternal record; having been the first Protestant Archbishop of
> this kingdom, and the greatest instrument, under God, of the
> happy Reformation of this Church of England . . . . He was a
> very rare person, and one that deserves to be reckoned among
> the brightest lights that ever shone in this English Church.
>   (Strype 1840, II, 1, 658)

What Lingard and Milner attempted to do was to strip Cranmer of the aura of spirituality with which he had been endowed by Burnet and Strype. Earlier we noted how he was vilified as a persecutor. Lingard and Milner went much further than this. Milner charged that, throughout his life, Cranmer 'exhibited such a continued scene of libertinism, perjury, hypocrisy, barbarity . . . profligacy, ingratitude, and rebellion, as is, perhaps, not to be matched in history'. The scandals regarding Cranmer's two marriages and the smuggling of his second wife into England in a chest; the tales of Cranmer's hypocrisy and the stories of his obsequious behaviour towards Henry VIII were all wheeled out as proof of the Archbishop's base nature (Drabble 1975). Lingard, whose account was much more influential than Milner's because it was less partisan in tone, indicated that Cranmer was given position in order to secure a divorce for Henry and that he duly kept his part of the bargain. H. J. Todd contradicted this view of Cranmer as sycophantic time-server, but Lingard insisted that Cranmer was but a mere lap-dog of Anne Boleyn, intent only on doing her bidding. Lingard similarly countered Protestant arguments that Cranmer remained loyal to his friends, especially Anne Boleyn and Thomas Cromwell, at great personal risk and that he opposed the Six Articles of persecution. Lingard's case was all the stronger because he used original documentary sources to prove his points. Cranmer's sycophancy and extreme personal ambition were emphasized (Lingard 1827, vi, 153, 77–80).

Although as we shall see, Protestant writers sprang to the archbishop's defence, the Roman Catholic critique had a pronounced effect upon the verdict of later nineteenth-century Protestants. For instance, both Canon Dixon and Dean Hook had absorbed the view that Cranmer had used the divorce as a route to preferment. It was now more difficult, given the evidence that Lingard adduced, to cast Cranmer as a plaster saint – if he was such then he certainly had feet of clay! (Hook 1868, iv, 467–8).

The defence of Cranmer immediately drawn forth by Lingard's *History* – H. J. Todd's *Vindication of the Most Reverend Thomas Cranmer*, 1831 – was very largely a restatement of Burnet. Todd insisted that Cranmer had been extremely reluctant to accept the see of Canterbury, despite Lingard's suspicion of Burnet's account. Todd felt that Cranmer's own account of the affair should be accepted at its face value. Similarly, Todd followed Burnet in maintaining that Cranmer had publicly protested against the oath to the papacy, whereas Lingard alleged that the protest was only made in private. Todd, like Lingard, produced manuscript sources to defend his interpretation of Cranmer's activities, but his work did not further the debate (Todd 1831, 50–3).

There can be little doubt that Cranmer's stature as a saintly reformer was imperilled by Lingard's work and that Todd and other Protestant writers were hard put to it to defend his reputation.

If they found it difficult to protect Cranmer's reformation standing, then they found it impossible to defend that of Anne Boleyn, a lady whose reputation was already besmirched. The issue of the Aragon divorce had long made historians uneasy. Catholics had tended to blame Cardinal Wolsey. Gilbert Burnet and David Hume saw that the issue was much more complicated than that: there had been problems in Henry's marriage to Catherine from the start; these problems intensified as time went on, especially as Catherine failed to produce a living heir male; Wolsey came to see Catherine as standing in the way of his vaunting ambition; and then Anne Boleyn captivated the king and monopolized him. Lingard, however, saw things in much simpler terms: 'The lust of Henry generated the independence of the English Church.' He revived the suggestion that Henry had had Anne's sister Mary as his previous mistress and he discovered the documentation to prove it. He alleged that Anne had been in England as early as 1522 and had been an early cause of Henry's dissatisfaction with Catherine of Aragon and not just the later catalyst of events – again he produced documentary evidence which supported this view. Lingard's character-assassination of Anne Boleyn was thorough. He maintained, like Cardinal Pole, that Anne 'artfully kept her lover in suspence, but tempered her resistance with so many blandishments, that his hopes, though repeatedly disappointed were never totally extinguished'. But her virginity was as tactical as that of her famed daughter, Elizabeth, much later. It served to make Henry scrupulous about his marriage with the wife of his late brother. It whetted his appetite and made him dream of marriage. Both Burnet and Hume had asserted that Anne maintained her chastity until her marriage to Henry in November 1532, ten months before Elizabeth's birth. Lingard shocked the public by alleging that Anne became Henry's mistress in 1529, months before the meeting of the Reformation Parliament. He even produced a letter, written by Cranmer, which suggested that the marriage did not take place until 25 January 1533, when Anne was already pregnant by Henry. And from the Vatican Archives he unearthed a dated letter from 1527 which contained the words: '*Ayant este plus qu'une anne attaynte du dart d'amours, non estant assure de faliere, trouver place en votre coeur et affection*' (Drabble 1975).

Lingard's account elicited a response from an anonymous author in the *Quarterly Review* which attacked the nature of Lingard's interpretation:

> Dr Lingard details the whole progress of the amour (between Henry and Anne) during five years, with the precision and accuracy of one of Marivaux' novels. His authorities for all this are a few dateless letters, and a furious invective by Henry's enemy, Cardinal Pole. The finished coquette, who, coldly and with ambitious calculation, for two years, refused a less price than a crown for her affection, who, by consummate artifice, wrought the amorous monarch to divorce his wife and wed herself, is stated, nevertheless, to have lived as Henry's concubine during three years. Now, in the absence of all authentic evidence, would it not have been more natural, evidently more charitable, to attribute her long resistance to her virtuous principles, perhaps to her previous attachment to Percy? her weakness to the seductions of Henry's ardent attachment, and to her confidence in his promises. All that is proved against her is, that she was married on the 25th of January . . . and that Elizabeth was born the 13th of September.
>
> (*Quarterly Review* 56, 13)

Such criticisms drew from Lingard a spirited reply in the form of his *Vindication of Certain Passages in the fourth and fifth volumes of the*

History of England (1826). One by one, he refuted the reviewer's arguments. There was, he said, a good deal of evidence that contemporaries regarded Anne as the king's mistress. Cardinal Wolsey had called Anne 'the night-crowe, that cries ever in the king's ear against me'; the French ambassador, Du Bellay, a man in both Henry's and Anne's confidence, looked on Anne as Henry's mistress; papal briefs stated the same. And the circumstantial evidence was surely devastating:

> We have the evidence of the facts. We find the king attempting to seduce a young and beautiful female. To overcome her objections, he promises her marriage, as soon as he can obtain a divorce from his wife. The cause is brought into court: but the delay of the judges irritates his impatience. He expels his wife; and sends for the object of his affection from the house of her father; he allots her appartments contiguous to his own, he orders his courtiers to pay to her all the respect due to the Queen; he suffers her to interfere in matters of state, and to claim a share in the distribution of favours. Thus they live for three years under the same roof. We find them taking their meals together; if the King ride out, we are sure to discover her by his side; if he hunt, he places her in a convenient station to partake of the sport; if he change his residence, she accompanies him; and, when he crosses the sea to meet the French king at Calais, he cannot leave her behind him. Let the reader couple all this with the amorous temperament of Henry, with his impetuous disposition, with his indelicate allusions and anticipations in his correspondence with her, and he will not want evidence to teach him in what relation they live together, nor feel any surprise, if her child was born within little more than seven months after the clandestine celebration of their marriage.

Then Lingard proceeded to rebut the claim that Pole's testimony regarding Henry's relationship with Mary Boleyn was by its very nature suspect. In fact, he urged, Pole assumed in his advice to Henry that the king's relationship with Mary was a known and undisputed fact. He assumed it when he sought to persuade Henry that he was divorcing Catherine not because of conscience but because of passion. The issue of consanguinity was not important, Pole argued, because Henry stood in the same relationship with Anne (the sister of his erstwhile mistress, Mary) as with Catherine (who had been his brother Arthur's wife).

Finally, he replied to the reviewer's charge that he had been unjust to Anne. Lingard claimed impartiality: he had recounted the rumours that Anne had been immoral and had taken servants as lovers, but he had refused to draw conclusions (Lingard 1826, 102–3).

It was indeed extraordinarily difficult to overturn Lingard's measured case against Anne Boleyn: contemporaries were quick to see that his work effectively besmirched the origins of the English Reformation. Sharon Turner's *Henry VIII* was by far the most ambitious Protestant attempt of the time to retrieve the situation. He tried to do this by diverting attention away from the embarrassment of Anne herself. He devoted an entire chapter to Cardinal Wolsey's part in instigating the royal divorce. Using Edward Hall and Polydore Vergil, he sought to demonstrate that the doubts about the legitimacy of the Aragon match originated not with Henry but with Wolsey, 'that Wolsey was the chief agent in the inception of the divorce; and that it was begun, and at first pursued, independent of Anne Boleyn'. To Turner, Anne was nothing more than 'an accidental and a temporary appendage' to a cause already under way and from which the king could not draw back. In an attempt to reassert the spiritual nature of the English Reformation, Turner emphasized the steady growth of Protestant ideas which were 'producing, every day, new stems and new fruit' and which formed a vital background to the passion and the politics at court (Turner 1828, ii, 179–80, 199–200).

But Turner *was* forced to deal with Anne's own tragic history. And there is no doubt that she was a severe embarrassment. As Lingard pointed out in the first edition of his *History*, even her daughter had made no attempt to clear her name, preferring rather to forget that there ever had been such a person as Anne Boleyn – as far as Elizabeth I was concerned, she was her father's and not her mother's daughter. She preferred to forget that she was a chip off the old block, when that block was located on Tower Green.

The main problem which Turner faced was that if *he* succeeded in clearing Anne's name of the charges made against her, he inevitably made Henry VIII the guilty party. He compromised. He withheld a verdict, claiming that the surviving evidence was immensely ambiguous, but he cast Anne in a favourable light. He was able to do this by consulting the commission for investigation into her behaviour and concluding that the commission and its findings suggested a fabricated accusation, and by maintaining that Anne herself acted throughout as someone would who believed that her indisputable innocence would save her. But Turner was worried by the nature of Mark Smeaton's confession and was unable to use evidence which later came to light to the effect that none of the five who were executed (Lord Rochford, Breton, Norris, Smeaton and Weston) declared their innocence or guilt at the execution. Turner's defence of Anne was not successful because he substituted mere assertion for documentary proof: his defence of the spiritual origins of the English Reformation suffered from the same defect.

Conclusion

In the late eighteenth and early nineteenth centuries the debate about the nature of the English Reformation became part of the language of politics. The controversy concerning Catholic emancipation preoccupied contemporaries. Features of the conflict between Catholic and reformer in the sixteenth century which illuminated this current debate were selected for attention. Were the Catholics traitors? Were the Catholics brutal persecutors of the adherents of the new religion? If so, were they any worse than the Protestants in this respect? Was persecution, in fact, a product of sixteenth-century society and culture rather than a necessary attribute of either Catholicism or Protestantism *per se*? Was the English Reformation really the act of spiritual cleansing which Protestant historians had proclaimed it? Had it not been an act motivated by lust, passion and greed? Had it not destroyed a pristine Catholic church, and a successful and caring social system, in the interests of a lustful monarch and his money-grubbing, capitalistic courtiers? All these questions were asked because they were seen to have a real bearing upon the current question – should the Catholics be accepted as full citizens or should they not? Nevertheless, the attempt to answer these questions had a profound effect upon the nature of the contemporary and future historical debate about the origins and nature of the Reformation in England.

How did it do this? The Catholic historians aired arguments about the nature of sixteenth-century Catholicism and Protestantism which had, in fact, appeared in many previous Catholic defences, but for the first time these arguments were widely read by non-Catholics and were actually countenanced by them. This owed much to the moderate approach of Butler and Berrington, and yet more to the measured, scholarly work of Lingard. These writers were not polemicists, slinging mud at their enemies, but historians expressing balanced points of view supported by evidence. When the evidence was uncertain – as, for example, respecting the guilt of Anne Boleyn – they would say so. The relative detachment of such writers from the events of which they spoke – despite their involvement in current controversy – made readers sit up and take notice. Lingard's work had an air of objectivity about it which appealed.

In addition, the controversy about the nature of Catholicism and early Protestantism raised a very important issue – that of historical specificity. If it could be proved that Catholics persecuted Protestants in the sixteenth century and vice versa, then why was this so? Was it because Catholicism was for all time and of itself a persecuting creed or was it because conditions in the sixteenth century – political, cultural, social, historical – made active intolerance the order of the day? This was a very pertinent question *and one which still absorbs historians today*: how far are particular features of the past part of the general human condition and how far are they contingent upon specific contemporary conditions? Reflection on this theme became part and parcel of the Reformation debate in the early nineteenth century. Reformation historians began to delve deeper for explanations: they were not content to chronicle events or to provide an entirely one-sided perspective upon them.

Wait a minute, you may well cry. What about Cobbett? He is scarcely an example of balanced historical argument! He is the polemicist writ larger than life! What shall we do with him? Ironically enough, Cobbett derived his view of the English Reformation and its impact upon society from a reading of Lingard's *History* – a measured and careful account. But Cobbett was no historian: he used the work of Milner and Lingard and others to produce a caricature of the English Reformation. This caricature has had a profound impact upon later interpretations of the Reformation because it presents the official Reformation as the brain-child of a lustful monarch and his capitalist courtiers, and as the originator in England of the oppression of the poor by the rich. It is an overdrawn picture, but in it we find the beginnings of the multitudinous social and economic interpretations of the Reformation characteristic of the late nineteenth and twentieth centuries.

In what other respects did these early nineteenth-century treatments of the Reformation help to shape the nature of the historical debate? Certainly they focused future attention on the official nature of the Reformation at the expense of the spiritual. Even ardent Protestants were converted to the view that the English Reformation was a political act first and foremost, and that the sanctity of Protestant heroes such as Thomas Cranmer and Anne Boleyn were not beyond doubt. If some attention was given to the spirituality of the Catholic church which was destroyed (by Milner, for example), the spirituality of the Protestant Reformation was merely attacked and demolished. Even Protestant historians such as Turner were able to give relatively little attention to the spread of the new faith which buttressed the official Reformation. Working with official state and church papers, and deprived of local materials, they were condemned to refute attacks on the spirituality of the Protestant Reformation with reiterations of Foxe and other histories and defences of the heroes of the Reformation based upon these. A corrective was not provided until the mid-twentieth century. For the time being, attention was concentrated upon the political leaders of the Reformation, be they lay or clerical. Henry VIII, Thomas Wolsey, Thomas Cranmer, Anne Boleyn – biographers abounded to explain and justify their Reformation roles.

Early nineteenth-century writings on the Reformation also drew attention away from the internal affairs of the Reformation church. Institutional history played little part in the debate: the focus was essentially political. This diversion from the path established by Strype in the early eighteenth century was, however, but temporary. The Church of England's family squabble of the mid-nineteenth century – when Anglo-Catholic and Protestant brethren fell out – revived this earlier interest in the nature of the Church of England both in terms of its institutional expression and also in terms of its creed and worship.

Catholics and Protestants alike openly used the historical past to support their contemporary political arguments. A study of the content and impact of the historical writings produced during the course of the debate about Catholic emancipation should, however, alert us to the fact that historical arguments produced to support contemporary political causes should not be casually dismissed – they may well have a profound effect upon historical debate, upon the issues selected for treatment and the interpretations proffered.

Chapter 4

The Church of England in crisis: the Reformation heritage

Nineteenth-century Britain saw the established Church of England in the throes of a major crisis of identity. Christianity itself was threatened simultaneously by the alienation of educated men as a result of the spirit of free enquiry into science, history and theology; by the belief of many that the Scriptures were incompatible with new high moral standards; by the suggestion that the Old Testament did not represent literal truth; by the militant unbelief of the secularists, among whom George Holyoake and Charles Bradlaugh were prominent; and by the failure to arouse the interest of the new urban working classes. All Christian denominations and sects were affected but the Church of England more than any or all of the rest. The Church of England claimed to comprehend all the Christians of England and Wales, yet it patently did not do so in a Britain in which the existence and practice of other religious organizations were formally tolerated and, moreover, in which their members were accorded civil rights. The crisis of the established church reached its climax with the repeal of the Test Acts (1828) and the emancipation of the Catholics (1829) but, when this crisis was past and the patient seemingly recovering, another and an uglier presented itself – attacks upon the church's temporal privileges. Militant dissenters assailed the church's monopoly over *rites de passage* (births, marriages and deaths), demanded freedom from paying rates to support a state church, claimed control over the education of their own young and the right to university degrees. Such agitation fuelled the activities of the Liberation Society, which campaigned for disestablishment.

Members of the Church of England reacted by attempting to locate afresh the source of the authority of the established church. Broadly speaking, Evangelicals sought this authority in the Scriptures; Broad Churchmen in the individual conscience which interpreted Holy Writ; High Churchmen within the church itself. This search for authority necessarily led to some rethinking of the relationship between state and church – a relationship which had been defined by the English Reformation of the sixteenth century and little refined since then. The Evangelicals were more or less contented with the status quo, preferring to be active in the parishes rather than to be active in politics. They were dragged into the debates about church organization, authority and relations with the state in the 1860s by the position of ritualists and rationalists, which seemed to threaten their own existence. The Tractarians, on the other hand, were far from content. Unlike the Old High Churchmen who had looked to the Reformation to delineate the nature of the church's authority in matters spiritual, Newman and others of the circle looked much further back to the powerful and authoritarian medieval church which had pronounced on all matters of doctrine and had directed the religious life of all believers.

The assault upon the Church of England's right to keep its own doctrinal house in order was highlighted by the transferral in 1832 of the power to judge ecclesiastical appeals from the Court of Delegates to a judicial committee of the Privy Council which contained laymen and included no ecclesiastical lawyers. When, in 1850, this judicial committee reversed the view of the church courts that Gorham's Calvinistic opinions on baptism were contrary to the church's doctrine, and when in 1860 it reversed the sentence passed upon the two beneficed clerical contributors to *Essays and Reviews*, battle was truly joined. Men of the Old High Church disliked this degree of intervention and hoped to counter it by measures such as the revival of Convocation and diocesan synods. The Tractarians adopted a more radical battle formation. They embraced the cause of disestablishment. They searched for historical support for their position.

The Oxford movement stressed the unbroken traditions of the English church – the Catholic faith, the Catholic heritage, the apostolic succession. Neither John Keble nor J. H. Newman was enamoured of the Reformation, but both hesitated to impugn it in public. Both men were influenced by a much bolder spirit – Richard Hurrell Froude (b. 1803). Froude was the eldest son of Robert Froude, Archdeacon of Totnes. He attended Oxford in the early 1820s and became a member of Keble's circle. Keble disliked Froude's expressed contempt for the reformers, but nevertheless shaped Froude's conviction that there was in the church a continuous Catholic heritage. When, in 1826–7, Froude studied under Dr Charles Lloyd, Regius Professor of Divinity, and traced development of the Anglican liturgy from Roman Catholic books, Froude's commitment to this view was absolute. Moreover, when he read about the Reformation and found the reformers themselves lacking in the integrity, reverence and moral courage which Keble so extolled, Froude became 'a less and less son of the Reformation'. His views appear to have been shared privately by Keble and Newman – Keble wrote to his sister in 1836 of the reformers: 'I have very little doubt that if we had lived in those times, neither my father, nor you nor Provost nor Harrison would have had anything to do with them' (Baker 1970, 243–59).

There can be little question that Hurrell Froude approached the story of the Engish Reformation as a moral critic rather than as a historian. The reformers, after all, had attacked everything about the Catholic church in England which he cherished – theirs was an iconoclastic, individualistic spirit entirely alien to his opinion that the church was the ultimate fount of authority. English churchmen should conform 'to the principles of the Church which has preserved its traditionary practices unbroken' and not those of the reformers. He found it unnecessary to consult many original documents. Instead he condemned the apologia for the new relations between state and church out of hand: 'I do not hesitate to say that his [Jewel's] Doctrine ought to be denied under pain of damnation.'

Hurrell Froude made of history polemic. Others joined in the battle fray. In an article on John Jewel for *The British Critic* in 1841 Frederick Oakeley declared the Reformation a 'deplorable schism' and called for the de-Protestantization of the Church of England; three years later, William George Ward styled the Reformation as political and unprincipled in his *The Ideal of a Christian Church*. Vilification of the reformers, protests against Protestant innovations, demands for autonomy in matters of doctrine became the order of the day. The construction of a supportive canon was under way. In 1842, for example, Lathbury published his *History of Convocation*. Samuel R. Maitland, 'the high and learned' librarian of Lambeth, sought with passionate zeal to discredit as historians both John Foxe, the martyrologist, and Stephen Reed Cattley, his editor. Many of the Catholic attacks upon the Protestant leaders provided additional valuable ammunition.

Those dedicated to the status quo had, of course, not bent their heads meekly to receive such blows. Far from it. The Religious Tract Society published the works of *The British Reformers* in twelve volumes between 1827 and 1831. Stephen Cattley's edition of Foxe's *Acts and Monuments*, complete with a life and vindication of its author, appeared in eight volumes between 1837 and 1861. This was conceived as a response to the traditional Roman Catholic attacks on the reputation of the great martyrologist (for example, William Eusebius Andrews, *A Critical and Historical Review of Fox's Book of Martyre, showing the inaccuracies, falsehoods, and misrepresentations in that work of deception*, which was reprinted in 1837).

In 1839 the Evangelicals had attacked Hurrell Froude directly from the pulpit. In April 1840 they went one step further in their attempt to canonize the English reformers. From the pages of the *British Magazine* they began the campaign to erect the Martyrs' Memorial, the form of which subscribers had decided upon in early March of that year. This lasting homage to the memories of Cranmer, Latimer and Ridley was designed by Sir Gilbert Scott and erected to the north of St Mary Magdalen in Magdalen Street, Oxford in 1841. It was as if, once a solid and imposing monument had been built, no one would again dare to assail the Protestant character of the English church.

The work of memorialization, and definition, was continued by the Parker Society, named after the first Elizabethan Archbishop of Canterbury, Matthew Parker. The Society endeavoured 'to make known those works by which the Fathers of the Reformed English Church sought to diffuse Scriptural truth. Their principles were clearly set forth in their writings, and their descendants are now called upon to manifest the same principles, with firmness and decision.' Accordingly, between 1841 and 1853, the Parker Society published fifty-three volumes of writings by sixteenth-century English divines, 'without abridgement, alteration, or omission'.

In their turn, the genuflections which the 'Protestants' made to the English reformers spurred the 'Catholics' in the Church of England towards ever greater extremes. The most notable of these attacks, and the one with the most lasting influence, was the onslaught staged by S. R. Maitland against the credibility of John Foxe (Maitland 1849). He attempted, again through the pages of the *British Magazine*, to undermine Foxe's centuries old reputation as 'faithful martyrologist of the church of England, skilful investigator of historical antiquity, stout champion of evangelical truth, remarkable wonderworker, who presented the Marian Martyrs like phoenixes revived from their ashes' (epitaph to Foxe at St Giles Cripplegate, London).

Maitland's works included a *Review of Foxe the Martyrologist's* '*History of the Waldenses*' (1837); 'Six Letters on Foxe's *Acts and Monuments*' (1837); 'Notes on the contributions of the Reverend George Townsend' (1841–2); 'Remarks on the Reverend S. Cattley's Defence' (1842); and 'Essay on . . . the Reformation in England' (1849). Maitland tried to show that Foxe was inaccurate, attacking the 'never-mind school of history' which 'cuts its way through matters of fact, with reckless slaughter of names, and places and dates, and with any translation or mistranslation of documents, in order to establish any point of faith, or opinion, which it may see fit to select'. Certainly he discovered in Foxe errors of Latin translation, plagiarism and a reluctance to cite his sources. He measured Foxe's work against the standards of contemporary historical scholarship and found him wanting – not surprisingly. But the allegation that Foxe *deliberately* falsified his account in order to glorify Protestants remained unproven.

Maitland's allies in the world of scholarship were no less unrelenting in their efforts to label Foxe as a falsifier of the evidence. Their opinion was absorbed into historical and reference literature. In his biography of Henry VIII, J. S. Brewer made no bones about it:

> Had Foxe the martyrologist been an honest man, his carelessness and credulity would have incapacitated him from being a trustworthy historian. Unfortunately he was not honest; he tampered with the documents that came into his hands, and freely indulged in those very faults of suppression and equivocation for which he condemned his opponents.
>
> (Brewer 1884, 1, 52)

Sidney Lee reiterated these sentiments in the influential pages of the *Dictionary of National Biography*. Small wonder it was that the *Encyclopaedia Britannica* of 1929 charged Foxe with 'wilful falsification of the evidence'.

Although there is no full-scale modern study of Foxe as a historian, some work has been done which suggests that these charges hold little water under closer examination. For example, in one place Foxe wrote that the Lollards preached against the concept of tithe; he later corrected this to read more accurately that they preached against the payment of tithe to wicked priests. Foxe's account of the Guernsey Martyrs (in both the 1563 and 1570 editions) has been attacked, but in fact it tallies with all surviving records. Foxe was castigated for including criminals and traitors among his martyrs, but in reality he was punctilious in denouncing the crimes of martyrs who had doubtful records. For instance, there was the case of William Flower, an ex-monk, who, on Easter Day 1555, struck a mass priest at St Margaret's Westminster. He proceeded to repent his violence, but spoke heresy against the mass and refused to recant to buy his life. Foxe, in recounting the story, denounced Flower's crime and praised only his refusal to recant what he believed to be the truth.

True or no, the blows struck against Foxe by Maitland and his allies travelled home. Foxe's reputation had to await the efforts of J. F. Mozley and William Haller to be partially reinstated.

And Maitland was carried away to destroy the credibility of all 'Puritan' sources. Buried away among the source materials of the English church, he was driven by his love of 'accuracy' to wage a very biased war against Protestant writers, ascribing to them the very worst of intentions and practices:

> For the history of the Reformation in England, we depend so much on the testimony of writers, who may be considered as belonging . . . to the puritan party . . . that it is of the utmost importance to inquire whether there was any thing in their notions respecting TRUTH, which ought to throw suspicion on any of their statements.
>
> The question is one which does not require much research or argument. There is something very frank (one is almost inclined to say, honest) in the avowals, whether direct or indirect, which various puritans have left on record, that it was considered not only allowable, but meritorious, to tell lies for the sake of the good cause in which they were engaged . . . [for] they did not hesitate . . . to state what they knew to be false.
>
> (Maitland 1849, 1–2)

In his essays on the Reformation in England, Protestants such as George Joye, Anthony Dalaber, John Knox, Christopher Goodman and Thomas Becon were held up as examples of this tendency.

Contemporary Protestants did attempt, of course, to protect the reputation of their Reformation heroes. George Townsend, the biographer of Foxe, made a detailed defence of his work in his 'Preliminary Dissertations' to the Cattley edition of 1837–41. He checked Foxe's use of documents against the British Museum manuscripts, emphasized Foxe's use of eyewitness accounts and especially his use of Grindal's assistance, and showed that Foxe might have been careless in his use of sources but that he had tried to include note of his authorities and to take account of fresh evidence as it became available in order to correct his narrative. But he, like Foxe's other defenders, made relatively little impression: it was Maitland's dart which reached home.

As it happened, the effective defence of the Reformation came, not from the friends of the martyrologist, nor yet indeed from those who built a memorial to his martyrs, but from the younger brother of that Richard Hurrell Froude who had led the attack. James Anthony Froude's *The History of England from the Fall of Wolsey to the Defeat of the Spanish Armada* (twelve volumes, 1856–70) was written from the perspective of a committed Protestant who saw religion as the determining force of history and was relatively uninterested in constitutional questions. Froude's was the history of the English Reformation and not of the Tudors. The terminal events of his history were chosen for their religious and not their constitutional import. The death of Wolsey signalled the birth of the Reformation; the defeat of the Armada its salvation.

In his history Froude portrayed the English Reformation as a moral victory in the struggle for human freedom and intellectual honesty. The Reformation was not political and unprincipled; the reformers were not frightened sycophants; the opponents of the reform such as More and Mary of Scotland were not heroes or heroines; there was no medieval Catholic Utopia destroyed by iconoclastic Protestants. Instead there were strong, good men fighting a strong, good fight. So Froude saw the Reformation as something not politically but morally necessary. The monasteries were dissolved not because Henry needed money but because they were offensive; the spoils went to serve educational and national defence purposes and not to line the pockets of Henry and his courtiers. England's independence of Rome was declared because she would govern herself and not be ruled by loathsome priests. Henry rid himself of Anne Boleyn because she was guilty. Lord Burghley was not simply a canny statesman but also a defender of the faith.

This is, of course, to caricature J. A. Froude's monumental work. The modern student may find strikingly familiar Froude's interpretation of the complex relationship between the official and the popular religious reformation. He wrote of the force of tradition, of habit as an inhibitor of change:

Healthy people live and think more by habit than by reason, and it is only at rare intervals that they are content to submit their institutions to theoretic revision. The interval of change under Edward the Sixth had not shaken the traditionary attachment of the English squires and peasantry to the service of their ancestors. The Protestants were confined chiefly to the great towns and seaports; and those who deprecated doctrinal alterations, either from habit, prudence, or the mere instinct of conservatism, still constituted two-thirds, perhaps three-fourths, of the entire people.   (Froude 1856–70, vi, 114)

He spoke of the dilemma facing the young Elizabeth on her accession:

Every course open to her was beset with objections, she would not stand still, she could move in no direction without offence to some one; and she herself in her own internal uncertainties was a type of the people who she was set to rule. She had been educated in a confused Protestantism which had evaded doctrinal difficulties, and had confined itself chiefly to the anathemas of Rome. Left to herself on her Father's death, while the Anglican divines had developed into Calvinism, Elizabeth had inclined to Luther and the Augsburg Confession. For herself she would have been contented to accept the formulas which had been left by her Father, with an English ritual, and the communion service of the first Prayer-book of Edward the Sixth. But the sacramentarian tendencies of English Protestant theology had destroyed Henry's standing ground as a position which the Reformers could be brought to accept. It was to deny transubstantiation that the martyrs had died. It was in the name and defence of the mass that Mary and Pole had exercised their savage despotism.
                    (Froude 1856–70, vi, 114–16)

One could be forgiven for expressing the view that modern scholars, for all their more careful scholarship and standards of textual criticism, have moved little beyond Froude. Presumably modern historians rarely look first to Froude's narrative: yet many a modern account could have been directly modelled upon his. It is in their preoccupation with the social foundations of the Reformation that later scholars parted company with Froude.

If, however, we read further in the same paragraph we will find evidence of the impact which earlier Protestant histories, and particularly that of Foxe, had upon Froude's interpretation. Again, the fundamentals of the narrative would meet with considerable agreement among modern Reformation scholars, but the 'tone' of the passage would be entirely foreign to historians of the later twentieth century:

> Elizabeth had borne her share of the persecution; she resented with the whole force of her soul the indignities to which she had been exposed, and she sympathized with those who had suffered at her side. She was the idol of the young, the restless, the enthusiastic; her name had been identified with freedom; and she detested more sincerely than any theologian living, the perversity which treated opinion as a crime. In her speculative theories she was nearer to Rome than to Calvinism. In her vital convictions she represented the free proud spirit of the educated laity, who would endure no dictation from priests of either persuasion, and so far as lay in them, would permit no clergy any more to fetter the thoughts and paralyze the energies of England. With such views it was impossible for her to sanction permanently the establishment of a doctrine from which the noblest of her subjects had revolted, or to alienate the loyalty of the party who in her hour of danger had been her most ardent friends.   (Froude 1856–70, vi, 116)

Froude's essentially nationalistic account of the Reformation has provided the counter to that version which sees the Reformation purely as an act of necessity for England's monarchy. J. A. Froude, unlike his brother, wrote from the archives and, although he often copied his sources carelessly, he does not seem to have deliberately falsified his tale. Yet, no less than Hurrell, he was using history to plead a cause. His was but a partial history. Hurrell denigrated the reformers; James Anthony whitewashed them. Neither case would find credence in a modern court. As the writer in the *Edinburgh Review* pointed out of J. A. Froude's history of the Reformation, he never thought to question the evidence, to look below the surface of Protestant propaganda, to query the stated positions of the protagonists. Froude thought that the 1529 Parliament was freely elected; he accepted the preambles to Tudor legislation as expressions of public opinion; he did not at all suspect the fact that not a single judge or jury acquitted a victim in a Crown prosecution. The processes which produced the documents available to him did not interest him at all. Froude's underlying purpose was to show that the Church of England was indeed Protestant – it had been created at the Reformation as a protest against a monstrous Catholic church. Monarchs had wanted a limited Reformation, perhaps, but religious reformers had in time taken over and moved the process of reform much further. The Church of England, therefore, did not and could not preserve in itself the traditions of the Catholic church. Hurrell, on the contrary, denied the religious character of the English Reformation and obstinately clung to the belief that the Church of England stood in an unbroken Catholic tradition, its record marred only by the sycophantic and heretical acts of sixteenth-century ecclesiastics.

Some much more scholarly works echoed the position adopted by Hurrell Froude, however. The detailed and learned history penned by Canon Richard Watson Dixon in the 1880s arrived at a similar conclusion: the English Reformation was a political act, the product of the legislation of the 1529 Parliament. Dixon's exceptional prose style and penetrating analysis warrant extensive quotation, the more so as his work has been sadly neglected:

> This was indeed the most memorable Parliament that ever sat. It was the assembly which transformed old England – the England of Chaucer and Lydgate – into modern England. At the time when it met, England herself resembled one of those great edifices, dedicated to religion, with which she abounded then, but which were soon to fall in ruin beneath the axe and hammer of the reformation . . . . The Parliament whose proceedings we are to consider laid the axe to the tree. A full generation at least of the fiercest hacking and hewing followed, ere the ancient system was spread upon the ground. The fury of a great revolution, which was designed to have been general, fell first, as in all such cases, upon religion and the Church.
>
> (Dixon 1884, 2–3)

He swept aside other explanations for the Reformation:

> As to what are commonly termed the causes of the Refor-
> mation, there seem to have been none which have not been
> exaggerated. Everybody knows what is said of the breaking up
> of the frost of ages, the corruptions of the old system, the influ-
> ence of German Protestantism, and the explosive force of new
> ideas generated by the Revival of Learning: and everybody has
> grown accustomed to set the old against the new, as if they
> were totally repugnant forces, which simply strove to destroy
> one another. Much of this may be dismissed as no more than a
> graphic contrivance for enabling us to comprehend a memor-
> able epoch, but historically untrue . . . . So far as England is
> concerned, there seem to have been no causes at work which
> had not been at work long enough, and with very much the
> same degree of activity, when accident precipitated the Refor-
> mation.   (Dixon 1884, 4)

Then he fixed upon that feature of the English Reformation
which he considered its most important characteristic. It was a
revolution and it was a revolution carried through by constitutional or legal procedure. It was precipitated by the presence of
Henry VIII on the throne: 'a man of force without grandeur: of
great ability, but not of lofty intellect: punctilious and yet un-
scrupulous: centred in himself: greedy and profuse: cunning
rather than sagacious: of fearful passion and intolerable pride, but
destitute of ambition in the nobler sense of the word: a character
of degraded magnificence' (Dixon 1884, 4, 6).

Why was Henry's role so central? The laity had always
opposed the clergy, envied them their wealth and eyed their patri-
mony. 'But the King of England had hitherto stood in the gate to
protect the one party from the other, and to preserve the rights of
all. Now he lent the sanctity of the Crown to an enormous devastation; and the elements which might have been controlled
became uncontrollable.' When the monarch called the people to
attack the clergy and their power, he 'had the nation at his back.
He had with him the needy and the greedy and the rich and the
noisy' (Dixon 1884, 5–6).

Dixon identified a revolution which struck first at the church but eventually undermined the entire system. His understanding of the nature of this revolution in government was astute.

> It was effected within the constitution, and not by the subversion of the constitution. It was effected by solemn procedure. Those who openly opposed it were made to take the position of rebels and traitors . . . we find a constant disclaimer of revolutionary violence, and repeated references, more or less justifiable, to some kind of precedent. This formal adherence to antiquity, this continued maintenance of the old constitution in all parts and branches, is the most characteristic and admirable feature of the English Reformation. But at the same time it must be carefully noticed that much of all this was no more than formal: that there was a real transfer of power made from one part of the old constitution to another: and that many things survived henceforth as shadows which had hitherto been of the force and activity of substance.   (Dixon 1884, 6–7)

Dixon's style is a delight to read but it is not only for his literary flourishes and unforced candour that he should be read. He reached his views after a careful examination of the available evidence, which he duly cited in the footnotes. He explored motivation, suggested the importance of social change, pondered the history of the surviving documentation and determined to look below the surface of proclamations and acts. Above all he penetrated to the heart of the matter: why was there an English Reformation? what was its nature? what role did the king play in it? And he laid the groundwork for many a later historian – as later chapters of this book will testify. As a result, Dixon's work is not without value for today's historian of the Reformation as well as for the student of Reformation historiography.

English historians of the Reformation exhibited a marked traditionary tendency – their aim was to show that their own current religious position, be it Protestant or Catholic or Anglo-Catholic – was securely founded on historical precedent. The dislike of innovation, apparently peculiarly characteristic of the English, fuelled an enthusiasm for the past and historical studies. At the same time there were some who found this absorption with precedent unhealthy. One such was Charles Beard, scholar, social worker, popular orator and preacher, an early light in the history of Liverpool University. Charles Beard (1827–88) was deeply interested by the relationship between past, present and future, but from a far different perspective than were the brothers Froude or librarian Maitland. Beard wanted above all to show that the Reformation occurred in a specific historical context – that it was a reformation for its own times – the sixteenth century – and not for the nineteenth century. In other words, the particular changes wrought by the Reformation – be it in Europe or in England – did not represent a blueprint for the future church. On the other hand, the *spirit* of the Reformation must be revived. Contemporaries had turned the truth upside-down. They treated the doctrine and dogma of the Reformation as sacrosanct and had, in the process, killed the motive force of the movement. For Beard, then, the Reformation was not a theological, religious or ecclesiastical movement at root but 'the life of the Renaissance infused into religion . . . a partial reaction from the ecclesiastical and ascetic mood of the middle ages to Hellenic ways of think-ing'. The Reformation stripped the church of the accretions of the Middle Ages. But it unfortunately crystallized doctrine – giving it a finality while the rest of human thought progressed. The church must think again and take account, for example, of the theory of evolution, of the concept of heredity, of heliocentric studies (Beard 1883).

Beard's brief discussion of the English Reformation has intrin-sic interest. He saw the English Reformation as a native product which, while it assimilated Lutheran, Calvinist and even Zwin-glian influences, yet 'followed no precedents, and was obedient only to its own law of development'. Yet he saw this 'native' reformation as a reaction to the same general situation as prevailed in Germany and Switzerland. But the actual inauguration of reform was not due to religious conviction at all. The Refor-mation did not reflect the beliefs of either the people or its leaders – 'the motive power was at least as much political as religious', 'the tone which it took and the rapidity of its progress depended more upon the caprices of a line of arbitrary princes than upon the serious convictions of the people'. 'All through these Tudor times the tide of Reformation ebbs and flows, as the monarch wills: now Henry is the Defender of the Faith against Luther, and now is urgent that Melancthon should undertake the task of the English Reformation: he is Protestant in the assertion of his own supremacy, Catholic in his adhesion to sacramental doctrine: the translation of the Bible is promoted or retarded as his royal caprice dictates: and when he has swept the wealth of the monasteries into his coffers, he issues the Six Articles, and burns the heretics who deny the Real Presence. I will not inflict upon you the familiar story of the fluctuations of religious policy under Edward, Mary and Elizabeth: the strange thing is, how little the nation counts for, how much the Prince.' The effect was to produce a Church of England which was both Catholic and Protestant, not out of design and commitment but out of accident. The settlement was politically constructed. This official Reformation was not the product of a religious movement. Yet the people of England were affected by a religious movement, and Protestantism gradually took a hold upon them. In this sense the 'Reformation in England was a case of arrested development, and Elizabeth's settlement, a compromise which came too soon'. Popular Protestantism was impatient with the settlement and strove to interpret it in a congenial way, but to no avail.

Seeing the Reformation in this way, Beard was able to show that 'from what has been said, it will be plain that from the first, two distinct elements have been present in the English Church, sometimes struggling for the mastery, sometimes living peacefully side by side, and that it is contrary to historical fact for either to insert itself in such a way as to exclude the other'. As to the Evangelicals and the Oxford Movement, both are correct. England's church is Protestant; England's church is Catholic. As such, the Church of England holds a middle and a mediating place in Christendom.

In Beard's view, therefore, the battles between rival religious parties have inflicted terrible and unnecessary wounds. The spirit of Reformation, if revived, will 'restore the unity which was shattered by the old'. A true understanding of Reformation history will bring reconciliation in its wake.

If Beard saw the Reformation as a case of arrested development, other Englishmen were more positive in their attitude, seeing it as

a key point in the evolution of civilized society. Social evolution-
ism, heavily influenced by the writings of Herbert Spencer,
provided a social complement to Darwin's theory of biological
evolution. Societies develop and mature. The good and strong
characteristics of these societies survive; the bad and weak are
defeated and diminish. It was left to a layman, Benjamin Kidd
(1858–1916), to locate in this scheme of things the Reformation, a purifying movement which represented the triumph
of all that was good of medieval culture and religion over all that
was bad:

> The importance of this movement, as we shall better under-
> stand later, is very great, much greater indeed than the his-
> torian, with the methods at his command, has hitherto assigned
> to it. Its immediate significance was, that while, as already
> explained, it represented an endeavour to preserve intact the
> necessary super-rational sanction for the ethical ideals of the
> Christian religion, it denoted the tendency of the movement
> which had so far filled the life of the western peoples to find its
> social expression. It liberated as it were, into the practical life of
> the peoples affected by it, that immense body of altruistic feel-
> ing which had been from the beginning the distinctive social
> product of the Christian religion, but which had hitherto been,
> during a period of immaturity and intense vitality, directed into
> other channels. To the evolutionist this movement is essentially
> a social development. It took place inevitably and naturally at a
> particular stage which can never recur in the life of the social
> organism. In his eyes its significance consists in the greater
> development which the altruistic feelings must attain amongst
> the peoples where the development was allowed to proceed un-
> interrupted in its course.   (Kidd 1906, 162)

Kidd's position led him to accentuate the bad in medieval Christianity and the good in Protestantism. He was, after all, committed to tracing a line of ethical progress. But, a-historical as he
often was in his treatment of this historical theme, Kidd, interestingly enough, did put his finger on one characteristic of the
Protestant Reformation which had been stressed by its agents.

It restored the individual to direct contact with God and with the teaching of Christ as expressed in the Scriptures:

> It is probable that the changes in doctrine which had principally contributed to produce this result were those which had tended to bring the individual into more intimate contact with the actual life and example of the Founder of Christianity, and therefore with the essential spirit that underlay our religious system and served to distinguish it from all other systems.
>
> (Kidd 1906, 301)

Individuals now felt responsible for their own actions; practical altruism was emphasized; family life was deepened and enriched; the commitment to industry was intensified. Small wonder, thought Kidd, for it may be noticed, consequently, 'how much farther the development of the humanitarian feelings has progressed in those parts of our civilisation most affected by the movement of the sixteenth century, and more particularly amongst the Anglo-Saxon peoples' (Kidd 1906, 303). He listed amongst these manifestations the crusade against slavery; the anti-vivisection movement; vegetarianism; and the enfranchisement of women. He went on to assert that in England all classes of society had been civilized by the Reformation and sensitized to the presence of evil in society. Because of this the movement towards adapting the old system to suit the new wants of the people was progressing 'as a natural and orderly development'. There was no need for revolution because there was evolution.

Of course, Kidd was not interested in the detailed history of the Reformation, either in England or abroad, but his work exhibited a tendency which should not go unnoticed. His view of the Reformation as a civilizing movement led him to underplay the politique aspects of the religious changes of the sixteenth century and to emphasize the spiritual and ethical content of the Reformation. Kidd was no historian, but the extreme popularity of his *Social Evolution* meant that his perspective on historical change was influential: his was certainly a 'basically Whiggish and ultimately "Protestant" view of things' and it probably had more effect upon literate Englishmen than historians have previously realized.

Nineteenth-century churchmen and involved laymen believed that the Reformation held the key to the crisis of identity which the contemporary church was experiencing. Unfortunately and, perhaps, inevitably they found it as difficult to agree in their analysis of the nature of the Reformation as they did to agree in their churchmanship.

Chapter 5

The Tudor revolution in religion: the twentieth-century debate

The figure of Henry VIII stands astride the Reformation century – a man of moods, at one moment terrifying and at another wooing his subjects, but always in command of the situation. But was he? At the very heart of the modern debate about the English Reformation lies the question – how far was the official Reformation the creation of the monarch?

During the past hundred years many historians have turned their attention to this question. In seeking to answer it, they have offered a variety of explanations for the official Reformation. Rather than seek to mention every work which touches on the topic (a gargantuan and not very useful task), we shall look here in some detail at the most important lines of interpretation.

Any such study must perforce begin with the work of Albert Frederick Pollard (1869–1948) for, whether the historians concerned like it or not, more recent interpretations of the role of Henry VIII in the shaping of the Reformation have been essentially reactive to Pollard's interpretation. Pollard began his writing career at a time when historians were seeking to develop a more scientific approach to history and were laying emphasis upon the use of original documentation, detailed research and objective analysis. In 1904 Pollard himself called for the establishment of a

London school of history, a post-graduate school of historical research and a London university press. During the First World War he paved the way, with his Thursday evening seminars for historians at London, for the future Institute of Historical Research, of which he was the first director, from 1921–39. The idea behind this venture was to provide a forum for the discussion of the practical and theoretical problems involved in the study and writing of history – the difficulties inherent in using properly the newly available documentation. When he wrote his biography of Henry VIII (1902), Pollard had at his disposal published editions of important categories of document – *The Letters and Papers of Henry VIII*, the reports of the Historical Manuscripts Commission, the volumes of the Camden Society and so forth (Galbraith 1949; Neale 1949).

In publishing the biography of Henry, Pollard declared that his prime aim was to present a balanced portrait of that monarch, yet he was acutely aware of the problems and even the impossibility of writing an objective account. The historian had to exercise his judgement when selecting the facts and the portrait which emerged must needs be shaped by this judgement. No one could put it better than Pollard:

> Mr Froude has expressed his concurrence in the dictum that the facts of history are like the letters of the alphabet; by selection and arrangement they can be made to spell anything and nothing can be arranged so easily as facts. *Experto credo.* Yet selection is inevitable, and arrangement essential. The historian has no option if he wishes to be intelligible. He will naturally arrange his facts so that they spell what he believes to be the truth, and he must of necessity suppress those facts which he judges to be immaterial or inconsistent with the scale on which he is writing. And if the superabundance of facts compels both selection and suppression it counsels no less a restraint of judgement . . . . Dogmatism is merely the result of ignorance; and no honest historian will pretend to have mastered all the facts, accurately weighed all the evidence, or pronounced a final judgement.   (Pollard 1905 edn, viii)

In short, Pollard realized the enormity of the problem facing the historians of the new breed. Unlike their medieval predecessors, they could not merely present chronicles or annals without analysis or arrangement. Unlike their more recent forebears, they could not blatantly take sides and make history support their current political or religious positions. They are committed to analysis and, simultaneously, to objectivity. Pollard decided that the dilemma was insoluble. No historian could present the absolute truth. He must settle for presenting, as honestly as possible, what he believed to be the truth after detailed and rigorous research and thinking. We do not need to agree with Pollard's interpretation of Henry VIII's part in the Reformation to appreciate the style and vigour of his writing, and the conviction which he brought to it.

Unlike more recent scholars interested in the official Reformation, Pollard assumed rather than argued the central importance of Henry's own views. Until he wrote, historians had been concerned to debate the morality of the English Reformation. The question foremost in their minds, as Pollard put it, was whether Henry was Attila the scourge of mankind or Hercules the cleanser of the Augean Stables (Pollard 1905, 1). Pollard, the historian's historian, was concerned not with morality but with explanation. With the documents at his disposal, he set out to explain how and why the Reformation occurred, rather than to argue that it was a good or a bad thing. And this intent led him to raise the whole issue of Tudor monarchy. Early in the biography he set before his reader the nature of the problem:

> What manner of man was this, and wherein lay the secret of his strength? Is recourse necessary to a theory of supernatural agency, or is there another and adequate solution? Was Henry's will of such miraculous force that he could ride roughshod in insolent pride over public opinion at home and abroad? Or did his personal ends, dictated perhaps by selfish motives and ignoble passions, so far coincide with the interests and prejudices of the politically effective portion of his people, that they were willing to condone a violence and tyranny, the brunt of which fell after all on the few? Such is the riddle which propounds itself to every student of Tudor history. It cannot be answered by paeans in honour of Henry's intensity of will and

force of character, nor by invectives against his vices and lamentations over the woes of his victims . . . the explanation of Henry's career must be sought not so much in the study of his character as in the study of his environment, or the conditions which made things possible before or since and are not likely to be so again.   (Pollard 1905, 4)

Was Henry a tyrant who rode roughshod over his people in the matter of Reformation or was he a despot who ruled by consent of his people?

Pollard, then, was not concerned primarily with *who* made Reformation policy – he assumed that by this time Henry was truly in control – nor yet with whether there was such a policy, but with a rather different issue: what enabled this policy to succeed? The early sections of his book, those which 'set the scene', should not be dismissed as mere background. They are crucial to Pollard's argument. They explain, to Pollard's satisfaction, why it was that the English people freely gave Henry the power which he wielded. The English, having seen their land torn apart by the civil wars and the administrative chaos of Lancastrian and Yorkist rule, declared: 'A plague on both your houses. Give us peace.' Stability and not freedom was what they most craved, for 'England in the sixteenth century put its trust in its princes far more than it did in its parliaments, it invested them with attributes almost divine' (Pollard 1905, 35). According to Pollard, both Henry VII and his son crystallized this tendency into 'practical weapons of absolute power' (Pollard 1905, 36) And Henry VIII's beauty, bravery, skill and learning, far from being 'mere trifles below the dignity of history', forged for him the most effective weapon of them all – a firm hold upon the popular imagination (Pollard 1905, 41). In truth, it is Pollard's appreciation of the importance of public opinion in allowing the English Reformation to take place that distinguishes his interpretation from other purely voluntaristic accounts of the Reformation. Yes, the Reformation was an act of Henry VIII's will; no, it could not have happened, had his people not allowed it.

Pollard, having established to his own content that Henry VIII had an all powerful armoury, sufficient to allow him to take all

England with him away from its allegiance to Rome, saw the key question as being when it was that Henry realized that he possessed this arsenal. ' "If a lion knew his strength," said Sir Thomas More of his master to Thomas Cromwell, "it were hard for any man to rule him." Henry VIII had the strength of a lion; it remains to be seen how soon he learnt it, and what use he made of that strength when he discovered the secret' (Pollard 1905, 41).

In this biography Pollard describes the processes by which Henry discovered his strength and the uses to which he put it. We are shown a slowly maturing lion, under the tutelage of Cardinal Wolsey, and then a fully grown lord of the savannah, the very personification of personal monarchy. In this work, as in Pollard's masterpiece, *Wolsey* (1929), Henry's long reign is seen as composed of two halves: from 1514 to 1529 the young Henry let Thomas Wolsey govern England; from 1529 (aged thirty-eight) until his death in 1547 Henry was his own prime minister. It followed that Pollard saw Henry VIII as the architect of the English Reformation.

The Reformation is presented as a movement 'not in essence doctrinal' but 'an episode in the eternal dispute between Church and State' (Pollard 1966 edn, 187). Later historians of the official Reformation have followed suit, seeing the break with Rome as motivated by secular concerns, be they Henry's desire for a divorce and a legitimate heir, the need to bolster Henry's authority in the state or the grand design for a reformation of government. As Pollard saw it, the church would not allow Henry VIII to divorce Catherine of Aragon and marry Anne Boleyn. For this reason, Henry withdrew England from the Roman Communion when he married Anne and assumed the headship of the Church of England. 'The divorce was the spark which ignited the flame, but the combustible materials had long been existent'; 'the divorce, in fact, was the occasion and not the cause of the Reformation' (Pollard 1966, 186–7). The cause was Henry's determination to be supreme in England. Pollard saw the Henrician Reformation as the culmination of the long struggle between spiritual and temporal powers in England: by it the English monarchy successfully asserted its authority over the church in England. '. . . the wonder is, not that the breach took place when it did, but that it was deferred for so long' (Pollard 1966, 186).

What does Pollard have to say about the immediate occasion? According to his account, Henry's desire for a divorce and remarriage stemmed from a succession crisis. He rejected the popular theories of the time: Henry's unbridled passion for Anne Boleyn and his doubts about the validity of his marriage to Catherine. Henry was convinced that there was a curse on his heirs – only one of his seven children by Catherine had survived infancy and that a girl, the Princess Mary. This alone made him begin to take seriously earlier doubts about the wisdom of marrying his brother's widow. The succession crisis was worsened by contemporary fears about the future succession of a woman and the existence of several rival claimants to the throne – the Duke of Norfok (via his wife, a daughter of Edward IV); the Duke of Suffolk (via his wife, the sister of Henry VIII); and the Duke of Buckingham, a descendant of Edward III. Henry was driven by fears for his succession to such lengths as ordering Buckingham's execution (1521) and publicly acknowledging the illegitimate Blount as his son and as Duke of Richmond in 1525. Blount was even made Lord High Admiral of England, Lord Lieutenant of Ireland and Lord Warden of the Marches, and it was rumoured that he would be made King of Ireland. But a peaceful succession was what Henry craved and such could not be secured save by a legitimate heir. A new wife was a necessity (Pollard 1966, 139–56).

Pollard's dismissal of the theory that Henry divorced Catherine and broke away from the Church of Rome because of his passion for Anne Boleyn is of some interest to us: as we saw in earlier chapters the theory was extremely popular both among those who sought to vilify Henry and Anne, and among those who sought to present Anne Boleyn as a Protestant reformer. Pollard was dismissive: Henry had already satisfied his sensual passion in 1529 and he could have had Anne as a permanent mistress just as he had had her sister, Mary, and Elizabeth Blount before her; it seemed possible that Henry had already commenced divorce proceedings *before* he became infatuated with Anne (Pollard 1966, 150). Moreover, Anne was no Protestant reformer, for no matter what John Foxe claimed, 'It had no nobler foundation than the facts that Anne's position drove her into hostility to the Roman jurisdiction, and that her family shared the envy of church goods, common to the nobility and the gentry of the time' (Pollard 1966, 154). The divorce was a political expedient. Anne's person was of little consequence – almost any able-bodied woman of child-bearing age would have suited Henry's purpose. At the most, Henry's passion for her drove a wedge between himself and Wolsey, and, to the extent that Anne was unpopular, between himself and his people.

For Pollard, then, it was Henry who diagnosed the problem (the need for a legitimate heir and, therefore, a change of wife), prescribed the medicine (divorce and remarriage) and insisted that the course of treatment be followed (break with Rome, removal of Catherine and remarriage to Anne). He stopped at nothing. A faithful wife was cast off; a daughter was declared a bastard; a minister was ruined; an ancient allegiance was deserted.

Pollard was astute enough to appreciate that no monarch could have implemented such a drastic policy peacefully had his people objected strongly. Henry had no standing army. Why then did he succeed both in obtaining the divorce and breaking with Rome – especially given the unpopularity of the divorce itself? Pollard believed that the answer lay in a coincidence between Henry's wishes and those of the ruling élite, as assembled in Parliament. 'By summoning Parliament, Henry opened the floodgates of anti-papal and anti-sacerdotal feelings which Wolsey had long kept shut; and the unpopular divorce became merely a cross-current in the main stream which flowed in Henry's favour' (Pollard 1966, 202). It was not necessary for Henry to pack the Parliament of 1529 because the interests of the king and the lay middle classes happened to coincide – peaceful government and opportunities for aggrandizement at the church's expense. An intriguing situation emerged: the king who seemed the embodiment of personal monarchy became the champion of Parliament and the enunciator of the principle of sovereignty vested in 'king-in-Parliament'. These were halcyon days for Parliament according to Pollard:

> Community of interests produced harmony of action; and a century and a half was to pass before Parliament again met so

often, or sat so long, as it did during the latter half of Henry's reign. . . . No monarch, in fact, was ever a more zealous champion of parliamentary privileges, a more scrupulous observer of parliamentary forms, or a more original pioneer of sound constitutional doctrine. (Pollard 1966, 207)

On occasion, it was even able to prevent some of Henry's plans being realized. For example, Parliament rejected the Statutes of Wills and Uses on two occasions (Pollard 1966, 211).

Pollard had a deep reverence for the British Constitution. He had much in common with Lord Macaulay. He certainly found evidences for the 'majestic growth' of the Constitution in places where later historians have found evidence of much less elevated motivation (Dickens 1966, xiv). In the pages of the biography, Henry appears as a king with an enormous respect for Parliament. The king did not force his will on Parliament: he exerted his will 'by his careful and skilful manipulation of both houses'. And it was Henry himself and not his ministers who managed Parliament. 'No one was ever a greater adept in the management of the House of Commons, which is easy to humour but hard to drive'; 'Henry VIII was very assiduous in the attentions he paid to his lay lords and commons'; 'From 1529 he suffered no intermediary to come between Parliament and himself. Cromwell was more and more employed by the King, but only in subordinate matters, and when important questions were at issue Henry managed the business himself' (Pollard 1966, 211).

If the divorce was the occasion for the Reformation, then the Reformation itself was, in Pollard's eyes, a manifestation of rising nationalism – a concern shared, not by the monarch alone, but also by his people and especially his Parliament.

The church in England had hitherto been a semi-independent part of the political community – semi-national, semi-universal; it owed one sort of fealty to the universal Pope, and another to the national king. The rising spirit of nationality could brook no divided allegiance and the universal gave way to the national idea. There was to be no *imperium in imperio*, but 'one body politic' with one supreme head. Henry VIII is reported by Chapuys as saying that he was king, emperor and Pope, all in one, so far as

England was concerned. The church was to be nationalized; it was to compromise its universal character, and to become the Church of England, rather than a branch of the Church Universal in England (Pollard 1966, 215).

The Reformation, then, was imposed upon the church by the civil power – king and Parliament. It was in no sense a spontaneous revolution on the part of the clergy against the Roman yoke nor yet a reformation of doctrine.

It is scarcely surprising that Pollard reached this view of the nature of the English Reformation. His book is based rather exclusively upon the printed *Letters and Papers of Henry VIII*, which summaries had been begun in the mid-nineteenth century by J. S. Brewer and which were to be completed in 1910 by James Gairdner and R. H. Brodie. Pollard looked upon the *Letters and Papers* almost as a Bible: on the one hand he would rely upon the printed summaries rather than consult the actual document; on the other he would neglect other perspectives on an issue, sometimes ignoring whole classes of relevant administrative and legal documents in the Public Records as well as documentary sources held elsewhere which supplied evidence of public opinion from another standpoint than that of the government. As a consequence his interpretation of the origins of the English Reformation is heavily slanted towards official policy and takes little or no account of other forces at work – such as the beginnings of Protestantism.

Pollard's *Henry VIII*, reissued as late as 1966 as a student text, is a masterly example of narrative historical writing. While Pollard was certainly conscious that he was breaking new ground by rejecting a 'moral' interpretation of the Reformation and seeking rather to explain its occurrence, he succeeded in weaving his analysis into a beautifully written and highly readable prose composition. This is something which no other modern Reformation historian – with the exception of A. G. Dickens – has been able to do. Pollard writes with such authority and conviction that it is easy to fall into the temptation of accepting too readily his version of affairs and, above all, his interpretation of Henry's role in them.

Because Pollard assumed that Henry governed England after Wolsey's fall, it was inevitable that he should see Henry as the sole creator of the Reformation. Until the 1950s this interpretation went unchallenged. One of the most popular and influential textbooks of the post-war years, and a book with a wide general readership – S. T. Bindoff's *Tudor England* – modified Pollard's account slightly but largely followed his interpretation. Bindoff wrote: 'The Henrican Reformation had begun with the fall of a minister and been quickened by the birth of a child; it was slowed down by the birth of another child and brought to an end with the fall of another minister' (Bindoff 1964 edn, 108). And he closed his account of the 1530s with this resounding paragraph:

> Supreme Head of his Church and master of its wealth, Henry VIII had everything that he had fought the Pope, killed More and Fisher, and looted the monasteries to obtain. He was monarch of all he surveyed and surveying it he found that it was good. Eleven years had he laboured to create this brave new world, and now he would have it remain just as he had fashioned it. But it was a living, not a dead, world that Henry had created. Cromwell he could kill, Latimer he could silence, Parliament he could persuade to frame an Act of Six Articles against the heresies which Cromwell and Latimer had fostered, and his Church he could trust to condemn those who went on dabbling in them. But could he lull back into spiritual and intellectual torpor a nation which he had so violently aroused? Would his power be as effective in checking thought as in stimulating it? Could Henry stop the revolution which he had begun?
> (Bindoff 1964, 110–11)

The Pollardian interpretation of the official Reformation has much indeed to commend it. While Pollard, and his disciples, did see the Reformation as a creature of Henry's will, they none the less modified their voluntaristic approach. Henry designed the Reformation, but he was allowed to create it by the nation and, more particularly, by Parliament. As historians, they were keenly aware of the need to understand the balance of power in the kingdom and the attitudes of contemporaries: it was not enough to study Henry himself.

But it is also an interpretation which poses more questions than it answers. This is because the issue of sovereignty was never faced. Bindoff, whose brief in writing a history of Tudor England forced him to take account of the unfolding story of the Reformation, gives us a king who governs but is not entirely in control. Henry set the Reformation in motion, but the Reformation overtook him. It took no notice of the red lights and rarely observed the speed limit. This interpretation was an expansion of, rather than a rejection of, Pollard's own version. For Pollard, Henry had been able to break away from Rome because the nation connived. It gave him licence to rule as a despot. 'Strictly speaking, he was a constitutional king; he neither attempted to break up Parliament, nor to evade the law . . . . He led his people in the way they wanted to go, he tempted them with the baits they coveted most, he humoured the prejudices against the clergy and against the pretensions of Rome, and he used every concession to extract some fresh material for building up his own authority' (Pollard 1966, 345–6). For Bindoff, the extent to which Henry was a successful manipulator of Parliament and people remained in doubt. But he skirted the issue by giving very little attention to the final decade of Henry's reign. And that little was contradictory. On the one hand he asserted that Henry held steadfastly to 'the via media of his own choosing' (Bindoff 1964, 148). He quotes Luther's comment: 'What Squire Harry wills must be an article of faith for Englishmen, for life and death' (Bindoff 1964, 148). On the other hand, he acknowledged that the decentralized nature of the state and the church made total uniformity impossible to realize, and religious discord remained close to the surface. And Henry was gradually moving towards the Protestant position. This, according to Bindoff, was because Henry appreciated the political wisdom of such a move. 'One thing alone could have prompted this change', the change from mass to communion which Henry contemplated but did not execute, 'his realisation that the old faith no longer satisfied enough of his people to serve as a bond of national unity' (Bindoff 1964, 150). Henry might remain the helmsman of the English people, but only if he steered the ship of England in an acceptable direction. Bindoff is able to reconcile the events of the 1530s with those of the 1540s only by expanding Pollard's view of the monarch as a devious constitutionalist. When Henry realized that his people would have nothing less than a thoroughgoing doctrinal reformation, he put aside his personal preference in order to remain in control.

But this means that the reader is left with a contradiction in terms: a king who is the embodiment of personal monarchy – a dominant personality who knows exactly what he wants and goes right out and gets it – and a king who can only have what his people will allow him to have. Moreover, was Henry a parliamentarian by conviction or because it was expedient to be so? If the former, he wears the guise uneasily; if the latter, then was he really anything other than a clever despot who used Parliament to rubber-stamp his personal choices? Both Pollard and Bindoff credit Henry VIII with the political acumen to be aware both of his personal limitations, and of the limits placed upon his actions by the mood of the nation and the will of Parliament. According to them, Henry modified his own plans according to what was politically possible. Yes, they are reluctant to dub Henry merely devious – he also respects Parliament and wants to work with it. Given the stage of development which Parliament had reached in the mid-sixteenth century, it is surely surprising that Henry VIII would think this way. A man of imperious nature and despotic temper, he does not seem a born constitutionalist, and yet we are asked to believe that he freely handed out to his Parliament, and especially the Commons, a share in government such as no monarch before him had acknowledged. Parliament had hitherto claimed rights and privileges; when these had been granted, it had been grudgingly. One is tempted to believe that Pollard and Bindoff were transferring to Henry VIII attitudes which belonged more properly to the late nineteenth and early twentieth centuries than to the middle years of the sixteenth. Their accounts stand in the tradition of Victorian progressive constitutionalism. Yet they offer no evidence sufficient to persuade us that Henry VIII was a constitutional monarch by design or that he freely accorded Parliament a role in the design of the English Reformation.

By the 1950s the time was ripe for a reinterpretation. The field of historical studies in Britain had undergone profound changes since 1902, in no small part due to Pollard's own endeavours. History was not merely the story of what happened in the past, it was a scholarly discipline, taught in the universities and highly

regarded. Although C. H. Firth and J. B. Bury had called for a
more scientific approach to history at the ancient universities in
the early years of the century, it had been the new universities
which espoused the cause enthusiastically. At Manchester, even
undergraduates wrote 'theses' in medieval history under the guid-
ance of the medievalist Tout, and the new degrees of Master of
Arts, Bachelor of Literature and Doctor of Philosophy (all by
thesis) were developed and attracted fresh interest. All the para-
phernalia of organized post-graduate research emerged. At
London, Pollard called for similar developments: the present Institute of Historical Research stands as a monument to his work and
to that of H. A. L. Fisher.

The years before the Second World War saw the further
development of the discipline of history. Herbert Butterfield's
The Whig Interpretation of History exposed the strengths and weak-
nesses of the tradition of progressivism. Historians became self-
conscious about their methodology and explored many different
approaches to the past. Lewis Namier, for example, used the
prosopographical method – conclusions based upon the compil-
ation and correlation of multiple biographies. The science of
validating historical documentation and then of assessing its value
to the historian asking particular questions also developed apace.
Detailed studies of institutions and administrations, laws and
policies, initiated by the great medievalists, were based upon the
available records in the Public Record Office and the British
Museum, the published calendars and collections, and the steadily
growing library of secondary works and reference books which
was now being listed by the bibliographers.

After the war, the post-graduate study of history became yet
more organized. It was thought necessary to delve into all the
minutiae of life in the past, whether it related to the national or
the local government, to institutions or persons, to power
relations or to custom, to society or to economy. This tendency
was to be accentuated by the influence of the French *annales*
school. At the same time, history became problem-centred. The
emphasis was now heavily upon asking questions about the past
and the methodology required to answer them. Following one
source was not smiled upon. The use of a wide variety of sources

was approved. Historians were, above all, taught to be critical of their sources. Some doctoral theses and books had more foot-noting than text.

The new history challenged the primacy of politics. Whereas for writers like Pollard 'the people' and 'Parliament' had been in the main abstractions, for the new historians the people lived and moved and had their being in the past. It became important to flesh the abstractions and to determine what changes occurred in the lifestyle of ordinary people. When political events were studied, it was now necessary to gauge the extent to which various social groups participated in and influenced them, reacted to them or ignored them.

At the same time, the new historians learned from other emerg-ing disciplines and methodologies – sociology, anthropology, demography, econometrics, statistics. The questions which they asked about the past were often the same questions, couched in the same language, that economists, statisticians, sociologists and anthropologists were asking about the present; the methodologies which they used were likewise borrowed. At their worst, the new histories sacrificed 'people' to 'problems'; at their best, they opened up new vistas and challenged the complacency of those brought up in the Whig tradition.

It was in the years just before and just after the war that the ideas of social theorists such as Karl Marx and Max Weber percolated through to English historical writing. There are, of course, Marxist and Weberian histories – for example, R. H. Tawney's *Religion and the Rise of Capitalism* and Christopher Hill's *Economic Problems of the Church* – but even historians who were by no stretch of the imagin-ation Marxists or Weberians owed much to their influence. This was, above all, because they drew attention to and lent definition to the major problems of modern capitalist and industrial societies; class struggle, bureaucracies and their influence upon government, exploitation of the workers by the capitalists, centralization of government; the emergence of the interventionist state and so on. Much historical writing tackled just this sort of issue, even or per-haps especially writing on the Reformation. There were certainly many historians who worked in the old empirical tradition rather than the new theoretical, but they too were children of their time.

After the war, Reformation historians began to ask new questions. Some wanted to know whether the official Reformation was Henry's own creation and what purposes he intended it to serve. Others suggested that someone other than Henry designed it or that it happened by accident. Still others questioned the primacy of the official Reformation and argued that the reformation from below was equally, if not more, important. Had the 'people' not wanted Protestantism, the Church of England would have remained Catholic if not papist. These questions all reflected contemporary concerns about the location of power in the nation – the nature of Tudor monarchy, the emergence of democracy. The historians involved in this debate often were not *religious* historians but *political* or *constitutional* historians. They either accepted or challenged Pollard's great thesis – that the Reformation was Henry's creation and that it originated in his desire to be king of his own castle and to drive out the foreigners who claimed the allegiance of his people. There were others (whose works are discussed in the following chapters) who identified different problems and questions.

The gauntlet was thrown down by Geoffrey Elton (b. 1921) in the late 1940s and early 1950s. He showed 'Henry in a very different light from that now normally shed upon him – from the lantern of Pollard's great book'. Elton, working in the English empirical tradition, came to a new view of the role of Henry VIII in the work of government and in the creation of the Reformation via a thesis submitted for the PhD degree at the University of London in 1948. He was not, in fact, really interested in the Reformation as such. The subject for his thesis was 'Thomas Cromwell: aspects of his administrative work'. Geoffrey Elton represented the new breed of scholar in that he boasted a knowledge second to none of the documents of central government and administration. His work is characterized by close attention to detail and penetrating textual criticism. His early work was important both as a discussion of the organization of government and as a contribution to the general debate on the balance of power in the Tudor state. Elton's 'new view' seems to have grown out of his conviction that Henry VIII was not interested in the day-to-day business of government – he was interested in the ends rather than the means – and that Thomas Cromwell, the quiet bureaucrat, took advantage of this fact to implement his own reform of government and administration. The reformation in religion was part of this process.

Down to the present day, Geoffrey Elton has produced a plethora of scholarly monographs and learned articles which contribute to the debate. These include *The Tudor Constitution: documents and commentary* (1960); *The Tudor Revolution in Government* (1953); and *England Under The Tudors* (1955). Yet nowhere is his challenging view of Henry's part in the Reformation more clearly and persuasively expressed than in a brief pamphlet produced for the Historical Association in 1962, *Henry VIII: An Essay in Revision*.

In this pamphlet, Elton questions the assumption made by Pollard that Henry's reign can conveniently be divided into two: a period from 1514 to 1529, when Henry let Wolsey govern and was Wolsey's apprentice; and a period from 1529 to 1547, when Henry assumed the reins of government and was thus the 'very embodiment of personal monarchy'. Elton suggests that there was no unity in the years 1529 to 1547 such as Pollard assumed. The 1530s were marked by a successful internal policy, the 1540s by unsuccessful foreign policies against France and Scotland, internal problems and economic crisis. Moreover, Henry had never left government entirely to Wolsey: he had, for example, managed state trials throughout the reign and he had been active personally in foreign policy early in the reign (the war of 1512–14). Elton is above all suspicious of the view that Henry was ever totally in control of his government and its policies. Certainly only he could make or unmake ministers; both Wolsey and Cromwell learned that to their cost. But Henry was often manipulated by his own councillors. And, while it is true that he was diligent in matters of business during Cromwell's ascendancy – reading and signing letters and papers – he did not initiate policy but relied upon Thomas Cromwell to devise and control policy. He was sufficiently intelligent to recognize in Cromwell gifts of industry and creative statesmanship and to delegate power to him. Naturally it was a power delegated on condition that Cromwell devised and executed policies broadly to the king's liking. Elton argues that Henry kept a more watchful eye upon Cromwell's activities with respect to theological and ecclesiastical affairs – he took a great interest in the Act against appeals to Rome in 1533, for instance. He rejects, however, the idea that, in all matters of moment, the king instructed Cromwell verbally to follow particular courses of action. As most of the business of government was normally carried on away from the court, oral communication between king and minister was impossible, and no letters survive to support this view of affairs.

For Pollard's bipartite division of the reign, then, Elton substituted a much more complex one (1511–14; 1514–29; 1529–31; 1531–41; 1541–7). He has argued consistently that each section of the reign differed markedly from the others, not as a result of the king responding in different ways to events and circumstances, but because the king was not in control. 'To some extent of course these differences were due to altering circumstances, but the indisputable fact that such problems as arose were tackled in a strikingly different fashion at different times cannot be so easily explained. Each section of the reign differed from the rest in a manner which can only rationally derive from changes in the men who directed affairs . . . . The King was always there . . . the differences lay in the men he employed' (Elton 1953; 1962 repr., 67). For Elton, the king's mercurial temperament offered no explanation for a changeable policy. The change in ministers helped to explain the contrasting attitudes towards Rome during the periods 1529–31 and 1532–4.

The reality of Henry's personal monarchy or his determination to pursue policies which would further his own interests is not questioned. What is denied is that Henry's interest in government extended to devising policies in detail and engaging in the administrative work involved. Moreover, he found it difficult to see Henry VIII as a constitutionalist. 'Henry was not, despite his over-powering personality and his ultimate control, the maker of his own policy; of course, he alone could turn it into his own, but he did not invent it and relied on others for the mind that must inform action' (Elton 1962, 67); 'in the day to day business of governing England, Henry VIII was not so much incapable as un-interested and feckless (Elton 1962, 68); 'the specific work of government, the ideas underlying it, and the possibilities put into effect at different times varied as Henry's ministers took over from one another' (Elton 1965, 24). Elton, then, sees Henry as 'a nimble opportunist, picking up ideas and suggestions from all around him and putting together a useable amalgam . . . without having to do the hard work himself' (Elton 1962, 25), 'an opportunist whose only real programme concerned the advancement of his own interests by whatever means seemed suitable and possible in terms of both law and politics' (Elton 1965, 26).

Geoffrey Elton, when he had read widely about Henry VIII, suspected that the monarch was not capable of the personal involvement in the detailed work of government which Pollard attributed to him. Elton usefully contrasted Henry VIII's style of personal monarchy with those of Henry VII and Elizabeth I:

> In the hands of Henry VIII personal monarchy did not mean personal attention to the business of government, though it had done so in the hands of Henry VII. Nor did it mean the constant weighing up of conflicting counsel and the pursuit of a personal policy based upon a personal assessment as it did for Elizabeth. It meant the putting of the king's personal force behind policies not of his devising. His greatness lay in the rapid and accurate interpretation of the immediate situation, in a dauntless will, and in his choice of advisers; but not in originality, and it is doubtful if he was the architect of anything, least of all the English Reformation.   (Elton 1966, 26)

Implicitly, Elton also doubted Pollard's vision of Henry as a monarch who not only worked with but respected Parliament. While there can be little doubt that the legislature was used to implement the Reformation, and that Henry concurred in this policy, Elton looked elsewhere than to Henry himself for the policy's origins: to Thomas Cromwell, the King's minister.

Thomas Cromwell, according to Elton, was the architect, the builder and the master craftsman of the English Reformation. The king only commissioned the work. Before Elton began to write, little attention had been paid in the modern age to this apparently colourless civil servant, largely because Pollard cast him simply as a builder's labourer. But Elton has put flesh upon his bones, breathed life into the cadaver of the architect.

If Elton has been correct in attributing to Thomas Cromwell the master plan for the English Reformation, then the minister's motivation is certainly debatable. In *England Under the Tudors* (1955) Elton ascribed to Cromwell a grand constitutional design:

> [Cromwell] offered to make a reality out of Henry's vague claims to supremacy by evicting the pope from England. To the king this meant a chance of getting his divorce, and a chance of wealth; to Cromwell it meant the chance of reconstructing the body politic.   (Elton 1955, 129)

Cromwell, according to Elton, wanted to set up a limited constitutional monarchy in which king and Parliament acted together. He was not working to construct an autocratic despotism. In support of this thesis Elton cited Cromwell's interest in the work of Marsiglio of Padua and Thomas Starkey, as well as his determined attempt to legitimate Henry's new authority through Parliament. He is portrayed by Elton as a man not only sympathetic to reform but dedicated to furtherance of the commonwealth through the reorganization of political structures. As A. G. Dickens observed (Dickens 1959b), Cromwell was also a committed patron of letters, of scholars, of evangelism. For Elton, his grand constitutional design was, however, essentially secular. The religious reformation – the break with Rome – was a political act and not an expression of Thomas Cromwell's dislike of Catholicism (Elton 1955, 160–2; 165–70; 175–9).

In *Reform and Reformation, England 1509–1558*, published in 1977, despite accommodating Dickens's position on Cromwell's Protestantism to some extent, Geoffrey Elton reached much the same conclusions regarding Cromwell's motivation in implementing the Reformation as he had done in 1955:

> Bible-worship could take very different forms in the many people whom it alone united. In Cromwell's case it supplied one of the driving forces to an essentially political temperament, the principled undertone and transcendental justification of labours that concentrated upon reforming the earthly existence of men

by reconstructing the state and using the dynamic thus released (rendered active in legislative potential – that is, in statute) to remedy the abuses and deficiencies for so long debated and identified. It was Cromwell's purpose to remake and renew the body politic of England, a purpose which because of the comprehensiveness of his intentions amounted to a revolution, but which proceeded by using the means inherited from the past. Not only did the practical statesman in him grasp the political advantage of introducing major change . . . under the guise of continuity, but Cromwell . . . also knew about the roots and long established realities of the polity he wished to transform. These realities lay in a general order embodied in the common law and in the making of a new law by discussion and consent, not edict. . . . Cromwell had a vision – a vision of order, improvement, the active removal of all that was bad, corrupt or merely inefficient, and the creation of a better life here and now in preparation for the life to come. To Cromwell, the reformed church was to serve the purposes of the reformed commonwealth. (Elton 1977, 172)

Upon what evidence rests Elton's argument that it was Cromwell who created the English Reformation? In 'King or Minister? The Man Behind the Henrician Reformation', Elton reiterated his view that Cromwell was no mere instrument in government and then attempted to ascertain whether it was Cromwell's mind or Henry's that originated the plan for obtaining Henry's divorce. Elton saw the Reformation as 'the definition of independent national sovereignty achieved by the destruction of the papal jurisdiction in England'. In other words, the break with Rome is the *essence* of the English Reformation. Whose idea was it? As we have seen, Pollard maintained that Henry had always known that it might come to a breach with Rome in the end – had hoped that it would not, had procrastinated but had prepared himself to take the risk. Pollard's contemporary, James Gairdner, concurred. Elton did not. If Henry had planned such a course of action, would it have taken six long, tortuous years for him to decide that the radical step was necessary? Moreover, neither Wolsey nor foreign observers suspected that the King had any such plan under his royal bonnet. Henry's actions do not indicate that he planned a break with Rome. In 1529 he called Parliament 'to overawe the Church': he wanted to bring the clergy to heel in anticipation of their being called upon to adjudicate in the divorce. In 1530 he uttered bold statements, but he did not *do* more than collect international opinions about the divorce. When the Pope refused to be moved, Henry appealed to General Councils, but threatened no schism. In 1531 he did not make any headway with the divorce; he did bring the English clergy under his control (when the clergy, threatened by praemunire, surrendered), but their acknowledgement of him as 'their singular protector, only and supreme lord, and as far as the law of Christ allows also supreme head' did no more than underline the pre-existent authority of the Crown and certainly did not undermine the spiritual authority of the Pope. '. . . the king's title does not expressly deny the pope's spiritual headship or justify the withdrawal of England from the papal jurisdiction. As yet there was no policy of a "break with Rome".' Throughout the negotiations at Rome in 1531–2 Henry was 'bankrupt in ideas. He knew what he wanted; that neither he nor his ministers knew how to obtain it is proved by those years of bootless negotiations' (Elton 1954, 223–9).

The advent of the policy of 'break with Rome' coincided with the advent of Thomas Cromwell to the king's inner council. The concept of empire (sovereignty) simultaneously entered the field. The hounds of Parliament were deliberately set upon the Pope. The Pope's authority over the church (with its lay as well as ecclesiastical membership) was the trophy handed over to the king. It was Cromwell who shaped the important Act in restraint of appeals to Rome, which pronounced national sovereignty and thereby signalled the breach with Rome and proclaimed the finality of the kill (Elton 1949, 174 ff.).

Dr Elton writes with such authority that relatively few have questioned the assumptions upon which his thesis rests, preferring rather to challenge the minutiae of his argument. For example, his contention that much of the proposed legislation originated not with the court, as had been thought, but with genuine lay grievances against the church and its courts which were deliberately brought to Cromwell's attention and were later used by him to bring the church to heel (Elton 1951, 507–34; Elton 1973) inspired several historians to reply (Cooper 1957, 616–41). The drafting procedures for new legislation were microscopically inspected. Yet the criticisms which Elton levelled at Pollard – those of assuming rather than arguing the truth of a case – could equally well be directed at Elton's own work. The case that he makes for Thomas Cromwell as the mastermind of the English Reformation is often plausible but incapable of proof. There is much circumstantial evidence, but little that would stand in a court of law.

The problem lies in the assumption behind Elton's detailed case. He challenges Pollard's belief that Henry was actively involved in government and an originator of his own policies; he replaces this with the assumption that Cromwell masterminded the Reformation, that he argued the invalidity of Henry's marriage to Catherine, that he toned down Henry's more extravagant claims for the Crown's spiritual jurisdiction and that he persisted in rooting the revolution in statute. Henry's reluctance to accept the break with the Roman jurisdiction as absolute and irreversible is, oddly enough, taken as evidence that Cromwell did not think likewise or hope likewise. Cromwell may well have realized that the move had to be permanent, given his analysis of affairs (and his own Protestantism), but this in itself is not proof that he had envisaged it as part of a grand plan for parliamentary monarchy. Dr Elton infers that Henry did not originate a policy of rejecting the Roman jurisdiction and locating the king-in-Parliament (as Pollard occasionally seems to have believed) on the basis of certain assumptions – that Henry would not have been acting in character had he planned a parliamentary or limited monarchy and that neither his words nor his actions prior to Cromwell's rise indicate that he had formulated any such policy. He then makes the leap, without looking, to the position that it was Thomas Cromwell and not Henry who originated this same long-term, revolutionary and very conscious policy. He shows us the wily Thomas hoodwinking Bluff King Hal. He does not seem to realize that this argument rests upon certain assumptions which he is unable to substantiate and which may be as erroneous as those which underpinned Pollard's thesis. Was there a long-term plan to locate sovereignty in the king-in-Parliament? (Hurstfield 1973 repr.; Stone 1951).

Joel Hurstfield (1911–80) sought to come to grips with this issue. Was there a Tudor despotism after all? (Hurstfield 1973 repr.). For those of us who want to know whether the official Reformation was a creature of Henry VIII's will or of the will of Henry VIII *and* his people, this is a crucial question. For those of us who want to ascertain the place of the Reformation in Cromwell's overall policy, it is no less important. Joel Hurstfield defined a despotism as 'authoritarian rule in which the government is resolved to enforce its will on a nation and to suppress all expressions of dissent; and if this is a society in which the people have few means of influencing decisions on major issues, then we may find despotisms – of varying degrees of efficiency – at many stages during the evolution of modern society' (Hurstfield 1973, 26). Historians in the twentieth century had previously denied that England's monarchy was a despotism. Trevelyan stated baldly: 'England was not a despotism. The power of the crown rested not on force but on popular support' (Trevelyan 1926, 269–70). Parliamentary consent for him implied that statute was the expression of the popular will. Elton went further:

> Thus the political events and constitutional expansion of the 1530s produced major changes in the position of Parliament. Long and frequent sessions, fundamental and far-reaching measures, revolutionary consequences, governmental leadership – all these combined with the Crown's devotion to statute and use of Parliament to give that institution a new air, even to change it essentially into its modern form as the supreme and sovereign legislator.   (Elton 1960, 234)

Moreover, in Elton's view this development was intentional. 'Whatever may have been the case before Cromwell's work . . . there was no Tudor despotism after it. Wittingly or not – and the present writer has no doubt that it was done wittingly – Cromwell established the reformed state as a limited monarchy and not as a despotism' (Elton 1955, 168). Joel Hurstfield challenged the fundamental assumptions of Elton's argument: that either Henry or Cromwell deliberately worked to establish a limited monarchy in England and that parliamentary consent is necessarily to be taken as indicative of active parliamentary participation in initiating law or policy. He adduced evidence to the effect that Cromwell held Parliament in contempt. He suggested that the Crown wished, by the Statute of Proclamations, to dispense with the need to work through and with Parliament. There is even evidence that Cromwell sounded out legal opinions as to the powers of proclamation. Had Cromwell succeeded in obtaining the enactment of the Statute of Proclamations in the form desired, argued Hurstfield, the situation would have been analogous to that in Germany when the Reichstag conferred upon Adolf Hitler in March 1933 the right to govern by proclamation. Hitler wished to buttress his destruction of German liberty with the law: he succeeded. Cromwell, no less, wished to use Parliament to give authority to the proclamations of the monarch. 'But is a thing less tyrannical because it is lawful?' and was the legislation of the Tudor Parliament the creature of that Parliament? (Hurstfield 1973, 33–40).

For Hurstfield, however, the problem of consent remained unsolved. He asked more questions than he answered, but the questions that he posed were penetrating. Did Parliament represent the people?

> On the basis of what we know, the House of Commons consisted of a minority of a minority of the population, while the members of the House of Lords, as contemporaries were aware, represented no one but themselves. Within the limits of such an institution we may, if we wish, speak of a partnership, provided that we see the House of Lords as becoming increasingly a pocket borough of the Crown, and the House of Commons as elected to a large extent under ministerial and aristocratic patronage.　　　　　　　　　　(Hurstfield 1973, 43)

What was the Crown's attitude to Parliament? 'Tudor monarchs behaved as though Parliaments were no more than regrettable necessities' (Hurstfield 1973, 44). What did Parliaments do? They did not initiate legislation (Hurstfield 1973, 43). Did Parliament reach its decisions regarding the Reformation legislation after a period of free discussion? '. . . the government held a tight grasp on Parliament, the pulpits and the press and strove, not always successfully, to silence the expression of dissentient opinion, in both the spoken and the written word' (Hurstfield 1973, 45). Did the people want the Reformation? The settlement certainly required powerful sanctions: the supremacy and the ideology were enforced by the government; the existence of nine treason laws during Henry's reign is 'hardly a demonstration of a secure government resting equably on the support of the people' (Hurstfield 1973, 44).

Geoffrey Elton may be dubbed the last of the great Victorians. He stands confidently with one foot in the tradition of progressive constitutionalism and the other in that of voluntarism. Parliament achieved a maturity during Henry VIII's reign such as it had never before possessed: one man willed this state of affairs and that man was Thomas Cromwell. Joel Hurstfield realized that it was difficult to belong to both camps. Either Henry was a constitutional monarch or he was not. Hurstfield sought to free himself and his readers from the shackles of the present: 'I have constantly to remind myself that, although a Tudor politician spoke our language, he did not think our thoughts' (Hurstfield 1973, 27). He used not only his detailed knowledge of the past but also his historical imagination to reach his conclusions about the nature of Henrician monarchy and the relationship between monarch and people.

> To understand the relationship between the Tudor people and their governments, it is essential to take into account that this was minority rule, an uneasy and unstable distribution of power between the Crown and a social élite in both the capital and the shires, and that this governing class, this élite, itself played a double role. It was under pressure to conform and was at the same time the channel of communication for a vast mass of propaganda in defence of the existing order, pumped out through press and pulpit, through preambles to acts and through proclamations read out in the market place, through addresses to high court judges in Star Chamber and by high court judges at the assizes, through all the pageantry and symbolism of royal progresses. All this functioned under a heavy

censorship which, for all its clumsy ineptitude, struck hard at independent thinking. . . . Here was a despotism in the making, sometimes of the Crown over Paliament, more often of the Crown in Parliament over the nation. This is what I mean by the dual role of the élite.   (Hurstfield 1973, 46)

Henry did not 'hold in submission the whole nation against its will and interests' (Hurstfield 1973, 47), but he and his ministers evolved a governmental machine which suppressed dissent, convinced, by propaganda, that the government's actions were just and right, established the Crown's control of foreign policy and religion, seized for the Crown enormous emergency powers and ensured that ministers were responsible to the Crown alone. All that Henry did was designed to serve one end – the establishment of despotism, the confirmation of his own power. When he worked with Parliament or in Parliament, it was to this end. When he worked without Parliament, it was to the like end.

Elton's own study of the enforcement of the Reformation during Cromwell's ascendancy, *Policy and Police*, his best book, explored the suggestion that dissenting opinion was suppressed by a reign of terror which disregarded the bounds of law and humanity. He demonstrated that there was certainly frequent resistance to the changes but that the government, in the embodiment of Cromwell, conducted an entirely legal campaign, which took careful account of the reports of informers, dismissing mere grudges and malicious complaints, before clamping down on dissent. There were no official spies. The government did not search out trouble: it dealt with resistance when it was brought to its attention. A vigorous propaganda campaign, aimed at enlisting the support of the people, was pursued. Clearly, Elton views this enforcement from a very different perspective to that adopted in Hurstfield's 1967 article (Hurstfield 1973, repr.). Elton attributes to Cromwell the very best of motives – he was trying to achieve stability and to convert opinion; Hurstfield, on the contrary, presents a far less roseate view: Cromwell's brief was to suppress contrary opinion in the interests of the King's power (Elton 1972).

All historians, when they write, make certain assumptions upon which their arguments rest. Often these assumptions are not only unstated but unrecognized by the author. Joel Hurstfield's searching intellect and ready wit fitted him for the task of questioning the assumptions upon which interpretations of the English Reformation and its origins rested. Whereas Elton and Pollard before him seemed to look at the events of the Reformation years through Victorian eyes, Hurstfield tried to remove the spectacles and to establish what contemporaries had meant by their words and actions. So he asked, 'How is it that this material . . . has somehow come to mean that this was government by consent? How can we call it consent when we know that the avenues of dissent were deliberately closed by policy?' (Hurstfield 1973, 48–9). To his mind strong central government was essential if England were to avoid civil war and foreign invasion. The public were aware of this and allowed Henry VIII to govern despotically. They consented to the advance of the state which rejection of the Roman jurisdiction implied. They did not initiate policy.

If we accept Hurstfield's argument that Henry VIII's rule was despotic in character it is, of course, still possible to maintain that it owed its character to the efforts of Thomas Cromwell and not to those of Henry himself. Instead of Thomas the Champion of Parliaments we have Thomas the Machiavellian supporter of absolute kingship. In either guise, he would be the bureaucrat who deliberately set out to revolutionize Tudor government and administration: the man with a blueprint for parliamentary democracy or despotism.

But there remain many who are unwilling to attribute such influence to Thomas Cromwell. Most notable of the critics of such an interpretation is J. J. Scarisbrick. In essence, Scarisbrick's biography of Henry VIII (1968) presents a modified Pollardian line. Whereas Pollard had claimed that Henry served an apprenticeship under Wolsey and only assumed the reigns of government personally after this minister's fall, Scarisbrick maintains that Henry had already been master during Wolsey's reign; that Wolsey's will rarely overrode Henry's when it came to matters of foreign policy. According to Scarisbrick, the wars, the divorce, the breach with Rome all originated with Henry (Scarisbrick 1968, 45–6). '. . . how far had Henry broken with his past by 1532, how deeply was he already committed to carrying out an ecclesiastical revolution? Were the three years, 1530 to 1532, years without a policy, years of aimless bombast and bullying, of makeshift and fumbling, as Elton would have us believe?' (Scarisbrick 1968, 287). Scarisbrick draws our attention to something which is oft forgotten – Henry's ability to hold two contradictory positions at once. He could, for example, claim the autonomy of each province of the Church and thus allege the validity of a local divorce while simultaneously suggesting judgement by three papal delegates (Scarisbrick 1968, 288). But by the autumn of 1530 it seems to Scarisbrick that Henry wanted national autonomy (Scarisbrick 1968, 289). Unlike Pollard, he believes that the idea that the pre-Reformation Church was autonomous is incorrect (Scarisbrick 1968, 263). Henry came to his position via a different route: he was irked by his inability to act without approval from Rome. Gradually he moved towards asserting Royal Supremacy. He claimed a pastoral role as early as 1529 and eventually required the clergy to acknowledge his cure of souls. By 1531 he was claiming overlordship of the national church by his attack on the Courts Christian and his editing of the decrees of Convocation. From the late summer of 1530 there was an atmosphere of mounting anti-papalism (Scarisbrick 1968, 287). But all of these would not have precluded a relationship between the English church and Rome such as that between the Gallican church and the Papacy. Henry could have claimed jurisdiction but granted the Pope primacy of honour and a limited spiritual authority, where heresy was concerned for instance. But Henry moved too far for that with the Praemunire campaign and with the attack on clerical privileges (Scarisbrick 1968, 295–301).

If it was with Henry that the revolutionary policies originated, what role did Thomas Cromwell play? Dr Scarisbrick does not quite demote him to the status of builder's labourer. Instead he is envisaged as a builder with flair and imagination who interprets the architect's blueprint in an original way. 'He was immediately responsible for the vast legislative programme of the later sessions of the Reformation Parliament'; 'He oversaw the breach with Rome'; 'He effected a new political integration of the kingdom and imposed upon it a new political discipline'; 'He left a deep mark on much of the machinery of central and local government' and he created a propaganda machine 'to shape public opinion' (Scarisbrick 1968, 303). But, he warns, Henry never gave any minister the sort of freedom which Cardinal Wolsey had enjoyed. Cromwell was not ultimately responsible for the Reformation (Scarisbrick 1968, 304).

The English Reformation, A. G. Dickens's general history (1964, soon to be published in revised form) looks at the respective roles of Henry and Cromwell from a somewhat different perspective. Unlike Scarisbrick, Dickens (b. 1910) believes that Protestantism was already a force to be reckoned with by the 1530s and that 'English Catholicism, despite its gilded decorations, was an old, unseaworthy and ill-commanded galleon, scarcely able to continue its voyage without the new seamen and shipwrights produced (but produced too late in the day) by the Counter-Reformation' (Dickens 1967, 108). Henry VIII, to his mind, could not have frozen the religious situation as it stood in 1530 (Dickens 1967, 108). Nevertheless, the divorce was important. It was one of the dangerous reefs that English Catholicism had to circumnavigate: it was the reef upon which this ship was wrecked at last. 'Without it the schism would not have been consummated by 1533–4' (Dickens 1967, 107). It was Henry who wanted the divorce and he was prepared to resort to radical policies in order to achieve it, but it was Cromwell who guided the Henrician ship of state into foreign waters, not Henry. For the Henrician ecclesiastical policy only becomes intelligible if viewed in the context of general administrative reform, if seen against the backcloth of Cromwell's vision of 'the sovereign state as transcending the turmoil and division inherited from both the defects and the death-struggles of feudal society' (Dickens 1967, 112). So, concludes Dickens, 'From this stage we cannot understand Crown policy if we continue to envisage Thomas Cromwell as merely a smart lawyer who made his fortune by solving the king's matrimonial problem. For good or ill, he is a figure of far greater significance in our history'. Dickens sees Cromwell pulling the Reformation forward – towing the Henrician ship into far deeper waters than the monarch had contemplated visiting. The demands for a single sovereignty and undivided allegiance, for Dickens as for Elton, smack of Thomas Cromwell's convictions and not those of the

King. Dickens's understanding of Cromwell's religious position reinforced this view (Dickens 1959b).

The debate which we have just revisited is, it must be admitted, in a state of deadlock. Short of a policy statement of extreme clarity from either Henry VIII or his minister, it is impossible to *prove* either side of the case. The individual contributions to the debate have been invaluable for the insights into Tudor rule and Reformation policy which they have revealed, but none has done what it set out to do – to answer the crucial questions: king or minister? despotism or limited monarchy? accident or design?

It might also be asked whether the participants in this debate chose their ground wisely. The argument as formulated belongs to a tradition of historical writing in which high politics is seen as central and the autonomy of politics taken for granted. Politics is the play. It fills the stage to the exclusion of all else. Of the authors whom we have discussed, only A. G. Dickens casts the 'people' in a real role – for the rest, the people are an abstraction, playing walk-on, walk-off parts. In this respect, Geoffrey Elton's view of the Reformation, influenced though his work is by modern political science, is as old-fashioned as that of A. F. Pollard. Only in *Policy and Police* does Elton consider the reception of the official Reformation at local and popular level. Both accept, without question, the centrality of politics. Both take, without demur, the view that the course of events was determined by the will of people in high places. Both are confused by the implicit contradiction between this voluntarism and the Victorian belief in a gradually maturing mixed constitution. Both refuse to face up to this contradiction and both proceed as if it never existed.

It is not only the relationship between policy-making and popular feeling that has escaped many of the historians of the Reformation of 'the old school'. In the main, they have little or no understanding of the interaction of socio-economic and religious factors with the world of politics. Of the authors quoted, only A. G. Dickens can correctly be dubbed a religious historian. None but he has any sympathy with the religious feelings which ran on the surface of Tudor society. For Elton, who is prone to see sixteenth-century men and women through twentieth-century or even nineteenth-century spectacles, religion is often ignored as a factor of importance. Even when he began to display Cromwell as an adherent of the new religion, he continued to insist that this man's thoughts were essentially secular. To be fair, Elton, Pollard, Hurstfield and Scarisbrick would not wish to be classified as anything other than political or administrative historians. But we may well pose the question: can one really solve the historical problems surrounding the official Reformation without also examining the religious perspective?

Since the end of the Second World War, the debate about the nature of the English Reformation has moved to new ground. Historians more acutely aware of the relationship between politics and society have reformulated the questions. Above all, historians interested in religion and in the church as an institution have moved in to chart the waters. In the next chapter, we shall examine the contributions to the social, economic and religious history of the Reformation made by the new generation of historians.

Chapter 6

The Reformation and the people

In the twentieth century, and particularly since 1960, the English Reformation has become prey to the *new history*. Historians, exhibiting their acquaintance with the methodologies of psycho-history, sociology, anthropology, demography, linguistics and economics have determined to write *histoire totale*. For this reason, it is often difficult to determine what are works of, strictly speaking, Reformation history at all and what are works of purely secular significance. Of course, the longstanding, if easily challenged, view that the Reformation was but the religious aspect of the Renaissance movement has always stressed the necessity for the religious historian to examine the Reformation in its context. That sixteenth-century intellectual life was imbued with religion is now a truism: every school student knows that God could not be left out of politics; that the clergy dominated education; that moral discipline was administered by the church courts; that the family was itself a 'church'. But now something has been added – an awareness that religion itself has a sociological, a psychological and an economic dimension. Concepts such as 'social control', 'professionalization', 'social mobility', 'class warfare', 'bureaucratiz-ation', 'capitalism', 'proto-industrialization' are bandied about. The historians, products of an age which if not anti-religious is certainly a-religious, approach the history of the Reformation in a less credulous spirit than did their predecessors. Indeed, some regard with incredulity any suggestion that 'man' could possibly have a pure, unmixed belief in the godhead; surely his economic interests, his upbringing, his ambition must have been the motivating force in his life? Marx, Weber, Freud – their ghosts stalk the land of the new Reformation history. The theories as well as the techniques of other disciplines are used.

The recent historiography of the Reformation is complicated. Of course, there is one level on which it can be made to look simple (Haigh 1982, 995–1007). The dispute over the *causes* of the English Reformation continues. On the one hand there is Geoffrey Elton claiming that the advance of Protestantism owed almost everything to official coercion, with the agreement of a few of the adherents of the new history and some adherents of the old (for example, Christopher Haigh himself and J. J. Scarisbrick). On the other there is the line pursued by A. G. Dickens that the new religion spread by conversions among the people and that it gained strength independently of the 'political' reformation. This view emphasizes also the debt owed by the English Reformation to continental Protestantism. Simultaneously there runs a debate concerning the pace of this religious change: Dickens's view that Protestantism made real inroads very early (so that it was a strong force by 1553) being challenged by Penry Williams, Christopher Haigh and J. J. Scarisbrick, who argue, from differing perspectives, that little permanent was achieved before Elizabeth's reign. Occasionally, there is no real disagreement between the historians involved: it is rather a matter of emphasis. Although Haigh cites A. G. Dickens and Patrick Collinson as proponents of quite opposing positions regarding the pace of change, it is far from clear that Patrick Collinson disagrees with A. G. Dickens's view of the strength of Protestantism in some areas during Mary's reign; what is clear is that Collinson's main interest is in the growth of Protestantism during Elizabeth's reign and beyond. But the debate is not as simple as Haigh maintains. There are other, underlying debates of greater subtlety and equal import which are often ignored because it is so very difficult to penetrate the forest to espy these particular trees.

The core debates about causes and chronology must be given their due, but we must also ask of the existing literature some other important questions: if, indeed, the Reformation was a popular movement rather than an official act, when and why did it begin and when did it end? How did it percolate through English society? Did it meet with resistance, and, if so, why? What implications did doctrinal, political and institutional changes have for 'secular' England and, indeed, for the church itself? Did the church as 'institution' change immeasurably? Were the functions of the church altered? Is it valid to pit an interpretation of the Reformation as springing from the localities against that which sees the Reformation as a 'national' and 'nationalistic' act?

Let's start at the beginning. But where is it? The historian of the English Reformation has always found this question problematic. The affinities of the doctrinal reformation with Lutheranism and Calvinism in Europe, with the ideas of the Northern Renaissance, with the popular reform movement of the Middle Ages are plain to see. Yet the English Reformation was also a political event – the reform of the church; the redefinition of its relations with the state; the creed which it professed were all shaped, at least in large part, by politicians and their collaborators, no matter what their motivation. Whatever Englishmen had wanted or now wanted, what they were allowed was legislatively defined. Some committed reformers found it very difficult to accommodate themselves to this state of affairs. And, while historians are able to trace earlier movements for reform, ideas which favoured and paved the way for doctrinal and political change, they find it ten or a hundred times more difficult to ascribe precise cause or effect and to discover necessary or contingent factors. They are left trying to reconcile the fact of the political reformation with the forces for reformation already present in society and of trying to assess their importance. It is worth quoting Horton Davies on this dilemma:

It would be entirely wrong to suggest that the Reformation in England was, as Hilaire Belloc has termed it, 'the English Accident'. For apart from the king's interest in securing his second-generation throne by male issue and his rapacity for the property of the church as was evident in the dissolution of the monasteries, there were two forces moving towards reformation, or at least spiritual renovation, in England. One was the secret brotherhood of Lollards who longed to see the 'dominion of grace' overwhelming the legal, institutional, and all too worldly external carapace of the church, of whom, since they were covert companies, we know very little. The other force was the band of Cambridge scholars who gathered from time to time in the White Horse Inn and who must have included Erasmians as well as Lutherans; from them the greatest Protestant episcopal leadership was to come in King Edward's reign. . . . Unquestionably . . . there were Protestants in England committed to a national Reformation while the king was still a 'defender of the faith' of Rome, and for whom his later turning from Rome was not quick or thorough-going enough.

(Davies 1970, 6–7)

It is certain that we must not ignore the debt of the English Reformation to continental – particularly Lutheran and Swiss – influences. William A. Clebsch wrote of the years 1520–35 as 'that initial and most difficult time . . . when the fountain of faith was a banned Bible, and when the gospel rediscovered by Luther rallied Englishmen to martyrdom' (Clebsch 1964, 10). Later, the Marian exiles were to be heavily influenced by their continental brethren, particularly in Geneva and Zurich (Garrett 1938). The religious rationale of Protestantism in England, as on the Continent, lay in the idea that the authentic teaching of Christ could only be ascertained from the contemporary sources in the New Testament. The methodologies associated with the textual and historical study of documents initiated by humanists were transferred to the study of the New Testament by Valla and Erasmus, and in their wake Martin Luther. This Pauline re-emphasis of Luther was accurately and exactly reproduced by William Tyndale, whom A. G. Dickens has dubbed the true father of the English Reformation. The rationale of Protestantism, its search for the authentic teaching of Christ, remained apparent – think, for example, of Hooper's teaching on the ministry; of the stand taken by the reformers both in exile and on their return under Elizabeth concerning vestments and ceremonial; of the debate concerning the meaning of the sacrament of the Lord's Supper. Just a glance at J. L. Ainslie's *The Doctrines of the Ministerial Order in the Reformed Churches of the Sixteenth and Seventeenth Centuries* (1940) will underline the common heritage of the English and continental reformed churches. Horton Davies's *Worship and Theology in England from Cranmer to Hooker 1534–1603* (1970) is one of the few modern books to draw welcome attention to the debt owed by English Protestantism to continental influences. Also worthy of attention is Derek Baker (ed.), *Reform and Reformation: England and the Continent c. 1500–c. 1750* (1979) and, in particular, Basil Hall's essay, 'Lutheranism in England, 1520–1600', therein.

Far and away the best account of the movement for religious reform in England and Wales in the later Middle Ages is A. G. Dickens's *The English Reformation* (1964). While his thesis has been embellished, and detailed points challenged, Dickens's account has not yet been superseded. He describes the popular religion of late medieval England. He asserts that the average Englishman was far less interested in religion or theology than most writers on the subject suggest, although atheism and agnosticism were absent. The mystical *devotio moderna* influenced but a few, and Dickens concludes that it entertained no 'solid chances of averting the Protestant Reformation or of capturing the forces and aspirations which made the latter possible'. Its demands were too exacting for most. Lollardy had a much wider appeal. The teachings of John Wyclif (d. 1384) were considerably modified as his Latin works were translated and vulgarized, and they had especial appeal for townsmen, merchants, gentry and some of the lower clergy. His teachings were too radical in their critique for the conservative peasantry and too revolutionary in their attacks on the social and political structure for the upper classes. By the fifteenth century, gentry support had diminished and the Lollard sects became more proletarian in character. Dickens maintains that Lollardy survived into Tudor Britain and was especially active in the Chilterns, in the City of London, in Essex, in parts of

Kent, in Newbury (Berkshire), in Coventry in the West Mid-lands, in Bristol and in the large diocese of York. Lollardy, according to Dickens's work, remained Wyclifite in inspiration at least until 1530, but the 'old heresy and the new began to merge together from about the time Tyndale's Testament came into English hands'. Although Lollardy had lacked any national organ-ization and, for this reason and others, was weak as a movement, there were active lines of communication between the various Lollard communities (which tended to coincide with important commercial centres on given trade routes). The ideas and literature of both Lollardy and Lutheranism were passed between the congregations. A detailed account of the links between Lollardy and early Protestantism is to be found in A. G. Dickens's *Lollards and Protestants in the Diocese of York* (1959).

More recently J. F. Davis has discussed the relationship between *Heresy and Reformation in the South-East of England 1520–1559* (1983). He has established that there were three localities in the south-east with well-developed Lollard traditions: part of north Essex; part of the Kentish Weald, between Rye and Hawkhurst; and the north-west of London (the wards of Coleman Street, Cripplegate, Cordwainer and Cheap). These were textile areas, relatively densely populated and characterized by independence and literacy on the part of their craftsmen. It was these areas which proved most receptive to early Protestantism. Foreign influences tended to reinforce native traditions of Lollardy – anti-clericalism; opposition to saint worship; evangelism; questioning of the sacraments; emphasis on the Scriptures. His detailed exam-ination of heresy trials throughout his period demonstrate the manner in which early Protestantism drew upon these earlier traditions of dissent, established itself in areas marked by religious heterodoxy and displayed similarly diverse positions. He has, thereby, considerably refined our knowledge of the com-plexity of the debt paid to Lollardy by Protestantism. 'Lollardy had proved a reservoir that flowed into many channels' (Davis 1983, 149).

This seems to confirm Dickens's earlier position that there were characteristic Lollard survivals in English 'heresy' during Mary's reign, but that Lollardy had already served its main purpose by 1530 in preparing the way for the Reformation. Dickens added two further ideas:

> fifteenth century Lollardy helped to exclude the possibility of Catholic reforms by hardening the minds of the English bishops and their officials into a sterile, negative and rigid attitude towards all criticism and towards the English scriptures.
>
> (Dickens 1964, 36)

And:

> The second and more important function of the Lollards in English history lay in the fact that they provided a spring-board of critical dissent from which the Protestant Reformation could overleap the walls of orthodoxy. The Lollards were the allies and in some measure the begetters of the anticlerical forces which made possible the Henrician revolution, yet they were something more . . . they provided reception-areas for Lutheranism. They preserved, though often in crude and mutilated forms, the image of a personal, scriptural, non-sacramental, non-hierarchic and lay-dominated religion.
>
> (Dickens 1964, 36)

Lollardy itself did not bring about the Reformation, because it shunned institutionalization and became negativist and incoherent. It was unable to capture the support of the ruling class; it was unable to gain command of the Press. Lollardy remained underground: in the 1530s it yielded 'the leadership to regular armies with heavier and more modern equipment'.

But not all would agree with A. G. Dickens's analysis of the effects of the Lollard tradition upon religious life in England. Regional studies completed in the years since he wrote have revealed that some of the bishops, far from setting their faces rigidly against reform, were active agents of reform in the period 1480–1530. Yes, they hated heresy; but they also recognized the truth of much of the critique of the behaviour of the clergy and the administration of the church. By the 1520s and 1530s even a conservative bishop might be involved in setting God's house in order at diocesan level (Bowker 1968; Bowker 1981). Other historians have also shown the pre-Reformation bishops in their guise as reformers (e.g. Lander 1976), but it was scarcely of a kind to satisfy the sort of religious dissent described by Dickens, Thomson and Davis.

The relative importance of other factors in shaping English religious life has also been assessed. In his stimulating story of *Reformation and Resistance in Tudor Lancashire* (1975) Christopher Haigh treated a county which remained resistant to Protestantism until the later sixteenth and seventeenth centuries. Protestantism did plant early roots in Manchester Deanery, however, and Haigh pinpoints several explanations for this early success. There was 'no more than the merest trace of Lollard and early Protestant heresy' because of the isolation of the county. It was only when Lancashire developed trading and other links with London and the southern towns from the middle of the century that 'those parts which were geographically closest to the capital' were open to wider influences. But Haigh makes the important point that evangelization was in the hands of university-trained theologians and not of the laity. The missionary efforts of Lancastrian preachers probably met with mixed success in a county where the work of Protestant missionaries found no support among the local beneficed clergy. No. 'The new faith was planted in Lancashire not by mass propaganda, but by personal links between the academic reformers and their families and friends' (Haigh 1975, 163–70). The tightly knit nature of the tiny Protestant connection is apparent, as is its 'foreign provenance'. Protestantism is something brought to Lancashire and not something arising out of a tradition of native dissent.

Preparedness for the introduction of Protestantism has been explained in other ways, too. D. M. Palliser wrote that 'the general pattern of early Protestantism can be explained largely in terms of accessibility to Continental influences. Areas receptive to the new ideas of the 1520s and 30s included London, East Anglia and Cambridge University, and (outside the south-east) districts centred on ports such as Hull and Bristol, which were, of course, in close touch by sea with the capital as well as with Europe' (Palliser 1977, 36–7).

The appeal of humanist propaganda, with its detailed critique of the spiritual and intellectual life of the church, coupled with lay anti-clericalism or, at least, lay attacks on parasitic priests, have also been praised or blamed for preparing the way of the king. But the whole concept of anti-clericalism in the sixteenth century has come under considerable attack recently (Haigh 1983). Haigh suggests that very few opposed the clergy as such, criticizing the unacceptable behaviour of some priests rather than the idea of a priesthood. He contends that anti-clericalism was a product of the clericalism which emerged after the Reformation. In some respects this is a persuasive argument: even after the Reformation the man on the proverbial cow path probably found the behaviour of the parish priest whom he knew far more interesting than the *idea* of a priesthood. Equally, though, the behaviour of this same parish priest probably coloured his view of the idea of a priesthood. People, especially those who are untrained as theologians, do tend to move from the particular to the general and we have no reason to believe that this was in any sense less the case before the Reformation than it was to be after. Certainly one cannot deny that anti-clericalism ran through the thought of early Tudor intellectuals nor that early reformers such as Hooper found it extremely difficult to reconcile the concept of a clergy with their extreme primitivism. And it may be an almost entirely academic argument. Whether one accepts that there was no early opposition to an order of clergy or not, it seems abundantly true that criticism of deplorable aspects of the behaviour of both regular and secular clergy did predispose the laity in favour of radical correction of such abuses and that a reading of the Scriptures led at least some to question the primitive origins of the priesthood.

There will always be disagreement about the balance of influences. A. G. Dickens's work was both sophisticated and important because it attacked the implicit voluntarism of so much Reformation history and because it reasserted the importance of the spiritual reformation which stood side by side with the legislative. C. S. L. Davies puts it very nicely when he writes:

Protestantism was to triumph in England, initially at least, because it was given a lead from above by the king . . . . Without that lead it is impossible to know what would have happened in sixteenth-century England. Almost certainly, there would have been a powerful Protestant party; very probably powerful enough to exploit particular political situations and bring about civil war. But there is no guarantee that a Protestant rebellion would have succeeded; any more than it succeeded in France . . . . In that sense the developments we have been describing did not make the Reformation inevitable. But we should also look at this the other way round: these developments made Henry VIII's break with Rome possible. One could, indeed, put the case more strongly; it was the dedication to Protestantism of a small but influential minority working on the discontents of their fellows which transformed what might otherwise have been a minor jurisdictional affray into a thoroughgoing change, not merely in the beliefs of the English people, but ultimately in their way of life.   (Davies 1976, 155)

The Reformation historian, while she or he must be aware that the existence of Lollardy, anti-clericalism or continental influence was not a necessary cause of the English Reformation, should appreciate also that such factors were important *contributory* causes of its eventual success as a popular movement. Because similar ideas already had a foothold in some parts of England, we should not wait for the reign of Edward the Boy King for evidence of the popularization of Protestantism (Cross 1976, 53).

But not all modern historians of the Reformation object to voluntaristic explanations. J. J. Scarisbrick's *The Reformation and the English People* (1984) sets out to reassert the view that the English Reformation was an official reformation and one that the people of England did not want.

> The English Reformation was only in a limited sense popular and from below. To speak of a rising groundswell of lay discontent with the old order, of growing 'spiritual thirst' during the later Middle Ages, and of a momentous alliance between the crown and disenchanted layfolk that led to the repudiation of Rome and the humbling of the clerical estate is to employ metaphors for which there is not much evidence.

This statement is intended as a body-blow to the work of A. G. Dickens and others of his school, but there is little power behind the blow. Scarisbrick is, for the most part, aiming his punches at straw men, for he would search a long time for a statement in any modern work which suggests that the Reformation did come from 'below' in the sense that he attacks here. Certainly, Dickens, Cross and Davies – perhaps the most eminent of the historians who discuss the 'preparedness' of the English people for the Reformation – could never be found guilty of such bald, unqualified statements. They may stress the factors which favoured the acceptance of Protestantism and those which provided a continuous tradition of radical critique of the church, but they nowhere state (or imply) that all Englishmen wanted Reformation, either before or after Henry's legislative extravaganza.

The assumptions behind Scarisbrick's latest book are worthy of notice because they are the same assumptions which govern the work of most Reformation historians who concentrate upon the world of high politics, of official policy. Scarisbrick accepts, quite simply, that the Reformation was, in England at least, a 'supreme event' and not a process. He seeks to restore 'voluntarism' and to throw out of the window all thought that past developments had prepared the English people to accept Protestantism and Protestantization of English life. He conceives of this latter view as typical of 'modern' approaches:

> Modern tastes have tended to prefer the grand, long-term explanations of big events (especially if they give pride of place to impersonal changes in social structures or aspirations) and partly from the fact that a basically Whiggish and ultimately 'Protestant' view of things is still a potent influence on our thinking. Diluted, residual and secularised that influence may now be. But we still find it difficult to do without the model of late-medieval decline and alienation – followed by disintegration and then rebirth and renewal – just as we still find it difficult to believe that major events in our history have lacked deep-seated causation or have ever run fundamentally against the grain of the 'general will'. (Scarisbrick 1984, 1)

So, in Scarisbrick's view, the Reformation was imposed upon the English people by the king and his counsellors. It apparently appeared out of the blue: Henry VIII was sufficiently powerful and original to remove England from the Roman Communion and change the fundamentals of church life without either help from or even the tacit consent of his people. Indeed, the people actively objected to Reformation; only very slowly did some of them accept it. This is a striking view and it raises a number of unanswered questions: whence came the 'Protestant' view of things if indeed it is true that the people objected to the Reformation? Is it true that the Tudor monarchy was so absolute in its power that it could pass successful legislation in the teeth of the active opposition of the nation? Is there nothing at all to be said for the 'gradualist' interpretation put forward by most other Reformation historians interested in the reception of the Reformation? Does the evidence really bear the construction which Scarisbrick has put upon it – that the English people were well-content with the Catholic church? How would J. J. Scarisbrick explain away the very real evidence of discontent in some quarters? He does not confront it here.

J. J. Scarisbrick's study of late medieval life and of the people's response to it both complements and corrects the studies of popular religion penned by others. His radical thesis is stated thus: 'I am not saying that all was well. I am not claiming that pre-Reformation England was a land of zealous, God-fearing Christians. . . . I am saying that, however imperfect the old order, and however imperfect the Christianity of the average man or woman in the street, there is no evidence of loss of confidence in the old ways, no mass disenchantment' (Scarisbrick 1984, 12), for the laity had a church 'which they wanted and found congenial', tolerant, easygoing, caring, non-interfering, community-conscious. Nevertheless, there were abuses which Scarisbrick does not hesitate to describe. But there was, he urges, little hostility towards the monasteries, the chantries, the wealth of the church. The kernel of his argument is that Englishmen did not want an attack upon the church's property, but, when the Crown attacked, the laity found that their own appetites were whetted by the opportunities for personal gain. The English people, then, accommodated themselves to a reformation which was neither of their doing nor their wanting.

What this book has to say about the religion of the laity is extremely valuable. There can be little doubt that the prevalent view of the effect of the Reformation is that presented by Claire Cross in her *Church and People* (Cross 1976, 9–52). According to this view the Reformation represents the *triumph of the laity*. Medieval laymen were discontented: jealous of the privileges of the clergy, they wanted to be able to participate in religious life and, above all, to read the Scriptures in the vernacular. They abhorred the abuses of the church – the squandering of wealth, the neglect of the poor, the abysmal pastoral performance of the priests, the waste and corruption associated with the monasteries. This assessment is balanced by an awareness that all was not lost in the medieval church – there *were* reforms and important ones at that. But Scarisbrick counters her argument with a detailed picture of lay participation in the pre-Reformation years which can be placed alongside Dickens's stimulating treatment of other aspects of medieval popular religion and which cannot fail to enrich our understanding of the reception of the Reformation. His discussion of the parish fraternities is especially fine.

Scarisbrick's medieval layman was not a second-class religious citizen, oppressed and put upon. He was a partner in religious life. Although not permitted an active role in public worship, the laity were intimately involved in the church's liturgical life and in the communal life of the local church. While there was anti-clericalism, this was directed against scandalous individuals and not against the office of priest (Scarisbrick 1984, 43–6). To prove his point, Scarisbrick has analysed the wills of late medieval laymen for evidence of their religious views and charitable bequests.

After reading this book the scholar and student must ask the question: if Scarisbrick is right and it is true that everything in the medieval garden was lovely, despite a few scattered weeds, does this defeat at one blow the view that the atmosphere in Tudor England was favourable to Henry VIII's religio-political reformation? Scarisbrick has no doubt that it does. He is then forced to plump for voluntarism. Henry VIII staged the Reformation. A few leading politicians, thinkers and ecclesiastics supported him, for a variety of reasons, and as a result the Reformation eventually took root. The English ruling classes had a vested interest in its continuance. The people did not want Reformation.

But we may well question this conclusion. Dickens, Cross and Davies emphasize discontent; Scarisbrick content. But the question is one of the balance between these forces. It is also one of influence, leadership, power. None of these historians is able to *quantify* his or her assertion. And even if such an exercise were feasible, it is far from clear that the case would be proven by superiority of numbers. Perhaps, for example, it is true that discontent, over and above a certain level, is more potent than content – especially when given strong leadership from above. Or perhaps we could posit that those who were discontented with medieval Catholicism, however 'wrong' they may have been, were in some way more influential than those who were happy – they were the intellectuals, the aspiring gentry and bureaucrats, the reforming spirits and, by the very nature of things, they were more aggressive than those who approved the status quo. In other words, cadres are decisive.

For this reason, the historian who seeks to determine whether the climate was favourable for reformation may need to look, not at relative content or discontent with the church in numerical terms, nor at the merits of the case against that church; rather he may need to discover who was discontented and how they displayed their disease. In this sense, both Scarisbrick and the historians he criticizes may well all be 'right'. Yes, the majority of the people were used to Catholicism, willing to live with it and participate in it on its own terms, even to enthuse about it. Nevertheless, there were significant pockets of discontent at popular level which provided those springing boards for early Protestantism; there were traditions of anti-clericalism, anti-papalism and veneration for the Scriptures which helped Protestantism make headway. Most important of all, there were numbers of very influential men, very vociferous individuals, who criticized the Catholic church.

If this is so, then Scarisbrick is directing his attentions to a different problem from that which exercises the minds of the historians with whom he disagrees. They search for the reasons for eventual Protestant success; he looks for the religious views of the man in the street. The former conclude that many of those with power and influence and organization favoured reformation; the latter that the English Reformation did not correspond to the desires of the average Englishman. These views are not in themselves contradictory. It is indeed important that we should know the extent to which the 'people' were carried along with the Reformation and the extent to which only particular groups welcomed it.

The question of the origins of the English Reformation clearly has a bearing upon the progress of that Reformation at popular level. If there was in the people a spiritual thirst which the Reformation quenched, then one would expect it to take on the character of a popular movement in at least some quarters. If the Reformation was a legislative act imposed upon a wholly reluctant English people, great and small, then it would not take on the appearance of a popular religion. Protestantization of the people would have to await other developments. As historians differ about the spirit in which the initial reformation was received, so they disagree about the progress of Protestantization – its pace, its geographical spread, its appeal to various groups in the country. The question remains: how quickly did a political act become a popular religious movement?

There has been much written on the attitude of Henry VIII himself to Protestantism. Commonly he is said to have remained a Catholic monarch for a good many years after the Reformation. A popular account is that of S. T. Bindoff in *Tudor England* (1950). In this book Bindoff saw Thomas Cromwell as pursuing a policy of cautious Protestantization (culminating in the publication of the English Bible in 1539) which was at odds with Henry's own conservatism. When Henry divorced Anne of Cleves and executed Cromwell, he had no wish to turn England into a Protestant country. He silenced the Protestant preachers; he had Parliament pass the Act of Six Articles, which spoke out against the Protestant heresies. But he was not able to halt the 'revolution which he had begun' (Bindoff 1950, 110). In the event, Henry sensed that the mood of the people did not favour the retention of thoroughgoing Catholicism. He left Cranmer in office, he did not enforce the Act of Six Articles; he allowed (in 1543) the 'middling sort' to read the vernacular Bible. Above all, he entrusted his son's education to the Protestants:

Had the reign lasted a little longer Henry might himself have been numbered among them [the Protestants]. It is fairly clear that before the end the King had come to recognise the need for a shift in officially-sponsored doctrine. He confided his son's tuition to three Reformers, Sir John Cheke, Dr Richard Cox and Sir Anthony Coke and in his last months he was meditating the crucial step of converting the Mass into a Communion.

(Bindoff 1950, 149–50)

In essence, Bindoff was reiterating here the belief first voiced by John Foxe the martyrologist that Henry was about to initiate a fresh revolution in religious life and thought when he died. It is a view which, with rather more caution, A. G. Dickens also accepted (Dickens 1964, 194).

In 1966 Lacey Baldwin Smith challenged this interpretation in an article 'Henry VIII and the Protestant Triumph'. Smith expostulated at Henry's outright hypocrisy in leaving the education of his son to Protestant tutors while systematically persecuting and burning 'heretics', forcing well-known Protestants to recant their opinions, ordering the burning of Protestant books and scorning his own queen's views. He found it impossible that an ageing monarch should initiate another and more radical revolution: 'there are few people quite so conservative as an elderly and successful revolutionist' (Smith 1966, 1238). Smith was not the first to identify these problems. Bindoff had credited Henry with Machiavellian prescience (Bindoff 1950, 150); Jasper Ridley thought that Henry underwent conversion (Ridley 1962, 255); Roger Lockyer believed that he bowed to the will of the majority (Lockyer 1964, 105); Geoffrey Elton doubted the reality of Henry's Catholicism rather than that of his final Protestantism (Elton 1962, 25–6).

But Smith approached the conundrum differently. Henry did not, in Smith's view, modify his own religious position. He was not inspired in the last years of his life by a conviction that the future lay with Protestantism. If we examine the education of Edward, that 'godly imp', when his father yet lived, its content will be recognized as neither specifically Protestant nor Catholic. Religious orthodoxy, however, prevailed in the prince's and the royal household down to and beyond Henry's death. Similarly, if we look carefully at Henry's flirtations with continental ('German') Protestants and also at Henry's outrageous suggestion to the French admiral d'Annebault in August 1546 that France and England both should convert the mass into a communion, break off with Rome and threaten the emperor with severance of relations unless he did likewise, we can see that these were reflections not of Henry's new love of Protestantism but of his understanding of the diplomatic and military needs of the kingdom.

Yet another view is presented by J. J. Scarisbrick (Scarisbrick 1968, 474–5). He accepts Smith's argument that Henry was not a convert Protestant by the end of his life. Cheke and Coke were humanists, not Protestants, at the time when Henry entrusted them with Edward's tuition; the fall of the Howards was not part of a systematic removal of Catholic influence from Henry's council; Hertford and Dudley were not the rising stars at court because of their religious affiliations but because of their proven loyalty and ability. The story of the abandonment of the mass, Scarisbrick accepts as 'diplomatic chicanery'. He dubs Foxe's analysis of Henry's long-term intentions as the 'babling of a hagiographer'. Henry was not a Protestant. He was a Catholic until his death, *but* he was no papist. Scarisbrick suggests that Henry feared a resurgence of popery (led by Bishop Stephen Gardiner) far more than he hoped for a 'Protestant triumph'.

But Henry's attitude to Protestantism and to Catholic doctrine remains problematic. Most modern commentators are uneasy about it. Before we accept either L. B. Smith's or J. J. Scarisbrick's solution too readily, we should recall Scarisbrick's own warning that Henry does seem knowingly to have permitted Cranmer to make plans for the replacement of the Latin mass by an English communion service, just as he had ordered the use of Cranmer's *English Litany* after its publication in May 1544. Certainly, he urged Cranmer to peruse the service books late in that year and he added 'creeping to the cross' to the list of forbidden ceremonies which Cranmer and his two co-workers drew up. Moreover, Cranmer was able to protect the English Bible against attack. Of course, these facts do not in themselves prove that Henry was sympathetic to Protestantism. (Scarisbrick thinks that the attack on the mass may have been the cover for an attack

upon the wealth of the chantries as much as an attempt to draw
Francis of France closer to him. This assumes that Henry already
had in mind the dissolution of the chantries, which did not occur
until the reign of his son.) But Henry's attitude to Cranmer and
to his liturgical reforms should make us hesitate before commit-
ting ourselves to a view which sees Henry as unswerving in his
dedication to Catholicism.

Interesting though the question of Henry's own religious
persuasion is, of late historians have occupied themselves more
energetically with the conversion of the realm to Protestantism.
Work in this area has been concerned, not only to assess how
speedily Protestantism took hold, but also to identify the factors
which facilitated or impeded this process. Several broad interpretations have emerged. A. G. Dickens leads the school of those
historians who believe that there was a rapid religious reformation, built upon the foundations laid by Lollardy and religious
discontent in the late fifteenth and early sixteenth centuries.
Another view is that the Reformation was imposed from above
and that the conversion of the people to Protestantism itself was a
slow process. Again, some emphasize the importance of the work
of the Elizabethan evangelists rather than the Edwardian in
spreading the new religion. There are flaws in each and every one
of these interpretations. Those who believe in early successes for
Protestantism often overstate their case. There is a tendency to
assume that the heresy cases which came to light were more
representative than they were, to overemphasize the importance
of the Lollard tradition and so on. But those who assert that
Protestantism had to wait for any real success until the reign of
Elizabeth sometimes neglect to observe that the absence of *recorded*
heresy (given the poor survival rates of many types of record) does
not prove that the population under Mary were content with the
restoration of Catholicism and that the length of the Elizabethan
recusancy returns is not necessarily indicative of intense loyalty to
the old religion.

Scholars have examined the religious history of different
regions in an attempt to settle the argument once and for all.
Margaret Bowker's *The Henrician Reformation: The diocese of
Lincoln under John Longland, 1521–1547* (1981) is one of the more

recent and important local studies. The pre-Reformation diocese of Lincoln was enormous, covering nine Midland counties. The diocese was relatively well administered. In theory, one might expect that the Reformation would have come early to this diocese: there was a university; there were important towns; there was an area of strong Lollard influence. Christopher Haigh quotes this diocese, on the strength of Margaret Bowker's work, as the classic case of 'slow reformation' from below. The clergy and the laity showed little inclination towards Protestantism until the late 1540s and effective evangelization came only in the reign of the first Elizabeth. Unfortunately, as Dr Bowker noted, the register which John Foxe used which recounted Bishop Longland's persecution of the Buckinghamshire Lollards no longer exists. Other court records are thin on the ground. So there may or there may not have been early heresy in the diocese. Margaret Bowker is cautious in her own conclusions: 'in 1529, in the diocese of Lincoln, all our evidence suggests that heresy was confined to the Chiltern area, at most fifty miles square, and to a few young scholars in the University of Oxford' (Bowker 1981, 64). We should follow her lead in being unprepared to push the evidence too far.

Christopher Haigh's own *Reformation and Resistance in Tudor Lancashire* (1975) takes not a diocese but a county as the unit for study. Haigh demonstrates the resistance which the Reformation encountered. The revival of traditional Catholicism in Lancashire prior to the Reformation had meant that the people had, for the most part, little quarrel with the Catholic church and no reason to welcome the Reformation with open arms:

> The fairly intensive efforts at conversion made in the reign of Edward had reaped only a meagre harvest, and Protestantism had gained very little support by 1559. Though habits of regular church attendance might give the Elizabethan church a period of grace in which Catholic opinion could be attacked and a reformed theology promulgated, success would only be achieved by a sustained campaign of propaganda and coercion.
>
> (Haigh 1975, 225)

And this was difficult in an impoverished county possessed of weak institutions and unsympathetic officials.

In his study of Sussex under Elizabeth, Roger Manning also high-lighted the importance of the institutional machinery of a diocese (this time that of Chichester) in imposing uniformity with the state religion and spreading its tenets. He observed that 'the predominant group among the gentry were more interested in protecting their political and economic interests than in carrying through a religious revolution' (Manning 1969, 279). Because the queen's prime aim was to create and preserve national unity, 'the enforcement of the Elizabethan religious settlement followed the middle road' and the ecclesiastical policy was therefore inconsistent.

Some other studies – such as those of Northamptonshire and Cambridgeshire – echo the view that Protestantism had made a relatively slight impact before the reign of Elizabeth.

Before we conclude that there was no popular Protestantism before 1558, we should note the evidence of very marked local variations. Margaret Spufford's *Contrasting Communities* (1974) indicates the considerable difference in religious feeling between the populations of three villages. Willingham had a secret Protestant conventicle as early as Mary's reign, an enthusiastic Protestant congregation thereafter, anti-episcopal spokesmen in the 1630s and, afterwards, a thriving Congregationalist church. Dry Drayton, on the other hand, despite having in its midst for twenty years the prominent Protestant evangelist Richard Greenham, remained resistant to Protestantism throughout.

The suggestion is that this variety of religious opinion could be copied on to a broader canvas. There is evidence that Protestantism did flourish early in some areas. Kent is the best-known example, but in Essex, Suffolk, Norfolk, Sussex and London, Protestantism had also made inroads. Peter Clark has shown how Cromwell, for strategic reasons, created through the skilful use of patronage a reforming group in Kent. The reformers took over the administration of the church and the task of evangelizing the county (Clark 1977). Clark's analysis of wills and the complexion of town governments indicates that the breakthrough to Protestantism had already occurred by the mid 1540s. M. J. Kitch argues that popular support for both Catholicism and Protestantism was geographically diverse (Kitch 1981, 78). Early Protestantism in Sussex flourished around Lewes (Kitch 1981, 94).

No recent scholar has claimed that England was Protestant prior to 1558. Clearly, the institutional machinery of the church and the personnel of that church simply were not geared to perpetrate a wholesale reformation before the middle of Elizabeth's reign. Reformation took root early in some places. The cause of the Reformation was not yet won. England might be described as Protestant in that she had protested against the Pope's authority and had sloughed it off, but doctrinally she remained predominantly Catholic.

The geographical spread of Protestantism seems, then, to have been slow until Elizabeth's reign. To say that the headway it did make was insignificant is, however, to say too much, for there is sufficient evidence to show that Protestantism was early gaining strength among the influential. Kent, after all, was by sixteenth-century standards a densely and highly populated county. The new religion seems to have spread quite early and easily in the towns of the kingdom (Sheils 1977a, 156–76). It also took hold at the universities. If the leading intellectuals and gentry who favoured the new religion were sent into exile and were therefore unable to influence directly the evangelization of Marian England, they, as it turned out, did ensure the future of English Protestantism by keeping the flame of the new religion ablaze (Garrett 1938). And it was surely important that there were some Protestant congregations within England itself upon which the Elizabethan church could build.

What were the factors which hastened the advance of Protestantism or hindered it? In an early essay David Palliser discussed this question (Palliser 1977, 35–56). Here Palliser drew a picture of a south and east broadly receptive to Protestantism during the crucial years down to 1570 and a north and west less so. But he sought to refine this 'crude textbook picture'. He observed that research has confirmed the outlines of the picture – areas such as London and the east coast ports were in frequent contact with the Continent; and the more prosperous lowlands of the country were apparently less bound to tradition than were the impoverished uplands. But he goes on to suggest that this form of geographical (or physical) determinism may be very inaccurate. If the north was less receptive to Protestantism it may have been for administrative rather than physical reasons. Detection of heresy and recusancy, eradication of old ideas, evangelization were all difficult to say the least in the huge reaches of York, Chester and Lichfield dioceses, especially when parish units tended to be large and unwieldy and personnel unsuitable.

David Palliser has reminded us that regional studies may have too coarse a mesh by far to be of much value in charting and explaining popular reactions to the new religion. Instead, perhaps we should look more closely at localities (Spufford 1974; Wrightson and Levine 1979) where the loyalties of the people might be swayed by individuals, local interests, the position of the local magnate, social and economic conditions. Dr Kitch in his discussion of the Reformation in Sussex points out that the arrest of so many Sussex Lollards in Mary's reign may well have been due less to the relative strength of Protestantism in Marian Sussex, and specifically Lewes, than to the Catholicism of its gentry and their total unwillingness to protect the heretics (Kitch 1981, 94). In York there were riots and quarrels before the Pilgrimage of Grace totally unrelated to the Crown's religious policy. And objections to the new beliefs elsewhere might be as much objections to the high-handed activities of a local clergyman as to the beliefs themselves. Margaret Bowker has drawn our attention to the fears of the laity during the Lincolnshire rising concerning the future of their own parish churches and endowments. Enough work has been completed to suggest that variables other than the region must be taken into account.

We are alerted to the fact that myriad influences determined the reactions of the English people to religious change in the sixteenth century. Even more, David Palliser underlined the fact that not only the nation but also its constituent communities, large and small, were far from homogeneous in their response to change. Diversity of opinion marked the inhabitants of towns and villages, social classes and occupational groups. So, of sixty-six peers in 1580, twenty-two were committed Protestants, twenty were recusants, twenty-four were relatively indifferent. According to Roger Manning, office-holding gentry in Sussex outnumbered Protestants two to one in the 1580s. Preachers such as Thomas Hancock actively sought to stir up dissension: he divided the people of both Salisbury and Poole by his evangelizing attempts and was forbidden to preach in Southampton lest he cause the same division there.

Work such as this has made historians aware that reactions to reformation were varied and has drawn attention to some of the factors which either favoured or hindered the progress of Protestantization. But, surprisingly, very little attention has been accorded the most important issue of all. How are we, as historians, to measure the process? What index are we to use? Rigorous treatment of this crucial question is required. Historians have concentrated, inevitably, upon evidence of the spread of Protestant ideas, upon manifestations of Protestant opinion, upon proof of the retention of traditional Catholic sympathies. But the question of the relative importance of these within the communities concerned and within the nation has been shirked. Measurement of religious opinion on either side is difficult and the more so because few agree on what it is that historians are seeking to measure. Moreover, only now are scholars trying to come to grips with the issue of religious apathy in Tudor England and Wales. There are implicit, and occasionally explicit, assumptions – either that people in that century were far more committed to active Christianity (in the sense of church-going) than were, say, the Victorians, or that there was considerable apathy but that this apathy was traditionalist. (If you were Protestant you were part of an enthusiastic minority; Catholics, on the other hand, were a residual category, including both enthusiasts and status-quoers.) But these assumptions are only now beginning to be tested in anything approaching a systematic manner. Nevertheless, until the answers are found, how shall we ever know what Protestantization implied?

Is it possible, given the surviving evidence, to measure the extent of religious commitment to either side or to quantify church attendance? Even contemporaries employed the preambles of wills as evidence of men's religious beliefs: in 1532 the corpse of a Gloucestershire man was disinterred and burned as a heretic by order of Convocation because in his will he denied the mediation of the saints (Froude 1856–70, I, 326 n.). More recently, A. G. Dickens, David Palliser, Peter Clark, Susan Brigden, Claire Cross, J. J. Scarisbrick, W. J. Sheils, G. J. Mahew and Elaine Sheppard have all examined the preambles to large numbers of wills in order to determine the religious persuasions of their authors. Most of these historians show a decrease in the number of conservative or traditionalist preamble formulae over time and commensurate increase in the number of 'reformist' or 'committed Protestant' formulae. J. J. Scarisbrick's intention is rather to show the satisfaction with the Catholic status quo which was present in the 1520s and 1530s. Is it wise to use wills in these ways?

There are serious difficulties in using will preambles as evidence of the precise religious beliefs of testators. Margaret Spufford has shown that scriveners were commonly employed to write wills for clients (Spufford 1971, 29–43). They used standardized preambles. The precedent books of the various dioceses contain early examples of such form preambles. Even more common was the employment of the clergyman to pen the will of the dying man. Very commonly the last will and testament was, literally speaking, just that – the dying wishes of the sick and weak. In such circumstances, it is unlikely that the words of the preamble closely reflected the creed espoused by the testator. And, if the testator were not knocking on the doors of death, he or she had to be extraordinarily committed to a form of words to risk the wrath of the parish priest and presentation to the visitation authorities which might accompany any ill-advised use of unacceptable doctrine. This does not mean that wills *never* revealed the deep-felt religious convictions of their makers – far from it. Some wills are marked in their preambles by strongly individual phraseology and it seems safe to say that *deviant* wills of this kind do reflect the individual testator's beliefs.

But, and this is the important point, will preambles cannot safely be used statistically to record the exact religious affiliations of the population:

> The evidence is not statistical. It is wrong for the historian to assume that if he takes a cross section of 440 wills proved over a particular period, he is getting 440 different testators' religious opinions reflected, unless, of course the wills also come from 440 different places. Even then the scribe might have a determining influence. One is still getting evidence on the attitudes

of the peasantry to whatever ecclesiastical settlement was in fashion, but it would take a much more stringent analysis to show *how much* evidence one is getting, and to eliminate more than one of a series of wills written by the same scribe. On the other hand when a testator had strong religious convictions of his or her own, these may come through, expressed in a variant of the formula usually used by the scribe concerned. If any local historian wishes to study the religious opinions of the peasantry, he should look for these strongly worded individualistic clauses which occur in any run of wills for a parish, which alone record the authentic voice of the dying man.

(Spufford 1974, 334)

Far from revealing the religious beliefs of the average testator, wills and their preambles hide them from the historian's gaze. Historians of the spread of Protestantism need to know what ordinary men and women believed. They have grasped at wills as a guide to such beliefs because most ordinary people left no other written record of their existence and wills are therefore our only large-scale evidence. But we must not use wills to prove what they cannot in fact prove (Zell 1977, 246–9).

What we can do is to examine large series of wills to indicate general trends, as suggested by the work of A. G. Dickens. It seems safe to assume that the residual tendency was that of conservatism. We would expect that it took an effort of will to write a decidedly Protestant testament when the establishment was Catholic and vice versa. While it may be true that a cleric or scribe would influence the form of the will's preamble, it seems probable that only the progressive would use the services of a Protestant and that traditionalists and Catholics would decline to do so. In this way, a long run of wills analysed statistically will reveal a percentage of committed Protestants and Catholics in a reasonably reliable fashion. The forces of conservatism were such that it may well be that statistical studies of this kind will always *underestimate* rather than overestimate the strength of Protestantism before the reign of Elizabeth.

Historians who have conducted surveys of wills of this kind have classified will preambles in differing ways, thus making direct comparison or collation impossible. Nevertheless, the results of their work are of great interest. In general, the research suggests that non-traditional will formulae were increasing in number from the late 1530s onwards. In Kent this was noticeable from 1538; in East Sussex from the mid 1540s (Clark 1977; Mahew 1983). Not surprisingly, this tendency gathered pace under Edward VI, when there were official attempts to convert the population to Protestantism. But under Mary, when, if this conversion had been merely skin deep, one might have expected a sharp swing back to the traditional formulae, the percentage in East Sussex rose to only 50 per cent of the Henrician rate. Protestant wills in East Sussex actually remained at 10 per cent down to 1557 and traditional wills never amounted to more than 50 per cent of the total. At the accession of Elizabeth, traditional preambles fell to a level of 19 per cent – only slightly higher than the percentage of Protestant wills at that time. Even in Yorkshire, non-traditional formulae were in the majority after 1549, with the exception of York, which long remained conservative (Dickens 1959a; Palliser 1971). A smaller sample of wills for the diocese of Peterborough suggests a similar pattern and indicates that at the beginning of Elizabeth's reign, before the Protestant future was determined, 5 per cent of wills were distinctly Protestant in tone and almost 25 per cent neutral in terminology (Sheils 1979). From 1535 onwards, Protestant influence showed itself in Norwich wills and there are indications that the spread of Protestantism was so entrenched by the end of Edward's reign that Mary was unable to restore the *status quo ante*, although there was the expected revival of traditional will formulae (Sheppard 1983). London wills of the period 1522–47 provide an index of the movement from Catholicism to Protestantism, particularly when the preambles are used in conjunction with the content of the wills themselves (Brigden 1977, 333–48).

So where does all this leave us? J. J. Scarisbrick asserts that a study of some 2500 wills demonstrates the devotion to traditional Catholicism prevalent in the population. Work done by Claire Cross on Hull and Leeds wills produces a like conclusion. But this does not, as Claire Cross would be the first to argue, remove the ground from beneath A. G. Dickens's feet. He and others do not argue that England was already Protestant in 1540, 1550 or, even, 1560. What they do say is that Protestantism had made substantial inroads, especially in given regions and localities, before 1558 and that the extent of this Protestantism is underestimated if we merely count martyrs or near-martyrs. The large-scale sampling of wills, even given the difficulties involved in their use, does point to the truth of their assertion.

Circumstantial evidence also points to this conclusion. Wills were made by those with property who died. In general they represent the older generations. If we accept that Protestantism had its greatest appeal for the young (Brigden 1977), then we would expect that there would be an inbuilt bias against Protestantism in any sample of wills before 1560. Similarly, if it is true that Protestantism was strongest among those groups who had been most open to Lollard influence – artisans, shopkeepers, lower clergy, etcetera – then we would again expect that any will sample would under-represent Protestantism as wills were made by the better-off elements of society. John Fines's index of 3000 known Protestants between 1520 and 1558 indicates a preponderance of 'workers' amongst early Protestants, which may have been obscured by the attention which historians have always accorded the Marian exiles.

The common-form dedicatory clause of most wills may hide positive religious convictions or apathy – which, we shall never know. A few historians, notably scholars who are not interested solely in religious history, have sought to establish the churchgoing habits and religious interests of the English people, using other types of evidence. In Europe, attendance at Easter communion during the Catholic Reformation is said to have reached 99 per cent of the qualified adult population. Levels of participation of this kind do not seem to have pertained in England and Wales. Towns in particular knew much absenteeism. As early as 1540–2 it was said that not half the qualified communicants of Colchester attended church on Sundays or holy days. Most of the evidence of church attendance, however, relates to the seventeenth century, especially to the later seventeenth century. Historians have tended to lump Tudor and Stuart times together – in a rather dangerous and incomprehensible manner – and it really is

not safe to assume that patterns and levels of attendance noted in
the 1670s bore any necessary similarity to those in pre- or immediately post-Reformation England. What we do know is that the
Church of England attempted, through the system of visitations
and consistory courts, to see that the confirmed received Easter
communion and that the church monopoly of marriages, baptisms
and burials was maintained. By the seventeenth century, it has
been hazarded, some 15 per cent of the qualified population in
some dioceses (this included heads of household with their families and servants) were hardened excommunicates (Laslett 1965,
70–3; Marchant 1969, 227). These people were, by definition, cut
off from the communion of the church. There were, perhaps,
other categories of people who absented themselves from church.

One prevalent view is that the poor were particularly lax in
their church attendance. Some scholars have suggested that the
church authorities actively shunned the poor and were almost
exclusively concerned to secure the attendance of independent
householders (Hill 1964, 1966 edn, 259–97, 1972, 32–45;
Thomas 1971, 189–90). Mervyn James, for example, believes that
those who could not afford to pay pew rents were excluded (James
1974, 123). Peter Clark draws a picture of pre-revolutionary Kent
in which 20 per cent of the population – the poor and vagabond –
were by the very fact of their poverty excluded from the church's
communion and community (Clark 1977). But there is little real
evidence of this and some of the sources employed can bear a very
different construction:

> That the lay people of every parish (as they be bound by the
> laws of this realm) and especially householders, having no law-
> ful excuse to be absent, shall faithfully and diligently endeavour
> themselves to resort *with their children and servants* to their parish
> church or chapel on the holy days, and chiefly upon the
> Sundays, both to morning and evening prayer and other divine
> service, and, upon reasonable let thereof to some other usual
> place where Common Prayer is used, and then and there abide
> orderly and soberly during all the time of Common Prayer,
> Homilies, sermons, and other service of God there used, rever-
> ently and devoutly giving themselves to prayer and hearing of

the word of God. And that the churchwardens and swornmen, above all others, shall be diligent in frequenting and resorting to their parish churches or chapels on Sundays and holy days, to the intent they may note and mark *all* such persons, as upon any such days shall absent themselves from the church, and upon such shall examine them upon the cause thereof.

(Nicholson 1843, 138–9)

In fact, the articles of visitation in post-Reformation English dioceses constantly repeated this exhortation to church attendance to all people and to vigilance on the part of churchwardens to enforce the policy. The emphasis upon ensuring that householders attend, if indeed such existed, was there because the household head commanded the obedience of his dependants: if he attended church so, in theory, would his children and servants (including farm labourers); if he held household prayers daily, so would they attend. In *The Religion of Protestants* (1983) Patrick Collinson called for more research into the attitude of the church to its poor (Collinson 1982, 216–20). He made it clear that the church itself, when it complained of the irreverent or the absentee, did not equate these troublesome elements with the poor (Collinson 1982, 220–1).

The church wanted full attendance by the laity at church service and extensive participation in communion. The ideal does not seem to have been attained. By the late seventeenth century, perhaps half the qualified were communicating at Easter – suggesting, as more emphasis was placed upon Easter attendance than any other, considerably lower church attendances on ordinary Sundays or holy days. The extreme ignorance of doctrine exhibited by Easter communicants in one parish certainly suggests that most were not regular attendants (Collinson 1982, 202). Work on the appeal of Puritan sermons indicates that the message of the Protestant evangelists was neither as popular nor as effective as some have thought (Haigh 1977). As Bishop James Pilkington wrote in 1560, the pull of the alehouse was a powerful counter attraction to that of the pulpit: 'For come into a church on the sabbath day, and ye shall see but few, though there be a sermon; but the alehouse is ever full' (Scholefield 1842, 6). The church authorities adopted holding tactics. Some of those who refused to attend church (but probably only a small percentage) were presented in the course of visitation. Occasionally the authorities would swoop down in an exceptional effort to extirpate non-attendance, as during Archbishop Grindal's visitation of York in 1575 (Sheils 1977b, 81–3). There were attempts, of course, to control or remove counter-attractions. But more and more the authorities and the enthusiasts realized that they would never secure full attendance and tried to use alternative means to reach the populace. House-to-house visiting had its place (although some Protestant preachers were doubtful about the propriety of their visiting 'the suspect places' (Usher 1905, 72).

Some scholars point to the possibility that those least likely to attend church were perhaps the unmarried young, who disliked the attempts of the church to control their social and sexual behaviour. Those under the age of twenty-five may have made up more than half of the total population. Patrick Collinson writes: 'Many would be removed from this class (of excommunicates) not so much by discipline as by the normal process of aging and entry to the married state' (Collinson 1982, 229). He might have added that many of the number would be removed by early death. This argument is indeed plausible, but there is as little solid, incontrovertible evidence to support it as there is to buttress the view that it was the poor who failed in attendance and stood in open hostility to the church.

The relationship between the young and the church is none the less a profitable area for future research. How did churchmen seek to reach the young population? There were three main approaches: catechizing of the young before confirmation; schooling of children and adolescents; the media (or what we might call, perhaps, an imposed popular culture). Historians have given some attention to the first of these – catechizing – but have relatively neglected the latter – schooling and popular culture. This is a mistake. The catechist had to capture his audience before he could captivate them; the teacher and the pamphleteer might captivate their followers first and *then* catch their minds. On the way to acquiring vital skills for making a livelihood, the child would be imbued with the values of the Christian church or, at the very least, of the Christian society with its moral and ethical standards. Imogen Luxton has examined the extent to which popular culture remained heavily religious in content after the Reformation, in addition to changes in the forms which popular culture took (Luxton 1977, 57–77). Patricia Took has dealt in detail with the use of print made by both Protestants and Catholics in the war for men's loyalties (Took 1979). But it is to more general studies that we must look for full-scale examination of the changing content and intent of popular culture during the period (Burke 1978; Eisenstein 1979).

Historians of the Reformation appear to regard *education* as a dirty word. Few of them do more than nod in the direction of acknowledging its importance. Contemporaries of the Reformation would have disagreed. They believed that where the parish priest and schoolmaster led, there would the people follow. They therefore attached the greatest importance to the education of the preacher and teacher, but they also put real effort into designing the content of education for the laity. General studies of early modern education sometimes discuss this concern (O'Day 1982; Simon 1970).

Scholars clearly have a long way more to travel in their attempt to chart the origins and chronology of the English Reformation. It seems reasonable to suppose that Lollardy and discontent with the medieval church and its personnel had prepared the ground to some extent for a religious reformation. It is important to recall, however, that this discontent was by no means predominant in English society. Large sectors of the population remained untouched; they may have been enthusiastic Catholics, conservatives or just plain uninterested. The Reformation itself was initially a political, legislative act. Influential sections of the community supported Henry's initiative for a mixture of political and economic reasons. His reformation also opened the door for a number of churchmen and others who were dissatisfied with the state of religion and who were influenced by early Protestantism or humanistic criticism. During the latter years of Henry's reign and during that of his son, Edward, it seems that Protestantism did take root in the universities and in some of the towns of the kingdom, especially the ports. A number of factors appear to have encouraged the growth of Protestantism: a Lollard heritage; contact with Protestants on the Continent; enthusiastic evangelism; the loyalties of a local magnate; and, under Mary, the example of the martyrs (Loades 1970). But it was not the case that the people of England were converted to Protestantism by the reign of Mary. There are numerous indications that traditional Catholicism remained strong, particularly in the north and west, but also in the south and east. It was not until the reign of Elizabeth that even cadres were decisive and that Protestantism began to flourish more generally. When it did so, this may have had much to do with the Crown's now continuous pursuit of a religious policy which assumed the permanence of Protestantism. But it also owed a good deal to the efforts of Protestant church officers, evangelists and laymen. Formal Protestantism must have been difficult to avoid once the parishes were staffed by Protestant clergy, schoolteachers and preachers. The establishment of a Protestant clergy was therefore of the utmost importance in ensuring the growth of Protestantism (O'Day 1979). The church authorities, for example, were convinced that Catholicism in the wastes of the north could be conquered only by a Protestant mission. They were willing to turn very blind eyes to Protestant practices and preaching in the north.

Beyond this general outline it is difficult to go. Historians are unable to chart the depth of Protestantism; to establish the extent to which the tenets of the new religion had the people in their grip; to make clear whether or not the majority of the people had any strong religious convictions or interests. Was Protestantism, even at its most popular, a religion which spoke to rather less than half of the population? Was it a religion of ministers rather than congregations?

Many of the questions which Reformation historians have posed and continue to pose about the Reformation in England demand *quantification*. To what extent was England Protestant? How quickly and widely did Protestantism spread? Historians have identified a number of variables which appear to have encouraged or hindered the reception of Protestantism. But they are not able, given the evidence, to place these variables in rank order of importance. The available documentation does not permit the historian to quantify. The temptation has been to skirt the issue – to use the language of quantification and to employ the surviving, rather scrappy evidence as if it were quantitative. In fact, we know where there were Protestant congregations, but we know precious little about their size, strength and social importance.

Is the answer, then, to be openly impressionistic? Not necessarily, but it is certainly evident that the historian must define the issues much more clearly than has so far been the case. Often it is unclear what the scholars involved are trying to establish – how many people attended church? how many people accepted the official Reformation as a *fait accompli*? how many people were enthusiastic about the doctrines of the new religion? how many people would have preferred to have retained the old ways? To date, the work in this area has been characterized by the shadows which it casts rather than by the light which it creates. Patrick Collinson's *The Religion of Protestants* has at length illuminated the path by looking at the church *in* society. He has asked questions about the religious involvement of the English people and about the very nature of English Protestantism itself. He has discussed the extent to which the established church comprehended English Protestantism. For can we measure Protestant commitment when a common definition of this phenomenon is so hard to find?

The broadening of the horizons of our work on the Reformation surely helps rather than hinders our efforts to answer very difficult and very important questions about the importance of religion to the people as a whole in that society as well as to its leaders. In this way, *histoire totale* can become our handmaiden instead of our taskmaster.

Historians, while rightly wary of the dangers of celebrating technique, should talk much more openly about the methodological difficulties involved in writing about the Reformation at the popular level – otherwise they are in grave danger of displaying a naivety about the use of sources similar to that characteristic of their predecessors.

Chapter 7

The church: how it changed

While they have been absorbed with the issue of the spread of
Protestantism during the English Reformation, historians have
given almost passing attention to an equally important question:
what impact did the Reformation have upon the Church of
England as an institution? To an extent, in the answer to this
question may lie the key to that concerning the rate at which Protestantism spread. For, if the church as an institution changed little
from its medieval predecessor, retaining the structure, organization and disciplinary mechanisms of Catholicism, its attempts to
plant Protestantism would be doomed.

There are many different facets to the church and it is not
feasible to examine all. Here the following questions have been
selected as crucial: what did the Reformation mean for church/
state relations? did the church as an institution preserve continuity with the medieval past or was it much changed? did the
church's function in society change as a result of the Reformation?

At one stroke, by the Henrician Act of Supremacy, relations
between church and state were put on a new footing. The fact of
the royal supremacy has long fascinated historians. By this declaration, the Crown claimed not only the headship of that English

state in which the church existed (thus demanding the allegiance of all secular or religious citizens) but also headship of the church, which existed within and of that state. The Crown, therefore, claimed rights within the church which exceeded those of claiming the loyalty of its personnel: rights of government, of direction and of initiation. The Crown's rights in the church were, in other words, active as well as passive.

Claire Cross has examined the theoretical relationship between Crown and church and has sought to demonstrate relations between Crown and hierarchy within this framework (Cross 1976, 15–34; 1969). For several generations, ecclesiastics tried to assimilate the fact of the royal supremacy and its practical implications. The reasoned justification for the Supremacy was well-developed by the reign of Elizabeth but churchmen and others had not been reconciled easily to the idea. It had been common to revile Henry VIII – he had cast out the Pope of Rome and set himself up in his stead. Some Protestants hoped that the Crown would eventually put into motion a thoroughgoing Protestant Reformation and then withdraw completely from the ecclesiastical stage. So they joined with the Catholics in regarding the Crown's pretence to supremacy as sacrilegious – and especially so when the person claiming allegiance was a woman. And, in practice, there were grave reservations on the part of the church's hierarchy about Crown control of the church. Many feared that a change of monarch might well mean a complete reversal of the Reformation, as it seemed to mean under Mary. Some, like Thomas Cranmer under Mary, were *so* loyal to the Crown that they came near to denying all their personal beliefs when the monarchy returned to Rome. Others went into exile rather than face up to the implications of this conflict of loyalties. Under Elizabeth, the conviction of the first generation of her bishops that she alone could secure the cause of Reformation in England persuaded them to accept otherwise unpalatable religious policies as adiaphora.

What, then, did this Oh-so odious royal supremacy entail? J. J. Scarisbrick described the position under Henry VIII:

The English Church was the King's Church. Its clergy were his ministers, his vicars, his servants; and if official statements never allowed it to be said that the *potestas ordinis*, the spiritual powers as distinct from the jurisdiction of the clergy, flowed from the Supreme Head . . . they were careful to state that the actual manner of election and appointment of clergy was a matter of local usage allowed by princes.

The King inspected the church (by visitation) either personally, through his viceregent or through his clergy. Convocation could assemble only when summoned by the king. Its president was to be a layman – the king's vicar-general. The clergy were to enforce discipline on an authority derived from the Crown and using canons produced by a royal committee. The ecclesiastical courts continued to operate, but appeals therefrom were now not to Rome but to the king in Chancery. The Crown would issue important dispensations and licences. The Crown would not only protect the church's doctrine against heretical onslaught, but also declare the nature of that doctrine and, by a series of injunctions, regulate the church's practices (Scarisbrick 1968).

The precise nature of the king's supremacy was problematic from the start. The Act of Supremacy was confirmatory of a grant of supremacy to the English Crown from God: it was not an act of creation. But other Acts, such as that restraint of appeals to Rome, were not simply declaratory: they authorized particular and new activities. Parliament (both Lords and Commons) were sharing in the supremacy. 'If the essential ingredients of the Royal Supremacy . . . were legalized by the parliamentary trinity, then clearly sovereignty in spiritual matters would seem to be vested in that trinity and not in any one member of it' (Scarisbrick 1968, 393). 'Descending' and 'ascending' theories for the authority of the royal supremacy were both argued. Probably Cromwell believed in the view that the royal supremacy was authorized by Parliament while Henry believed that his authority came direct from God. No matter what their personal opinions, the instruments which declared the supremacy were confused in the extreme.

Elizabeth's revived supremacy was rather different from that of her father. When her first Parliament restored the supremacy it did so against a background of discontent with the Henrician model. Probably the government had wanted Parliament simply to assert the supremacy and to wait before defining the religious settlement. In fact, the queen ensured that Parliament pass an Act of Uniformity to the Second Prayer Book of Edward VI as well as an Act of Supremacy. The Act of Supremacy repealed the Marian ecclesiastical legislation, revived the Henrician laws against Rome and restored to the Crown the ecclesiastical powers that Henry VIII had enjoyed. All ecclesiastics were to swear an oath of allegiance to the royal supremacy – this enabled Catholic clergy to be deprived. But Elizabeth was dubbed Supreme Governor and not Supreme Head – probably in an effort to appease Catholic subjects.

G. R. Elton's *The Tudor Constitution* (1960, 333–5) usefully compares the Elizabethan supremacy with that of Henry. Henry, says Elton, saw himself as a lay bishop within the church; Elizabeth rejected this semi-ecclesiastical role, and disciplined her clergy from outside the church. Elizabeth like her father refused to accept that her Supremacy derived in any way from Parliament but, in fact, it depended much more than his upon Parliamentary authority. The 1559 Act of Supremacy declared that the powers of Henry over the church should be restored 'by the authority of this present parliament'. It was the queen-in-Parliament who ruled the church.

But how did churchmen assimilate the royal supremacy in their thought? When John Jewel penned his *Apology of the Church of England*, it seemed that the monarchy was indeed the bulwark against the threat of a restored Catholicism. To Jewel the question of whether a subject should disobey his prince in religious matters appeared academic: the settlement of religion in 1559 had been based upon general consent. He believed that the church would be protected by the Crown, but would be left free to perform its spiritual functions without interference. Jewel's views were very influential. Richard Hooker adopted much the same position in *The Laws of Ecclesiastical Polity*, portraying the monarchy as the guardian of the church. But by 1593 Hooker was implicitly critical of the way in which Elizabeth herself was exercising this royal supremacy. The queen (and her Archbishop of Canterbury, Whitgift) maintained that the Act of Supremacy had declared her authority to rule the church through her bishops and Convocation; Hooker set out to demonstrate that Parliament had a continuing right to legislate in ecclesiastical matters. The royal supremacy of the church was not to be seen as part of the monarch's prerogative power. As such a defence of the royal supremacy would have been anathema to the queen, small wonder that Hooker did not publish Book Eight. In fact this part of his work did not appear until 1648.

The practical implications of the royal supremacy, as they emerged, deeply affected thinking on the subject. Many churchmen were content with the supremacy for as long as the monarchy seemed to be the bastion of true religion; when the queen appeared to be pursuing hostile policies these men began to quarrel with the concept. Obviously, members of the hierarchy differed widely on what we might call the 'breaking point' of their tolerance: what were things indifferent to one bishop were things tremendously important to another. The Elizabethan bishops of the first generation did not hesitate to remind Elizabeth of the limits of her influence and of their obligation, in the final instance, to obey a higher power than she. Best known of all is the stand taken by Archbishop Edmund Grindal over Elizabeth's suppression of the prophesying in 1576 – when Grindal refused to do the queen's bidding because he felt it to be contradictory to the will of God, and when he justified his action with an outspoken rebuke, he was suspended from the exercise of his archiepiscopal duties:

> Remember, Madam, that you are a mortal creature. . . . And although ye are a mighty prince, yet remember that he which dwelleth in heaven is mightier. . . . Wherefore I do beseech you, Madam, *in visceribus Christi*, when you deal in these religious causes, set the majesty of God before your eyes, laying all earthly majesty aside: determine with yourself to obey his voice, and with all humility say unto him, *Non mea, sed tua voluntas fiat*.

The working relationship between the royal Governor of the established church and her bishops now at length came under close scrutiny. The fact of the supremacy certainly threw into question the authority of the bishops. Patrick Collinson asks, 'What was the competence of a bishop under a monarchy held to be supreme in all causes, ecclesiastical no less than civil? Was it a distinct competence in any way, or merely an extension of omnicompetence, royal government through commissioners or superintendents bearing the courtesy titles of bishops? Certainly, some scholars have seen the bishops under Henry's Supremacy as an emasculated breed' (Collinson 1982, 3). Margaret Bowker concluded that, as Henry VIII claimed the cure of his subjects' souls, the bishops 'one and all became civil servants. They were the king's men, strengthened in their office by his power and impotent without it' (Bowker 1975, 227–43). These civil servants did not initiate policy. Patrick Collinson accepts this indictment (although he does not comment upon whether the Henrician and Edwardine bishops shared this new interpretation of their role) but suggests that the position differed under Elizabeth, who was Supreme Governor and not Supreme Head. Collinson draws a distinction, admittedly somewhat blurred, between the supremacy and the jurisdiction. So Richard Hooker had argued that the monarch had supreme authority to uphold the laws and liberties of the church but not to undermine them. And it was the church itself which should define what these laws and liberties were – only specialists were capable of defining the doctrines, rites and ceremonies of the church. (Hooker went on to argue that these laws were given authority by the consent of Parliament, something which both Crown and hierarchy would dispute.) In general the Crown and the episcopate shared identity of purpose after the translation of Whitgift to Canterbury (1583–1603) and harmony was threatened only in specific areas. Patrick Collinson singles out 1559, 1603 and 1625 as moments of crisis.

Awareness of the potential for conflict, however, fed a tradition in which some of the bishops stressed that they were bishops *jure divino* (by divine right) – that is, that their spiritual jurisdiction derived from God – rather than by the grace of the monarch. James Cargill Thompson observed that the bishops aroused the animosity of many laymen by behaving as though their authority was 'knytte to theyre byshoprykes jure divino directlye' (Dugmore 1980, 94–130). Such bishops believed that they *were* bishops and not mere civil servants: they acted in accordance with this belief. In *The Religion of Protestants* we are presented with the complexity of the situation: there was an 'ideological framework' for church government 'within which the leading if unequal forces of monarchy and episcopacy manœuvred, sometimes together but often in subdued contention, for a controlling interest' (Collinson 1982, 38). It was only when the hierarchy identified itself with the monarchy and conceived of the Crown as its greatest protector against onslaughts from Puritans and Catholics that Bishop Richard Neile was able to say of his translation to the bench of bishops and, in consequence, to the House of Lords, 'When the king gave me this honour and laid his hands upon me'.

In theory and in practice the Reformation altered the relations of church and state and cast doubt upon the competence of the church's hierarchy. It was not only the theoretical relationship between Crown and bishops which changed: the recruitment, role and reputation of the episcopate also were subject to change. The survival of large numbers of diocesan records in a relatively good state of repair and organization has encouraged the post-war generation of scholars to explore this rich field of enquiry.

And such investigation assumes a background of the Crown's deliberate plunder of the church. Once, historians were deceived into believing that the suppression of the monasteries was haphazard because so small a part of the total of confiscated monastic property was permanently annexed to the Crown's estate, most of it being sold or granted away within a generation of 1536–9. The work of Joyce Youings and others, however, has demonstrated the moderate, orderly and methodical means by which the monasteries were suppressed and pillaged. It is clear that Thomas Cromwell intended that the monastic lands should become part of the Crown's estate – his plan was confounded. Some thought that the wealth of the secular bishoprics should also be seized. The great survey of ecclesiastical wealth, the Valor Ecclesiasticus of 1535, catalogued the wealth of bishops, deans and chapters, archdeacons, rectors and vicars as well as monasteries. In the autumn of 1534 it was being suggested that the bishops should become stipendiaries, with the state collecting most of their revenues (Stone 1951). A petition of both Houses was composed in 1536–7 to roughly the same effect. Everyone was very much aware of such projects. During the Pilgrimage of Grace, clergy and laity in Lincolnshire feared that Cromwell would turn his attention to the wealth of the parish churches. And among the bishops there was a feeling that it was necessary to propitiate Cromwell with gifts and obsequious behaviour in an attempt to forestall his plunder.

But, in fact, it appears that neither Cromwell nor Henry was wholeheartedly behind such a project. Henry was prepared to mulct the existing sees in order to found new, more modestly endowed sees on a county basis, if he had the support of the episcopal bench. In the event, six of the proposed thirteen new bishoprics were established. But Henry opposed a draft bill of 1539 which proposed an outright attack on episcopal wealth. Henry's reluctance arose from his awareness that the bishops needed wealth if they were to command the respect and allegiance necessary for them to do their jobs – as essential propagandists for his policies. Yet he could stoop to piecemeal and damaging plunder of the resources of the episcopate. He depleted the endowment of the see of Canterbury by £277 per annum, during a period of rising prices and heavy responsibilities (Robin Du Boulay 1952).

Indeed, there is agreement that Henry's inconsistent attitude to the financial position of the English church set a pattern for his successors. There was no fundamental reorganization whereby episcopal lands were centrally administered and the bishops paid a salary by the state. Equally, Crown and courtiers did not hesitate to plunder the church of its inheritance. And, as a result of Cromwell's past policies, the Crown did improve its revenues at the church's expense. From 1535 to 1540 the revenues from First Fruits brought in £16,000 per annum – more than the Duchy of Lancaster or the Court of Wards. This sum dropped to £9,700 per annum with the Great Dissolution of 1539 – the king could not have his cake and eat it. The Crown received also an average annual subsidy from the clergy of £18,000. Approximate figures for the total income of the Court of First Fruits and Tenths are £52,200 per annum, plus a subsidy of *circa* £18,000. When one recalls that the Crown's pre-Cromwellian income totalled only £100,000 per annum, it is clear that adding a sum equal to half that amount was by no means insignificant. And it left the clergy as a body more heavily taxed after 1535 than they had been previously (Scarisbrick 1960, 41–54).

But the image of the Crown as *the* great predator of episcopal resources has come under attack. The total annual income of sees remained almost the same throughout Elizabeth's long reign – it fell from £27,250 to £23,000. Of course, in a time of inflation, this did not mean that the receipts remained unaltered in real terms, but this was due to circumstances outside the Crown's control and certainly beyond its comprehension (Heal 1980, 265–311). What can fairly be said is that Elizabeth was in general (but not always) unsympathetic to the need for *augmentation* of episcopal revenues in those hard times. In addition, a certain levelling of episcopal incomes was achieved whether by accident or by design. The value of rich sees such as Winchester and Durham was lowered while that of impoverished Welsh dioceses was left intact.

Did the Crown use other ploys to exploit the wealth of the church? Traditionally, Elizabeth has been alleged to have left sees vacant for considerable periods of time in order to reap their profits, legitimately, *sede vacante*. But, in fact, delays were normally caused by the difficulty of finding suitable candidates. Only three vacancies were of long duration and may have had a financial motivation – Bristol, Oxford and Ely. If so, Elizabeth did not choose her victims all that wisely, for both Bristol and Oxford were among the poorly endowed Henrician sees and only Ely was a plum. Of the five other sees which were left vacant for more than two years, only Salisbury was relatively wealthy. If this charge does not stick, then it is none the less true that the Crown was made aware of ways in which its church patronage could be used to financial effect. In 1575 a list was prepared to demonstrate how frequent translations from one see to another might increase the profits to the Crown from first fruits. Lord Keeper Puckering showed how the successive moves of just five bishops would bring in a welcome profit. But none of these suggestions was implemented: not until the nineteenth century did the rate of translation from one see to another fall so low. Stuart monarchs could much more fairly be accused of indulging in this practice.

So Christopher Hill's charge that Elizabeth was the 'Supreme Plunderer' as well as the 'Supreme Governor' of England's church has been shown to be exaggerated. The threat to some sees was real under Henry VIII but it was often, as in the case of York, removed by Henry's death (Cross 1969). Evidence for the dioceses of Lincoln, Exeter, and Bath and Wells indicates that they suffered their worst period of depredation under Edward VI. During Elizabeth's reign, the church suffered more at the hands of the queen's courtiers than at those of the monarch herself. The plan for a rationalization of episcopal finance in 1559 failed. Ely is the sole outstanding example of Elizabeth's deliberate plundering of the church. During a nineteen-year vacancy of this see from 1581–1600, the fruits of the bishopric supported an expensive foreign war. When Martin Heaton was finally appointed, the price of his elevation was a massive exchange of episcopal property, involving thirty-four of the see's remaining manors. But it is also clear that the see suffered less from this plunder than might have been expected. Ely had escaped lightly under Edward VI, so there was much fat left to pare. And Elizabeth did release the bishops of Ely from the requirement to pay tenths on their property after 1559 – a gesture which saved the see £207 a year. So the income from the see shrank by about £200 only between 1535 and 1608. Of course, the real value of episcopal revenues had fallen, but this was scarcely Elizabeth's doing.

For the historian of the Reformation the question of the reputation of individual monarchs is probably of less relevance than the question of the sufficiency of episcopal incomes. And, in order to know whether or not episcopal incomes were adequate for the job, we have to know just what that job was and what its demands were. Richard Hooker, the great apologist of the English church, wrote:

A Bishop is a minister of God, unto whom with permanent continuance there is given not only power of administering the Word and Sacraments, which power other Presbyters have, but also a further power to ordain ecclesiastical persons and a power of chiefty in government over Presbyters as well as Laymen a power to be by way of jurisdiction a Pastor even to pastors themselves.

But, apart from this responsibility for the spiritual well-being of his charges, the bishop needed to be able to defend his church (in speech and/or in writing); to administer the church and its temporal estates efficiently and responsibly; to recruit personnel for that church wisely and well; to give political advice when called upon; to act as a wise and just judge in his courts of correction and instance; and to accord hospitality and charity to the great and to the lowly to the greater glory of God. Different ages, different parties, and different bishops have lent varying emphases to these responsibilities. The first generation of Elizabethan bishops, for example, were convinced of the primacy of their duty to preach the Word – they were the evangelists. Many of these men deplored the papistical trappings of episcopacy, hesitated about accepting bishoprics and declared progressive intentions. The second generation of bishops – characterized by Whitgift, Aylmer and Freke – saw their position as one of defending the church and its status quo against all comers, Catholic and Puritan alike. They stressed the bishop's disciplinary role – he was to enforce conformity – and they paid considerable attention to the church's administrative problems. Under James I, the bishops sought to prove their usefulness to the Crown, under a monarch who respected the *jure divino* status of the bishops and saw the need to support them in matters of administrative reform. These are, of course, broad generalizations – in fact, the traditions often coexisted, but there were marked trends in episcopal thinking. So it would be very difficult, and perhaps unwise, for the historian to suggest which of these responsibilities was the most important.

One thing is certain. Even those bishops who were much about the court in James's time – when the social status of bishops probably reached a new peak – were not expected to be princes of the church on the model of, say, Wolsey or Gardiner in pre-Reformation times. The bishops had to maintain a certain magnificence in order to command the respect of the lay ruling classes and they had to finance their active episcopates, but there was not the need to impress with pomp and circumstance. Indeed, there was every incentive to play down the wealth of the church as it aroused lay jealousy and tempted the greedy.

The most exhaustive of the studies of the changes which befell the episcopate during the period of the Reformation is that undertaken by Felicity Heal in *Of Prelates and Princes* (1980). The import of the study is political, but it argues the case for the changing material circumstances of the church succinctly and well, and attempts to assess whether the bishops had the wherewithal to fulfil their responsibilities adequately. The pre-Reformation bishops are portrayed as 'spiritual noblemen', possessed of all the trappings of authority that church and Crown could provide. Chief among these accoutrements was land. Some of this land had been donated to the church by Saxon monarchs and nobles; other had been granted as a reward for services to the Norman kings. The bishops continued to serve the Crown – their functions were similar as tenants-in-chief to those of the lay nobility. But they also had responsibilities to their laity arising from the many pious donations of land to the church – obligations of hospitality and charity. The bishops were prominent local patrons and overlords as a result of their land holdings. And many of them held secular offices which yielded significant additional income and, of course, political power. The bishops also had the power of the purse and they exercised it by maintaining often alarmingly great households and retinues. Sometimes it was necessary to maintain a household in order to fulfil a military function: Rowland Lee complained that he had to have two hundred men in livery because he was President of the Council of the Marches. Usually, a large household was required to provide hospitality: Nicholas West, for example, provided two hundred hot meals a day and Thomas Ruthal would feed up to eighty beggars at his gates on his visits to his diocese. And the bishop had to entertain his flock – the maintenance of his household allowed contact with great and small, enabled the housing of the bishop's chaplains, and permitted the bishops to educate and nurture the sons of the county gentry and nobility. In the late fifteenth century, the Bishop of Winchester ran such a school – one that emphasized scholarship in contradistinction to the schools in noble households which emphasized martial arts. Sizeable episcopal households were common and made huge demands upon the finances of the bishops. Maintenance of the accommodation itself was a major expense, to which had to be added wages and provisions.

If the services which individual bishops rendered the Crown reaped dividends, then the Crown exacted its own reward in the form of enormous benevolences and loans extracted from these spiritual lords. In 1491 John Morton, Archbishop of Canterbury, paid no less than half the income of the see to the Crown as a benevolence. After this date the bishops did not grant benevolences but were asked for substantial loans. Individual bishops raised such sums by a sale of plate and other valuables. It is sometimes suggested that the need to keep a substantial reserve of wealth available for the Crown's use may have deterred the bishops from making charitable endowments before their last years.

After the Reformation the bishops were still regarded as 'a fount of hospitality and charity and as the essential centre of systems of local patronage' (Heal 1980, 238). Many of the conflicts between the gentry and the bishops had their origin in the bishops' failure to 'oil the wheels of local patronage' by buying the loyalty of the gentry with leases and offices. And, with the advent of the legitimate episcopal family, the bishops found it yet more difficult to meet their obligations of hospitality, charity and patronage. There was no 'private income' allocated to the bishops, as distinct from 'public income' designed to support the administration of the diocese. The bishops used the same revenues to support their wives and families as they did to maintain the official household, to endow charitable bequests and to administer the episcopal estates. There was much less money to give away. The bishops left a mere £6,255 for learning, the poor and pious works, while bequeathing £22,000 to their families (Berlatsky 1978, 19). There seems to have been a definite correlation between size of charitable bequest and size of or absence of family. The bishops had other problems associated with their private lives: now they lived in their dioceses they had to live up to the expectations of the surrounding gentry and to maintain their families in appropriate style. They were criticized if they lived opulently – such a lifestyle coexisted uneasily with the claims of Protestant bishops to be the descendants of the Apostles; at the same time they were also often despised because they were insufficiently magnificent. The bishops found it more and more difficult to please any of the people for any of the time.

The precarious financial state of the episcopate during the early years of Elizabeth's reign is well illustrated by the *Letter Book of Bishop Thomas Bentham* (O'Day and Berlatsky 1979). Bentham was already in personal debt before he entered the see of Coventry and Lichfield in 1560 and he had no private fortune with which to pay off his creditors. (More of the bishops now came from relatively humble backgrounds than had been the case with Henry VIII's bishops (Heal 1980, 245). Bishop Bentham was greeted immediately with a claim for first fruits and subsidy payments, and for the repayment of some of his predecessors' debts. This was bad enough, but the situation was made yet more parlous by the fact that the full revenues of the see were not at his disposal and would not be so for some time. He was unable to collect rents from various properties and the collector denied him rentals for the period of vacancy. Bentham's approach to these *temporary* difficulties had long-term repercussions for the finances of the see. He succeeded in reclaiming his property, but at great cost. The parsonage of Hanbury which he regained was laid waste and he had to lease it for twenty-one years. Although Bentham succeeded in persuading the Crown to forgive him some of his debt, his financial predicament forced him to grant long leases to the Crown for the rest of his episcopate. The situation of the post-Reformation bishops of Coventry and Lichfield, like that of so many of their colleagues on the bench, was perilous because it was one of cumulative indebtedness. Quite apart from this worsening financial position, the bishops now had an unwelcome call upon their time and energies at the very moment when they wished to devote more attention to pastoral duties than ever before. Forty-six per cent of Bentham's surviving correspondence was entirely devoted to financial problems.

Dr Heal warns that it was in the interests of the bishops to claim abject poverty when dealing with the Crown and, in fact, there were a number of strategies available to them still which enabled most to live comfortably and to leave respectable estates to their heirs. Nevertheless, when the Elizabethan episcopate is compared with that of the years before the break with Rome the contrast is very evident: the bishops had lost most of the 'proud concentrations of land', both temporal and spiritual revenues had been depleted. And their relative position had deteriorated even more than their absolute position. Inflation had cut into their ability to shoulder the responsibilities assigned them. And their new obligation to their families had further eroded their capacity to fulfil these existing duties.

Criticisms of the episcopate were frequent and were complicated by the different understandings of the role of bishops mentioned earlier – one opinion was that the bishops should devote themselves to pastoral work and be married to apostolic poverty; another was that bishops must maintain lavish hospitality and charity; yet another was that the bishops must live extravagantly in order to command respect of high and low as they imposed law and order on local society. Whether or not the bishops had the wherewithal to do the 'job' depended upon one's understanding of what that 'job' was. Undoubtedly Reformation thought about the ministerial order had added complications to this picture – there had always been criticism of the wealth of the bishops, but now such criticism was acceptable even in established circles.

These differences of opinion about the bishop's function also have a bearing upon any assessment of the success of episcopal recruitment. Before and during the Reformation, the bishops were often drawn from among the upper ranks of society, from administrators and lawyers; after the Reformation, the bishops more commonly came from among the gentry than from among the nobility, from the theologians and preachers than from among the administrators and lawyers. The bishops in Elizabeth's reign, then, were much better equipped to be pastors and evangelists than to administer episcopal estates and husband resources. They were more designed to work with the humble gentry than with the magnates who sat on the queen's councils. Bishop Toby Matthew, for instance, had a prodigious preaching record and many bishops did emphasize their pastoral role – preaching throughout their dioceses, confirming children, supervising their clergy, becoming personally involved in the work of correction (Collinson 1982, 48–9; O'Day 1972; O'Day and Berlatsky 1979, 116–20). To the extent that the episcopate had sloughed off earlier obligations, the new bishops were suited to fulfil the function of the office; to the extent that the old obligations lingered, they were not.

Patrick Collinson sums it up:

> the economically and socially diminished episcopal order was required to perform functions which had not been radically redefined and which the enhanced demands of the Tudor state had rendered in many ways more onerous. It was political necessity, not personal vanity, which dictated that their house-keeping should still be consistent with the life style of mag-nates.

But the pressures upon them made this difficult if not impossible to achieve. 'When a new bishop of Norwich arrived in 1603 many gentlemen flew in "like butterflies in the springe" but moved on when they found "little hope of benefit".' It was not only that the bishops had no official resources for the adequate performance of their role. They had been recruited from among those without personal fortunes, without local influence and without local patronage. Most of the bishops lacked local roots. If they attempted in the course of their episcopate to attack one of the dominant gentry 'affiliations' within the diocese, the absence of a commen-surate 'church'-dominated faction spelt disaster for episcopal policy. Bishop Curteys of Chichester found himself in just such a predicament: an enthusiastic evangelist, he yet roused the detes-tation of the ruling élite of Sussex (and of the Privy Council) by calling many wealthy families before his consistory court on charges of recusancy (Manning 1969, 91–125). Edmund Freke came to grief when he set himself against the combined strength of powerful local patrons (MacCulloch 1977). The successful bishop co-operated with local gentry and dealt tactfully with the diocesan clergy (Collinson 1982, 78). Historians have judged bishops who worked harmoniously with their county notables to be somewhat un-newsworthy. But the bishops were aware of the need for co-operation if Protestantism were to be established successfully. In the early years of Elizabeth's reign, commissions of clergy and laity with power to fine and imprison offenders were often suggested as the means to co-operative government of the church at local level. Some were even set up. But they did not work as well as the bishops had hoped. Oft-times the commissioners fell out among themselves. Occasionally they made the bishop himself the prisoner of a faction. On other occasions the commissioners actually opposed the bishop. Later in the reign the commissions were dominated by clergy and so lost their initial purpose. Again during the early years of Elizabeth's reign the bishops attempted personal government of their dioceses, with frequent meetings with local gentry and yeomanry to judge petty offences and settle disputes. Certainly, where such contact was possible, relations between the bishop and his people were improved, but it was simply impracticable for most bishops to administer and discipline their dioceses personally. The dioceses were large and communications were frequently difficult. The Reformation had stripped the bishops of many of their episcopal residences and, where it had not, had robbed them of the means to maintain the remainder in habitable condition. No longer was it feasible for the Bishop of Lichfield to conduct a progress through his large, unwieldy diocese, lodging in episcopal residences *en route*, preaching to and disciplining the multitude and conducting congenial conversation with leading notables. There were proposals to create more and smaller diocesan units, which would have permitted more personal government, but these came to nought (Collinson 1966, 91–125).

In short, the Reformation laid fresh obligations upon the church's bishops – both civil and ecclesiastical – but it did nothing to prepare the bishops or to provide them with the wherewithal to fulfil the same. Indeed, the financial position of the bishops deteriorated and the age-old machinery of diocesan organization and administration did not receive the necessary overhaul to permit the bishops to perform their duties adequately. Had these faults been corrected it is conceivable that the English bishops would have overcome the undoubted problems caused by their background and lack of local connection. Problems of recruitment there were, but these were not insurmountable.

The choice of bishops could certainly affect markedly the complexion of the church, but to speak of recruitment perhaps suggests that the Crown – in whose gift all bishoprics lay – had a deliberate policy which it pursued in appointing to the episcopal bench. Closer inspection shows that this was far from the case. In *theory* the Crown selected bishops. In *practice* the Crown rarely made a personal choice in the reign of Elizabeth. The Crown permitted others to exercise its patronage at this level – because different individuals were granted this favour during the reign, the choice of bishops did reflect rather accurately the queen's current position regarding ecclesiastical politics. Early in the reign, Lord Burghley was paramount among the distributors of episcopal patronage, although Leicester, Bedford and Huntington all made their mark. The queen had excluded her first Archbishop of Canterbury from direct influence. Elizabeth had been forced to work with the reformers before 1580; at that point, drawing her own conclusions from Archbishop Grindal's blatant insubordination, she selected her own archbishop, John Whitgift, against advice and determined the direction which her church was to take. Now the queen's men took over. Christopher Hatton and Archbishop Whitgift influenced the choice of bishops. A general willingness to follow the Crown's conservative ecclesiastical line was now the principal criterion for selection, other things being equal. Whereas some work has been done to explore the selection procedure under James I, and to assess the rank order of the criteria adopted, little has been done to describe episcopal recruitment under Elizabeth. At the start of the reign, the Crown largely had to work with what was available. Although the returning exiles were often not the queen's personal taste, she had little alternative but to use them. After a generation of the production of university-educated, Protestant clerics, the pool of potential recruits was considerably improved and the choices made accorded broadly with the queen's sympathies. While Elizabeth seems to have preferred conservative clerics and James I to have been influenced by the quality of a man's preaching at court, neither monarch appears to have paid much attention to the need to recruit able administrators, pastors or theologians. Instead, they were more concerned with the value of their ecclesiastical patronage in terms of secular politics. The right to select a bishop was granted as a mark of royal favour in the world of secular politics. This said, neither monarch allowed matters to get out of control. The Crown retained an active veto on all appointments,

which had to be reconcilable to the broad sweep of current ecclesiastical policy.

After the Reformation, then, bishops were selected with but
little regard for the needs of the church as an institution. Churchmen might seek to draw the Crown's attention to the need for
carefully selected church personnel, but the Crown paid no heed.
It goes almost without saying, also, that the bishops were chosen,
not to implement radical Protestant policies of diocesan organization and pastoral care, but to execute those policies of the hierarchy which the Crown found congenial and, in the main, to
preserve the status quo. In short, the bishops were not *chosen* for
their Protestantism.

At any one time, there were 26 bishops and 2 archbishops; there
were perhaps 9000 beneficed clergymen and auxiliaries. The
layman probably rarely had contact with his diocesan; he encountered his parish priest almost daily. When we consider the question
'Did the clergy change fundamentally as a result of the Reformation?' we meet with many of the same problems which were
present when we spoke of the episcopate. In a real sense the
religious Reformation had robbed the clergy of its theoretical
raison d'être. The priest was no longer necessary as a mediator
between man and God. The acceptance of the doctrine of the
priesthood of all believers meant that the clergy had to find a new
justification for their continued existence because by implication
the Reformation was anti-clerical. Yet its leaders were prominent
churchmen and it is unsurprising that such men found a need for a
clergy. The people did not need *priests* – clergy who by their
sacrifice of the mass mediated between man and God – but they
did need *pastors* – clergy who cared for the flock, taught them
about God, and exercised a fatherly discipline in order to bring the
people to God. This distinction between the priest and the pastor
became the staple of Protestant teaching on the ministerial order;
even so, reformers such as John Hooper found it very difficult to
reconcile their views about the direct relationship between the
individual soul and God with the existence of a full-time, paid
clergy. This difficulty had still not been resolved in the mid-
seventeenth century. The doctrinal reformation, then, involved a
rethinking of the clergy's functions, but this revolution was

unacceptable to many. The Crown and many clergy and laity resisted such change. Indeed, it was inevitable that those who resisted the spread of doctrinal Protestantism would also resist this, its concomitant.

The manner in which the English clergy discovered a new role makes a fascinating story. It is clear that not all of the clergy themselves shared the Protestant view of the function of a clergy in a reformed church. (J. Ainslie, *Doctrines of the Ministerial Order* (1944), gives a good account of the various continental clergies and makes clear some of the links between English and continental thought on this issue.) The many good, recent accounts of the Reformation in the provinces illustrate this simple but oft overlooked fact. Patrick Collinson's *The Elizabethan Puritan Movement* (1967) is a good place to start. But, while theory was important, the role of the English clergy was also defined by circumstances. Before the Reformation the clergy formed an estate of the realm (the others being the nobility and the remainder of lay society) whose members dedicated their lives to God but followed a number of occupations – there were both regular and secular clergy (monks and friars; parish clergy); there were clerks and teachers; scholars and lawyers; civil servants and politicians; preachers and prayers; pastors and priests. With the dissolution of the monasteries, the entire regular clergy were swept away. Monarchy and laity preferred in future to exclude the clergy from political office. Canon law was no longer taught at the universities. When the chantries were dissolved, the mass priests disappeared. The destruction of minor orders removed that pool of clerks from whom administrators and clerks might be recruited. The numbers of laymen who attended the fast-expanding universities now staffed the expanding bureaucracies of the Tudor church and state without first entering orders. Of course, theory and practice fed off one another. There were theoretical justifications for the abolition of minor orders and the dissolution of monasteries and chantries. Nevertheless, as I shall demonstrate in a forthcoming study, it is true that the role of the clergyman in the Church of England was *de facto* redefined and narrowed during the Reformation period.

The English clergy changed in response to diverse forces. The changes were not always conducive to the spread of Protestantism among the laity. One approach is to regard the clergy as a professional group, with a developing *esprit de corps*, hierarchical structure, internal recruitment and educational policies, and expertise. This view (argued in O'Day 1979 and in my forthcoming book) sees the post-Reformation clergy as different from their pre-Reformation forbears. It does not deny the professional features of the medieval Catholic clergy, but urges that the post-Reformation clergy were united by a common occupation and that they professionalized as a result of their deep awareness of the importance of this occupational/vocational bond. The function of pastor dictated a powerful emphasis upon expertise, training, recruitment and performance. Some historians have found it difficult to accept this argument, perhaps because they are unused to dealing with the concept of professionalization. Clearly it is unwise to overdraw the extent to which the clergy professionalized or to claim that the post-Reformation clergy was entirely dissimilar to the pre-Reformation clergy. But it is only by exploring and analysing the occupational group, using as many approaches as possible, that we will reach a full understanding of the implications of the Reformation for the church's personnel.

Work done so far suggests that the clergy were marked more by change than continuity. In the place of an estate of men and women performing a variety of functions, there was a single occupation. In place of a celibate personnel, there was a married clergy. In place of priests, there were pastors. Now, the once relatively uneducated *resident* clergy had been replaced by resident university graduates. Now, it was accepted that all clergy in the parishes, and not simply a group of theologians in the universities, should have biblical expertise.

But the picture was a complicated one. Some features of the church before the Reformation, had they been retained, would have given the clergy more control than they now possessed over organization, training and recruitment. The power of the church to legislate for itself was questioned. The powers of Convocation shrank. The Crown's position as Governor spelt increased external interference. The further distribution of patronage rights among laity after the dissolution reduced clerical control of recruitment. The expansion of the universities to cater for the secular interests of laymen diluted the professional content of a university education and removed control of the curriculum still further from ecclesiastical control. The financial organization of the church (lack of organization might be a more appropriate description) made the establishment of a clerical career structure using criteria of vocational excellence impossible. These features of the post-Reformation clergy made it difficult for the hierarchy to follow a policy, whether their own or the Crown's, consistently and effectively. Attempts to Protestantize the clergy were, as a result, *ad hoc* and piecemeal. And some features retained from the medieval church made it even more difficult to move in a Protestant direction. The primitivists lost their battle against the wearing of clerical uniform. Ceremonial remained a part of the church's worship. Neither the recruitment nor the financing of the clergy was completely overhauled in line with Protestant thinking.

Given the existence of these factors which made it difficult for the church, should it so wish, to consciously reform its ministry, the 64,000 dollar question remains: how quickly and completely were the clergy converted to Protestantism? or, perhaps more pertinently, how quickly were sufficient Protestant clergy put into the parishes? Historians have tackled this question in several ways. Some have looked at the clergy as part of the entire scene when studying the pace of Protestantization; others have examined the clergy as a discrete group. The extent to which the clergy were Protestant themselves clearly has considerable bearing upon the pace and extent of the Protestantization of the laity. But there are particular problems in assessing the Protestantism of the clergy.

The response of the parochial clergy to the Henrician and Edwardian Reformation over the country as a whole remains to be charted. We do however have valuable indicators. A. G. Dickens argues that the parochial clergy in general offered little resistance to the new measures – they were prepared to obey their bishops and archbishops, and to enforce government policy even when if conflicted with their private views. It was not the break with Rome which upset individual clergy, but the sacramental, ceremonial and property changes which accompanied it – such worries led a few to participate in the Pilgrimage of Grace or the Western rising of 1549. Michael Zell added considerably to our knowledge of the way in which the clergy expressed their discontent and in which the church authorities handled it. In Kent, opposition to the new practices and doctrines in Henry's reign 'was common but not constant . . . usually disorganised but occasionally found support in more powerful quarters; . . . and it involved a scattered collection of parochial clergy and some zealots among the religious'. The Archbishop of Canterbury was able to control this opposition but not to eradicate it, because the Protestant laity reported the clergy who gave voice to their opposition. The government, in fact, was remarkably tolerant of clerical opposition: there were no large-scale deprivations of recalcitrant clergy and only those who actively sought martyrdom were allowed to find it. It seems to have been both important and relatively easy to control the Catholic clergy in Kent. It was far less so in Lancashire, a county characterized by large parishes, poor communications and unsympathetic laity. Detection of the seditious was problematic. Organized opposition became a reality (Zell 1974a, *passim*; Haigh 1975, *passim*).

Clerical opposition under Henry was scattered, but the overall impression is one of clergy unenthusiastic about reform or even covertly hostile. Even unstated opposition provided an environment conducive to conservative rather than reformed religious life at parochial level. Positive enthusiasm in the shape of a definite evangelical effort was necessary if Protestantism were to survive and thrive. Nevertheless, because the official Reformation was not itself Protestant, it was natural that there should be no radical purge of conservative priests during the early Reformation. The period, down even to the 1570s and 1580s, was marked by continuity of personnel.

Clerical enthusiasm for the Edwardian church also seems to have varied from region to region. Admissions to the ministry were low, perhaps because of the uncertainty which now surrounded it, perhaps because Protestant bishops refused to accept conservative or uneducated candidates. If the number of clergy who chose to marry is indicative of a favourable response to Protestantism, the clergy of London, Essex, Suffolk, Norfolk and

Cambridgeshire were more markedly Protestant than those of Lancashire, Lincolnshire or Yorkshire (Palliser 1977, 42), but there are problems involved in using marriage as an indicator. The enthusiasm of individual bishops in persecuting married priests (under Mary) may have influenced the figures considerably. And marriage did not necessarily imply acceptance of Protestantism, although it may seem to go hand in hand with a rejection of conservatism. It is much more difficult to locate positive Protestantism among the parish clergy – there are isolated examples of clerical enthusiasm for the new ideas and some of the bishops (Hooper at Gloucester, for instance) were trying hard to re-educate their parish clergy. On the whole, however, significant results at parochial level were not achieved until Elizabeth's reign. Mary I felt obliged to deprive only 2000 (about one fifth) of her beneficed clergy and of these many were promptly instituted to other churches.

It may seem that the lie is given to this argument when we reflect that Elizabeth herself deprived only a few hundred clergy at the start of her reign. But in fact Elizabeth wanted a conformable clergy rather than a Protestant one and she was willing to accept the services of all but the most enthusiastic of Catholics. And she had no objection to the celibate priesthood which Mary had re-imposed – on the contrary, she opposed clerical marriage. At any one point between the reign of Henry and the early years of Elizabeth, the body of the parochial clergy appear to have been conservative priests, anxious to maintain a low profile (and thereby their jobs), exercising themselves little with doctrinal and political questions, with a minority caring desperately about the religious settlement. When Elizabeth ascended the throne the problem was less one of a nonconforming than of an absent clergy.

The period 1536–80 saw a turning away from the church as a career – partly owing to the uncertainty of the religious settlement and partly to the slurs cast on the status of the ministry in the early years of the Reformation. The acute shortage of clergy could not be remedied immediately because of the new emphasis upon educated and resident clergy. This shortage was more acute in some regions than in others.

As the status of the ministry improved, so recruitment rates recovered markedly. The emphasis now laid by both hierarchy and others upon university education ensured that by the early seventeenth century most ordinands were graduates and that many held further degrees. It remained difficult, however, for the church to control the placement of 'approved' clergy. The bishops held some but by no means all church patronage. Although organized attempts to build up clerical factions within the church by the use of patronage were few and far between, the exercise of church patronage by the Crown and large numbers of laymen stood in the way of church control of church personnel. The law of the church and of the land prevented the bishops and other ecclesiastical officials from intervening habitually to block the placement of unsatisfactory ministers in the parishes (Calder 1948, 1957, *passim*; O'Day 1977; Sheils 1974; Hill 1956, 245–74; O'Day 1975a, 247–60).

The Protestantism of the ministry, therefore, in the absence of central control over placement, depended upon the supply of Protestant ministers and upon the accidental matching of enthusiastic Protestant patrons with like-minded clergymen. There is a consensus that the parochial clergy, while generally conformable, were not 'reformed' until the middle or later years of Elizabeth's reign. There also is agreement that enthusiastic Protestantism was contained within the Church of England, notwithstanding Elizabeth's objections to its more radical expressions, until Archbishop Laud forced it into the cold. Thus many of the beliefs, attitudes, assumptions and practices which have become associated in the popular mind with 'separatism' and 'Puritanism' were in fact part of the life of the established Church of England prior to Charles I's reign (Collinson 1982; Collinson 1975, 182–213; O'Day 1979, 66–74). The main areas of debate remain the difference (in terms of ideology and practice) between the Catholic clergy and the post-Reformation clergy and, therefore, the impact of Protestantism and Reformation upon the ministers' roles and functions.

The church in society was an institution which disciplined its members and acted as a force for the preservation of law and order. Not only its ministers but also its judges, proctors, advocates, registrars and apparitors played important roles in the maintenance of ecclesiastical discipline. Historians have asked whether the nature of the ecclesiastical discipline altered as a result of the Reformation. They have asked whether ecclesiastical discipline retained its old importance in society as a whole.

There was Protestant criticism of the idea of administering discipline through impersonal courts, but unless such criticism made its impact upon the practice of discipline it would remain nothing more than a voice crying in the wilderness.

It would be all too easy to indulge in a chalk-and-cheese comparison of ecclesiastical discipline before and after the break with Rome. In fact, all was far from well with the Courts Christian prior to the event. 'The spiritual welfare of a diocese depended to a large extent upon the efficiency and authority of its church courts, especially those of the bishop' (Lander 1976, 215). But this 'efficiency and authority' was very variable. In many dioceses there were rival jurisdictions which tended to limit the authority of the diocesan ordinary (bishop). In the city of Chichester alone, the Archbishop of Canterbury, the Bishop and Dean of Chichester, and the Bishop of Exeter all exercised jurisdiction. In late fifteenth-century Sussex there were no fewer than nine distinct ecclesiastical courts in operation. Peculiar jurisdictions, such as that of the Dean in Chichester, presented a particular challenge to the bishop's overall authority. Battle Abbey was exempted from episcopal jurisdiction: as a result the priest who served the parish of Battle became its ordinary and settled all but matrimonial causes. The existence of the distinct jurisdictions made it very hard to bring an offender to justice – it was such a simple matter to escape to an exempt area. Disputes were also common where jurisdictions clashed. If the diocese of Chichester was typical, which is far from established, measures were being taken by diocesan bishops to remedy the situation prior to the Reformation. Bishop Sherburne of Chichester took steps to eliminate some of the diverse jurisdictions by amalgamation: the archdeacon in one case became the bishop's commissionary; the consistory assumed jurisdiction over the dean's peculiar court in another. (There is some evidence that similar steps were being taken in the Lincoln diocese. The bishops of Ely, Norwich and Winchester were also taking active interest in their spiritual jurisdiction.) The diocesan administration in Chichester was completely reorganized, with the appointment of trusted officials to implement a reform of the bishop's own courts. Simultaneously the Chichester courts were marked by increased efficiency and effectiveness. The bishop's consistory court sat far more frequently in the third decade of the sixteenth century than it had in the first; matters were dealt with with far greater dispatch; the attack on abuses appears to have been successful – for example, the court prosecuted those responsible for church dilapidation and, what is more, succeeded in getting the necessary repairs carried out; discipline of the clergy was pursued energetically: non-resident clergy were sought out and compelled to reside. While all this had much to do with the reorganization of the courts, it also owed a good deal to Sherburne's personal interest in the success of his reforms.

So, there is evidence for some dioceses at least that the abuses which had bedevilled the efficiency and effectiveness of church discipline were being eradicated in the early sixteenth century – confused jurisdiction, corrupt and inefficient personnel, cumbersome processes, delay. In those areas where reforms were successfully carried out, the business of the ecclesiastical courts probably increased in volume. For example, in Chichester diocesan consistory the number of office (disciplinary) cases pressed rose from 65 in 1506/7 to 195 in 1520 – a threefold increase. But this rise was confined to official use of the courts to discipline clergy and laity: the spiritual and moral functions of the courts were being revived, but the level of use made by laity and clergy of the courts for party v. party cases remained approximately the same. This suggests that the instance courts of the church did not assume a more important place than previously in the lives of laymen. Yet the bishop did improve the service to plaintiffs in instance cases – he introduced arbitration, for example, and even the normal processes were less costly and time consuming. The business of probate in particular was expedited. In dioceses where reform was not implemented, it seems probable that the bishops did not employ their courts to enforce energetically the necessary spiritual discipline and that parties in instance cases did not receive a value-for-money service. And such unreformed dioceses may have been in the majority. This number may well have included the diocese of London. Here the diocesan courts are said to have been in full decline by the 1520s. Methodological problems beset a systematic and full-scale survey of the ecclesiastical courts in this important diocese, however, and more work is necessary before we can accept unreservedly the conclusions drawn by Richard Wunderli (1981). But clearly more local studies are necessary before we can be certain that the entire system of ecclesiastical discipline had been overhauled successfully before the Reformation.

The enthusiasm, enterprise and energy of individual bishops clearly made a good deal of difference to the functioning of the church courts. This makes it nearly impossible to attribute any identifiable change in the use of ecclesiastical discipline wholly to the Reformation or, indeed, to any other national 'event'. The diocese of Chichester forms a good case study because it was marked by a revival of the court system immediately before the break with Rome, but even here we can see that the role of individual bishops contributed to the changed style of discipline. Bishop Sherburne had supervised personally the exercise of discipline: Bishop Sampson neglected his see for work in London. There is no indication that a reform of the courts was 'official' hierarchical policy.

The Reformation period was marked by direct attacks on the spiritual jurisdiction of the bishops. Whatever reforms had been implemented had been insufficient to prevent this. There was violent anti-clerical feeling among members of Parliament in 1529. More specifically, plans for a far-reaching reform of the courts was circulated and a draft bill in 1532 proposed the abolition of office cases (discipline cases using the ex-officio oath – which compelled the accused to incriminate him or herself – brought by the bishop and his officers) in all but heresy cases. A separate spiritual jurisdiction was itself challenged and the planned reform of canon law was a cause for concern among church lawyers. The future of the Courts Christian hung in the balance. Then the bishops had to face other, more insidious challenges to their authority: in 1534–5, for the first time in over a century, the Archbishop of Canterbury staged a metropolitical visitation, during which the jurisdiction of the diocesans was suspended; then, in the autumn of 1535, episcopal jurisdiction was again inhibited when the Crown's visitors toured the country. In

Chichester the bishop and his officials appear to have been panicked by contemporary attacks on their spiritual discipline and to have reduced their activity in this area very considerably. Similarly, they reduced the number of court days available for instance business. Only probate remained unaffected.

In the event, the jurisdiction of the ecclesiastical courts remained untouched and the courts themselves survived in their old shape. The vicegerential court was not revived under Edward or Elizabeth. Although royal visitations were still conducted under Elizabeth, the practice of issuing royal commissions to the bishops was dropped – from 1535 to 1553 such royal commissions had underlined episcopal dependence upon royal authority. But the efficacy of the ecclesiastical discipline was dealt more than a glancing blow. On the one hand, the business of the courts revived but slowly. In Chichester for example, even in the 1550s office and instance business had not reached their pre-Reformation levels. This suggests either that energetic diocesans were a rarity or that they were disciplining their flocks through different agencies. On the other hand, respect for spiritual sanctions had been seriously undermined – a legacy of the attacks on ecclesiastical jurisdiction encouraged during the 1530s. Prior to the Reformation, the threat of excommunication had in general been sufficient to enforce obedience; even the lesser excommunication (suspension) had frightened offenders enough to make them want to escape sentence. After the Reformation, the greater excommunication was much more frequently pronounced. Both penalties seem to have been debased. Perhaps the inability of the church to enforce the economic isolation attached to excommunication contributed to this debasement. (No one was to do business with an excommunicate person.) But more important yet was the inability to enforce excommunication over so many persons, for apparently trivial reasons.

The Crown and Parliament did little to improve the position of the diocesan courts. When the Crown did attempt to tackle the problem, instead of giving the bishops the right to imprison and fine offenders (thus providing effective punishment for those who were godless and cared not a tittle if they were forbidden the church's communion), it created a High Commission with these powers – thus overriding the diocesan structure and further undermining the bishops' independent authority within their sees (Houlbrooke 1979, 14–16). This High Commission was designed to enforce and uphold religious uniformity, but after a while it attracted a good deal of other business. This left the bishops with the unenviable task of enforcing spiritual discipline in other areas without new sanctions. Nevertheless, the bishops probably regarded the High Commission as a source of support – where an offender was obstinate the case could now be referred to this court.

By the reign of Elizabeth, the Courts Christian were involved in a new function – that of maintaining and enforcing the new religious settlement. Of course, the courts had always been there to see that the church's rules regarding worship, doctrine, morals and so on were observed, but there had been a real difference. Then, the rules had been accepted if not obeyed: now, the rules were hotly contested (by both conservatives and radicals) and many saw an opportunity of changing them. The Crown used the bishops to enforce its rules concerning church attendance and to see that the churches were equipped for Protestant worship. The bishops were required to ensure a conformable clergy (despite inadequate powers to control recruitment, training and place-ment) and to ensure nonconforming laity. The disciplinary busi-ness of the ecclesiastical courts increased considerably. At the same time, a growing litigiousness in society meant that the instance work of the courts also rose to the levels of the early sixteenth century and beyond.

There was, then, at the very time when the sanctions of the church courts were being challenged, a revival of activity. The ecclesiastical courts were in the business of enforcing conformity and uniformity – of imposing a royal supremacy. They were certainly not involved in the 'Protestantization' of the provinces in any sense which the reformers would have understood and accepted. The reformed church, despite plans to the contrary, was not given a revised code of law. The *Reformatio Legum Ecclesiasti-carum*, designed to improve the efficiency of the courts and tighten up their discipline, which was drawn up in Edward's reign (1551), found no official approval when it was published in

1571. Articles, orders, injunctions and statutes modified the ecclesiastical law throughout the period, giving statutory force to the new liturgy, for instance, but, at core, the ecclesiastical law in 1570 was that of the medieval church.

But, even had the courts been given a new code, it is doubtful whether the discipline they administered would have found favour with the more radical Protestant spirits. For the reformers objected to the whole concept of impersonal discipline administered through a system of courts. The discipline which they favoured was one of fatherly correction by the pastor of his flock. It was a congregational and personal discipline. If a diocesan system had to be employed, then the reformers objected to the fact that the courts were run by professional lawyers and that spiritual sanctions were imposed by far from spiritual persons – law judges. And the abuses which afflicted the system convinced them yet more of its iniquity – corruption, escalating costs, delay.

The reforming bishops and officials of the first years of Elizabeth's reign favoured the abolition of the medieval dioceses and their replacement by much smaller units under the care of superintendents. This would have facilitated a fatherly discipline (Collinson 1966). In the absence of thoroughgoing reform, these men involved themselves personally as much as possible in the work of their diocesan courts – taking particular care to sit in consistory when spiritual offences or grave disciplinary matters were before it; holding courts of audience (Lincoln, Winchester and Norwich); acting as arbiter in intractable cases (Houlbrooke 1979, 23–4.) This tradition was pursued right down to the Civil War. Conscientious bishops continued to employ these means of supervising the courts and ensuring that lay officials did not pronounce sentence in grave spiritual cases. In some dioceses, Coventry and Lichfield for example, clergy were used as regular surrogates in the consistory courts, thus supplementing, if not replacing, the professional judges. In other dioceses, and Norwich is a case in point, synods of the clergy went some way towards compensating for regular direct episcopal supervision of the clergy through the courts, although we do not know how active the synods were. At Lichfield, during the episcopate of Thomas Morton in the 1620s, the bishop made a practice of hearing cases involving his clergy in person. The archidiaconal courts which might have helped to make discipline less remote seem to have lost much of their disciplinary function by the reign of Elizabeth. In the northern province, rural deaneries and their courts supplied an invaluable smaller unit of administration and discipline which helped make discipline more immediate. There is some evidence that they were used in at least two of the dioceses of the southern province – Coventry and Lichfield and Worcester.

To the radical Protestant, however, all such measures involved compromise of an unacceptable nature. By definition, unreformed institutions (i.e. basically Catholic although denying the Pope's authority) could not exercise a reformed discipline or be the agent of further reformation. In the 1580s the intolerance towards Protestant nonconformity displayed by the Archbishop of Canterbury, John Whitgift, and the markedly still unreformed nature of the church as an institution appears to have fed a revival of Presbyterianism, on a national scale, under the leadership of John Field. In the 1570s the university teacher Thomas Cartwright had expounded a series of sermons at Cambridge in which he set forth a church government based upon a system of congregations ruled by pastors and elders, under district assemblies or *classes* (representative of the congregation and, in their turn, under provincial and national synods). Cartwright had no flair for organization and it was John Field who became the movement's leader. During the 1570s Presbyterianism attracted little support in the nation – it was by no means clear that reform could not be achieved within the state system laid down by Elizabeth and, in any case, the threat from Rome seemed far more important than that from the hierarchical organization of the Church of England. But, with Whitgift's rise, Field had some success in co-ordinating the movement from London. In some parts of the country regional district assemblies did meet regularly to supervise the exercise of discipline. For several years the leaders of these *classes* did meet on a provincial and even a national basis. Although it is clear that earlier historians (particularly R. G. Usher) overestimated the significance of the Presbyterian movement in Elizabethan England, it is still an important indication of the discontent felt by many reformed clergy with the organization of the new state church and their attempts to substitute a different kind of discipline.

We are fortunate that the records of one of the *classes* of the 1580s have survived. A set of rules was drawn up at Dedham in Essex on 22 October 1582 by twenty ministers, to govern the behaviour of the *classis*. The first meeting was held on 3 December 1582 and the eightieth and last on 2 ? 1589. A three-hourly meeting was held on the first Monday of each month. The frequency and regularity of the meeting is in itself a point of some significance – they were designed to replace or, at the least, supplement the discipline offered by the church. The *classis* discussed and reached decisions on points of discipline, doctrine and ceremonial. For instance, it rebuked absentee ministers, looked into the qualifications of neighbouring ministers, ordered catechizing of children, discussed the propriety of baptizing the children of the unmarried and so on. The weakness of the discipline lay, inevitably, in its voluntary nature. The *classis* advised a member not to leave one parish for another: it could do nothing when he ignored this advice.

The Presbyterian movement collapsed when Field died in 1588 and when the leaders of the movement, including Cartwright, were prosecuted in Star Chamber for attempting to overthrow the established church. In fact the Presbyterians had never conceived of themselves as separatists – they had wanted to further reform the Church of England, not to exist alongside and outside it. When separatist churches emerged in London the Presbyterians admitted their allegiance to the idea of a comprehensive national church. Moreover, their fear of being convicted of seditious activities, brought them into line (Cross 1976, 138–52; Collinson 1967, 333–55).

Why did not the Presbyterian attempt to introduce a godly discipline gain more support from the laity? One explanation is that most laymen of Protestant leanings (and perhaps most clergy too) felt that the degree of further reform which they desired could in fact be achieved within the framework of the existing national church – grand, articulate schemes provoked the opposition of the authorities and ultimate suppression, and came to nothing. Far better to work quietly within the system, taking advantage of the sympathetic attitudes of so many bishops and so many patrons. Fear of the Crown was undoubtedly important. Too few people cared sufficiently strongly for radical reform to stand fast against charges of sedition and the death penalty. Reformation in practice, covertly achieved, was preferable to Reformation in theory, overtly argued but denied.

Let us turn now to the question with which this chapter began: what impact did the Reformation have upon the Church of England as an institution? Outwardly, the institution looked remarkably similar to the medieval church. The ecclesiastical hierarchy was retained. The organization of the church into provinces, dioceses, archdeaconries and rural deaneries persisted. The system of ecclesiastical courts, with a few additions, continued. It was small wonder that radical Protestants under Elizabeth alleged that this church was but halfly reformed. As we have seen, the relationship between Crown and hierarchy was fundamentally altered by the assertion of the royal supremacy. The Crown saw the episcopate as a protection against radical change in the social and religious framework. Not all the bishops or other officers of the church agreed with this conservative position, but, as the reign of Elizabeth progressed, the queen found archbishops and bishops whose views coincided with her own. Under such leadership, a more fundamental Protestantization of the Church of England was indeed unthinkable. Adoption of the Book of Discipline of the English Presbyterians was an unrealizable pipe-dream. For as long as the Crown was content with the settlement, and for as long as many clergy and laity were prepared to live with it, no further reformation was possible. And a large number of individuals and groups had a vested interest in the retention of the old form of the church – even including Protestant clergymen and Puritan lay patrons.

It is both easy and incorrect to move from this position to another – that the Church of England, apart from its relationship with the Crown, remained totally unreformed. But this is untrue. New ideas about the role of the bishops and the clergy, for instance, had their impact upon the working relationship between Crown and hierarchy, upon the manner in which individual bishops administered their dioceses and disciplined their clergy, and upon recruitment, training and placement of parochial clergy. The church courts, themselves relics of the medieval Catholic church, underwent a revival. Unpopular they might have been. Disregarded they almost certainly were by many of the laity. Nevertheless, their business increased, their disciplinary function became more important and the attempt to impose a fatherly discipline, through the greater involvement of the parish clergy and the bishops, became more noticeable. Some of these changes might well have occurred had there been no official reformation, but others are more directly attributable to Protestant ideology. The Church of England was not the same as the church in England. The positive aspects of its half-reformation should be remembered. Because of the Reformation its surviving institutions were often altered fundamentally from within.

The import of this assessment cannot be ignored. The retention of the institutional apparatus and framework of the Catholic church has been seen as a force for conservatism. The Crown clearly saw it as just that. In so far as the Crown and sympathetic ecclesiastics managed to enforce this conservative line, the status quo would be protected. But, equally clearly, the Crown and hierarchy had but imperfect control. A variety of forces coincided to produce a half-reformation. Crucial was the reformation of the ministry. By the end of Elizabeth's reign so very many of the clergy and bishops of the church conceived of their role as different from that of the Catholic priests that the institutions of the church were inevitably also seen differently. Subtle the changes may have been, uneven their pace and spread; real they nevertheless were. An emphasis upon the institutions of the church must be balanced by an appreciation of the importance of the personnel who staffed them and ruled them.

Bibliography

This bibliography provides a listing of printed works mentioned in the text and a selection of other works which the reader may find helpful, especially items treating the period before 1570. It is not intended to be a complete bibliography of works on the English Reformation. For works published prior to 1930 details of publication are not given unless the work is part of a series.

Arber, E. (ed.) (1868) *English Reprints*, 8 vols, London.
Aston, M. (1964) 'Lollardy and the reformation: survival or revival', *History*, 49, 149–70.
Aston, M. (1965) 'John Wycliffe's reformation reputation', *Past and Present*, 30, 22–51.
Aston, M. (1973) 'English ruins and English history: the dissolution and the sense of the past', *Journal of the Warburg and Courtauld Institutes*, 36, 231–55.
Aston, M. (1977) 'Lollardy and literacy', *History*, 62, 347–71.
Ayre, J. (ed.) (1843–4) *Thomas Becon. Works*, 3 vols, Cambridge, Parker Society.
Ayre, J. (ed.) (1840–50) *Works of John Jewel*, 4 vols, Cambridge, Parker Society.
Babbage, S. S. (1962) *Puritanism and Richard Bancroft*, London, SPCK.
Bailey, D. S. (1952) *Thomas Becon and the Reformation of the Church in England*, Edinburgh, Oliver & Boyd.

Baker, D. (ed.) (1979) *Reform and Reformation: England and the Continent, c. 1500–c. 1750*, Studies in Church History, Subsidia, 2, Oxford, Blackwell.

Baker, W. J. (1970) 'Hurrell Froude and the reformers', *Journal of Ecclesiastical History*, 21, 243–59.

Bale, J. See Christmas, H.

Bateson, M. (ed.) (1895) *A Collection of Original Letters from the Bishops to the Privy Council, 1564*, Camden Miscellany, 9, London, Camden Society.

Baumer, F. L. V. (1937) 'Christopher St German: the political philosophy of a Tudor lawyer', *American Historical Review*, 42, 631–51.

Beard, C. (1883, 1927 edn) *The Reformation of the Sixteenth Century in its Relation to Modern Thought and Knowledge*, London.

Becon, T. See Ayre, J.

Berlatsky, J. (1978) 'Marriage and family in a Tudor élite: familial patterns of Elizabethan bishops', *Journal of Family History*, 3, 6–22.

Berlatsky, J. (1981) 'The Elizabethan episcopate: patterns of life and expenditure', in R. O'Day and F. Heal (eds), *Princes and Paupers in the English Church 1500–1800*, Leicester, Leicester University Press, 111–27.

Berlatsky, J. and O'Day, R. (eds) (1979) *The Letter Book of Bishop Thomas Bentham, 1560–1561*, Camden Miscellany, 27, London, Royal Historical Society.

Berrington, J. (c. 1792) *Appeal to the Catholics of England*, London.

Berrington, J. (1793) *The Memoirs of Gregorio Panzani*, London.

Berrington, J. (1799) in *Gentleman's Magazine*, 69, 654.

Bindoff, S. T. (1950, 1964) *Tudor England*, London, Penguin.

Black, J. B. (1926) *The Art of History: A Study of Four Great Historians of the Eighteenth Century*, London.

Blench, J. W. (1964) *Preaching in England in the Late Fifteenth and Sixteenth Centuries*, Oxford, Oxford University Press.

Blunt, J. H. (1869) *The Reformation of the Church of England, its History, Principles and Results*, 2 vols, London; (1878–82), 2 vols, London.

Booty, J. E. (ed.) (1963) John Jewel, *An Apology of the Church of England*, New York, Cornell University Press, Folger Shakespeare Library.

Bossy, J. (1962) 'The character of Elizabethan Catholicism', *Past and Present*, 21, 39–59.

Bowker, M. (1964) 'Non-residence in the Lincoln diocese in the early sixteenth century', *Journal of Ecclesiastical History*, 15, 40–50.

Bowker, M. (1968) *The Secular Clergy in the Diocese of Lincoln, 1495–1520*, Cambridge, Cambridge University Press.

Bowker, M. (1971) 'The commons supplications against the ordinaries in the light of some archidiaconal acta', in *Transactions of the Royal Historical Society*, 21, 61–77.

Bowker, M. (1972) 'Lincolnshire 1536: heresy, schism or religious discontent?' in D. Baker (ed.), *Studies in Church History*, 9, Oxford, Blackwell, 195–212.

Bowker, M. (1975) 'The supremacy and the episcopate: the struggle for control, 1534–1540', *Historical Journal*, 18, 227–43.

Bowker, M. (1977) 'The Henrician reformation and the parish clergy', *Bulletin of the Institute of Historical Research*, 50, 30–47.

Bowker, M. (1981) *The Henrician Reformation in the Diocese of Lincoln under John Longland, 1521–1547*, Cambridge, Cambridge University Press.

Brewer, J. S. (ed.) (1845) Thomas Fuller, *The Church History of Britain*, 6 vols, Oxford.

Brewer, J. S. (1884) *Henry VIII*, London.

Brigden, S. E. (1977) 'The Early Reformation in London, 1520–1547', unpublished PhD thesis, University of Cambridge.

Brook, V. J. K. (1957) *Whitgift and the English Church*, London, English Universities Press.

Brook, V. J. K. (1962) *A Life of Archbishop Parker*, Oxford, Clarendon Press.

Brooks, F. W. (1945–7) 'The social position of the parson in the sixteenth century', *Journal of the British Archaeological Society*, 10, 23–37.

Brooks, P. (1965) *Thomas Cranmer's Doctrine of the Eucharist*, London, Macmillan.

Brooks, P. (1980) *Reformation Principle and Practice: Essays in Honour of A. G. Dickens*, London, Scolar Press.

Bruce, J. (ed.) (1853) *The Correspondence of Matthew Parker*, Cambridge, Parker Society.

Burke, P. (1978) *Popular Culture in Early Modern Europe*, London, Temple Smith.

Burnet, G. (1679–1715) *History of the Reformation of the Church of England*, 3 vols, London; (1865) see Pocock, N.

Burrow, J. W. (1981) *A Liberal Descent*, Cambridge, Cambridge University Press.

Butler, C. (1819) *Historical Memoirs of the English, Irish and Scottish Catholics Since the Reformation*, 2 vols, London; (1822) 3rd edn, 4 vols, London.

Butler, C. (1822) *Reminiscences*, London.

Calder, I. (1948) 'A seventeenth century attempt to purify the Anglican Church', *American Historical Review*, 53, 760–75.

Calder, I. (1957) *Activities of the Puritan Faction of the Church of England, 1625–33*, London, SPCK.

Cardwell, E. (1839, 1844) *Documentary Annals of the Reformed Church of England*, 2 vols, Oxford.

Cardwell, E. (1842), *Synodalia*, 2 vols, Oxford.

Carr, S. (ed.) (1843) *Early Writings of John Hooper*, 2 vols, Cambridge, Parker Society. See Nevinson, C.

Cattley, S. R. (ed.) (1837) *The Acts and Monuments of John Foxe*, London.

Christmas, H. (ed.) (1849) *Select Works of John Bale*, Cambridge, Parker Society.

Clark, P. (1977) *English Provincial Society from the Reformation to the Revolution. Religion, Politics and Society in Kent, 1500–1640*, Hassocks, Sussex, Harvester.

Clebsch, W. A. (1964) *England's Earliest Protestants, 1520–1535*, New Haven, Yale University Press.

Cobbett, W. (1824–7; 1850 edn) *A History of the Protestant Reformation in England and Ireland*, London.

Collier, J. (1708–14) *An Ecclesiastical History of Great Britain*, 2 vols, London; (1852) See Lathbury, T.

Collinson, P. (1966) 'Episcopacy and reform in England in the later sixteenth century', in G. J. Cuming (ed.) *Studies in Church History*, 3, Leiden, 91–125.

Collinson, P. (1967) *The Elizabethan Puritan Movement*, London, Jonathan Cape.

Collinson, P. (1975) 'Lectures by combination: structures and characteristics of church life in 17th century England', *Bulletin of the Institute of Historical Research*, 48, 182–213.

Collinson, P. (1979) *Archbishop Grindal, 1519–1583. The Struggle for a Reformed Church*, London, Jonathan Cape.

Collinson, P. (1982) *The Religion of Protestants*, Oxford, Oxford University Press.

Collinson, P. (1983) *Godly People*, London, Hambledon Press.

Cooper, J. P. (1957) 'The supplication against the ordinaries reconsidered', *English Historical Review*, 72, 616–41.

Corrie, G. E. (ed.) (1844–5) *Hugh Latimer. Works*, Cambridge, Parker Society.

Coverdale, M. See Pearson, G.

Cox, J. E. (ed.) (1844–6) *The Works of Thomas Cranmer*, 3 vols, Cambridge, Parker Society.

Cranmer, T. See Cox, J. E.

Cross, M. C. (1960) 'Noble patronage in the Elizabethan church', *Historical Journal*, 3, 1–16.

Cross, M. C. (1969) *The Royal Supremacy in the Elizabethan Church*, London, Allen & Unwin.

Cross, M. C. (1976) *Church and People 1450–1660*, London, Fontana.

Cross, M. C. (1977) 'Churchmen and the royal supremacy', in F. Heal and R. O'Day (eds) *Church and Society in England, Henry VIII to James I*, London, Macmillan, 15–34.

Cross, M. C. (1979) 'Parochial structure and the dissemination of Protestantism in sixteenth century England: a tale of two cities', in D. Baker (ed.) *Studies in Church History*, 16, Oxford, Blackwell, 269–78.

Cross, M. C. (1981) 'The incomes of provincial urban clergy, 1520–1645', in R. O'Day and F. Heal (eds) *Princes and Paupers in the English Church 1500–1800*, Leicester, Leicester University Press, 65–89.

Cross, M. C. (1982) 'The development of Protestantism in Leeds and Hull, 1520–1640: the evidence from wills', *Northern History*, 18, 230–8.

Davies, C. S. L. (1968) 'The pilgrimage of grace reconsidered', *Past and Present*, 41, 54–76.

Davies, C. S. L. (1976) *Peace, Print and Protestantism 1450–1558*, London, Paladin.

Davies, H. (1970) *Worship and Theology in England from Cranmer to Hooker, 1534–1603*, Princeton, Princeton University Press; London, Oxford University Press.

Davis, J. F. (1983) *Heresy and Reformation in the South-East of England 1520–1559*, London, Royal Historical Society.

Dickens, A. G. (1947) (ed.) 'Robert Parkyn's narrative of the Reformation', *English Historical Review*, 62, 58–83.

Dickens, A. G. (1957) *The Marian Reaction in the Diocese of York*, 2 pts, York, St Anthony's Hall Publications, xi–xii.

Dickens, A. G. (1959a) *Lollards and Protestants in the Diocese of York 1509–58*, Oxford, Oxford University Press.

Dickens, A. G. (1959b) *Thomas Cromwell and the English Reformation*, London, English Universities Press.

Dickens, A. G. (1964) *The English Reformation*, London, Batsford.

Dickens, A. G. (1966) Introduction to A. F. Pollard, *Henry VIII*, New York, Harper Torchbooks.

Dickens, A. G. (1967) 'Secular and religious motivation in the pilgrimage of grace', in G. J. Cuming (ed.), *Studies in Church History*, 4, Leiden, 39–64.

Dickens, A. G. (1971) 'Heresy and the origins of the English Reformation', in J. S. Bromley and E. H. Kossmann (eds), *Britain and the Netherlands*, II, Groningen, 120–5.

Dickens, A. G. (1982) *Reformation Studies*, London, Hambledon Press.

Dickens, A. G. (1985) Review of J. J. Scarisbrick, *The Reformation and the English People*, *Journal of Ecclesiastical History*, 36, 123–6.

Dixon, R. W. (1878–1902) *History of the Church of England*, 6 vols, London.

Dodd, C. (1737–42) *The Church History of England from 1500 to the Year 1688, Chiefly with Regard to Catholicks*, 3 vols, Brussels; (1839–43) ed. M. A. Tierney, 5 vols, London.

Douglas, D. (1951) *English Scholars, 1660–1730*, London, Eyre and Spottiswoode.

Drabble, J. (1975) 'The historians of the English Reformation, 1780–1850', unpublished PhD thesis, New York University.

Du Boulay, F. R. H. (1952) 'Archbishop Cranmer and the Canterbury temporalities', *English Historical Review*, 47, 19–36.

Dugmore, C. W. (1958) *The Mass and the English Reformers*, London, Macmillan.

Dugmore, C. W. (ed.) (1980) W. D. J. Cargill Thompson, *Studies in the Reformation. Luther to Hooker*, London, Athlone.

Eisenstein, E. (1979) *The Printing Press as an Agent of Change*, 2 vols, Cambridge, Cambridge University Press.

Ellis, H. (ed.) (1807–8) Raphael Holinshead, *The Chronicles of England, Scotland and Ireland*, 6 vols, London.

Elton, G. R. (1949) 'The evolution of a Reformation statute', *English Historical Review*, 64, 174–97.

Elton, G. R. (1951) 'The commons' supplication of 1532: parliamentary manoeuvres in the reign of Henry VIII', *English Historical Review*, 66, 507–34.

Elton, G. R. (1952) 'Parliamentary drafts, 1529–1540', *Bulletin of the Institute of Historical Research*, 25, 117–32.

Elton, G. R. (1953, 1962 repr.) *The Tudor Revolution in Government*, Cambridge, Cambridge University Press.

Elton, G. R. (1954) 'King or minister?: the man behind the Henrician reformation', *History*, 39, 216–32.

Elton, G. R. (1955) *England under the Tudors*, London, Methuen.

Elton, G. R. (1960) *The Tudor Constitution*, Cambridge, Cambridge University Press.

Elton, G. R. (1962, 1965 repr.) *Henry VIII. An Essay in Revision*, London, The Historical Association.

Elton, G. R. (1972) *Policy and Police: Enforcement of the Reformation in the Age of Thomas Cromwell*, Cambridge, Cambridge University Press.

Elton, G. R. (1973) *Reform and Renewal: Thomas Cromwell and the Common Weal*, Cambridge, Cambridge University Press.

Elton, G. R. (1974) *Studies in Tudor and Stuart Politics and Government*, 2 vols, Cambridge, Cambridge University Press.

Elton, G. R. (1977) *Reform and Reformation, England 1509–1558*, London, Arnold.

Firth, K. R. (1979) *The Apocalyptic Tradition in Reformation Britain, 1530–1645*, Oxford, Oxford University Press.

Foster, A. (1976) 'The function of a bishop: the career of Richard Neile, 1562–1640', in R. O'Day and F. Heal (eds), *Continuity and Change*, Leicester, Leicester University Press, 33–54.

Foxe, J. See Cattley, S.

Frere, W. (1896) *The Marian Reaction*, London.

Frere, W. H. and Kennedy, W. M. (eds) (1910) *Visitation Articles and Injunctions of the Period of the Reformation*, 3 vols, London, Alcuin Club Collections, 14–16.

Froude, J. A. (1856–70) *History of England from the Fall of Wolsey to the Defeat of the Spanish Armada*, 12 vols, London.

Fuller, T. (1655) *The Church History of Britain*, London; (1845) See Brewer, J. S.

Gairdner, J. (1902) *The English Church in the Sixteenth Century*, London.

Gairdner, J. (1904) 'Bishop Hooper's visitation of Gloucester, 1551', *English Historical Review*, 19, 98–121.

Galbraith, V. H. (1949) 'Albert Frederick Pollard, 1869–1948', *Proceedings of the British Academy*, 35, 257–74.

Garrett, C. H. (1938) *The Marian Exiles*, Cambridge, Cambridge University Press; (1961 repr.) Cambridge.

George, C. H. and George, K. (1961) *The Protestant Mind of the English Reformation, 1570–1640*, Princeton, Princeton University Press.

Gooch, G. P. (1952) *History and Historians in the Nineteenth Century*, London, Longman.

Greaves, R. L. (1981) *Society and Religion in Elizabethan England*, Minneapolis, University of Minnesota Press.

Greenslade, S. L. (1960) *The English Reformers and the Fathers of the Church*, Oxford, Oxford University Press.

Grieve, H. E. P. (1940) 'The deprived married clergy in Essex, 1553–61', *Transactions of the Royal Historical Society*, 22, 141–69.

Grindal, E. See Nicholson, W.

Habbakuk, H. J. (1958) 'The market for monastic property, 1539–1603', *Economic History Review*, 10, 362–80.

Haigh, C. (1969) *The Last Days of the Lancashire Monasteries and the Pilgrimage of Grace*, Manchester, Manchester University Press.

Haigh, C. (1975) *Reformation and Resistance in Tudor Lancashire*, Cambridge, Cambridge University Press.

Haigh, C. (1976) 'Finance and administration in a new diocese: Chester, 1541–1641', in R. O'Day and F. Heal (eds), *Continuity and Change*, Leicester, Leicester University Press, 145–66.

Haigh, C. (1977) 'Puritan evangelism in the reign of Elizabeth I', *English Historical Review*, 92, 30–58.

Haigh, C. (1981) 'The continuity of Catholicism in the English reformation', *Past and Present*, 93, 37–69.

Haigh, C. (1982) 'The recent historiography of the English Reformation', *Historical Journal*, 25, 995–1007.

Haigh, C. (1983) 'Anticlericalism and the English Reformation', *History*, 68, 391–407.

Haigh, C. (ed.) (1984) *The Reign of Elizabeth I*, London, Macmillan.

Haller, W. (1938) *The Rise of Puritanism, or the Way to the New Jerusalem*, New York, Columbia University Press.

Haller, W. (1963) *Foxe's Book of Martyrs and the Elect Nation*, London, Jonathan Cape.

Haugaard, W. (1968) *Elizabeth and the English Reformation*, Cambridge, Cambridge University Press.

Heal, F. (1974) 'The bishops and the act of exchange of 1559', *Historical Journal*, 17, 227–46.

Heal, F. (1976) 'Clerical tax collection under the Tudors: the influence of the reformation', in R. O'Day and F. Heal (eds), *Continuity and Change*, Leicester, Leicester University Press, 97–122.

Heal, F. (1980) *Of Prelates and Princes. A Study of the Economic and Social Position of the Tudor Episcopate*, Cambridge, Cambridge University Press.

Heal, F. and O'Day, R. (eds) (1977) *Church and Society in England. Henry VIII to James I*, London, Macmillan.

Heath, P. (1969) *The English Parish Clergy on the Eve of the Reformation*, London, Routledge & Kegan Paul.

Hembry, P. M. (1967) *The Bishops of Bath and Wells 1540–1640*, London, Athlone.

Heylyn, P. (1661, 1670, 1674) *Ecclesia Restaurata or the History of the Reformation of the Church of England*, London; (1849) See Robertson, J. C.

Hill, C. (1956) *Economic Problems of the Church. From Archbishop Whitgift to the Long Parliament*, Oxford, Oxford University Press.

Hill, C. (1958) *Puritanism and Revolution*, London, Martin Secker & Warburg.

Hill, C. (1964, 1966) *Society and Puritanism in Pre-revolutionary England*, London, Martin Secker & Warburg.

Hodgett, G. A. J. (1962) 'The unpensioned ex-religious in Tudor England', *Journal of Ecclesiastical History*, 13, 195–202.

Holinshead, R. see Ellis (1807–8).

Hook, W. F. (1860–76) *Lives of the Archbishops of Canterbury*, 12 vols, London.

Hooper, John. See Carr, S. and Nevinson, C.

Hoskins, W. G. (1939) 'The Leicestershire country parson in the sixteenth century', *Transactions of the Leicestershire Archaeological and Historical Society*, 21, pt. i, 89–114.

Houlbrooke, R. A. (ed.) (1974–5) *The Letter Book of John Parkhurst*, Norwich, Norfolk Record Society, 43.

Houlbrooke, R. A. (1976) 'The decline of ecclesiastical jurisdiction under the Tudors', in R. O'Day and F. Heal (eds), *Continuity and Change*, Leicester, Leicester University Press, 239–57.

Houlbrooke, R. A. (1977) 'The Protestant episcopate, 1547–1603', in F. Heal and R. O'Day (eds) *Church and Society in England, Henry VIII to James I*, London, Macmillan, 78–98.

Houlbrooke, R. A. (1979) *Church Courts and the People during the English Reformation, 1520–1570*, Oxford, Oxford University Press.

Hudson, A. (1985) *Lollards and their Books*, London, Hambledon Press.

Hughes, P. (1950–4) *The Reformation in England*, 3 vols, London, Hollis & Carter.

Hume, A. (1963–) 'English Protestant books printed abroad, 1525–1535: an annotated bibliography', in *The Complete Works of St Thomas More*, 8 vols, New Haven, Yale University Press, vol. 8, pt. ii, appendix B, 1063–91.

Hume, D. (1861 edn) *The History of England from the Invasion of Julius Caesar to the Abdication of King James II, 1688*, Boston.

Hurstfield, J. (ed.) (1965) *The Reformation Crisis*, London, Arnold.

Hurstfield, J. (1973) *Freedom, Corruption and Government in Elizabethan England*, London, Jonathan Cape.

Ingram, M. J. (1976) 'Ecclesiastical justice in Wiltshire 1600–1640, with special reference to cases concerning sex and marriage', unpublished DPhil thesis, University of Oxford.

Ives, E. W. (1972) 'Faction at the court of Henry VIII: the fall of Anne Boleyn', *History*, 57, 169–88.

James, M. E. (1974) *Family, Lineage and Civil Society: A Study of Society, Politics and Mentality in the Durham Region, 1500–1640*, London, Oxford University Press.

Jewel, J. See Booty, J. also Ayre, J.

Jones, N. L. (1982) *Parliament and the Settlement of Religion*, London, Royal Historical Society.

Kidd, B. (1894; 1906 edn) *Social Evolution*, London.

Kitch, M. J. (1981) 'The Reformation in Sussex', in M. J. Kitch (ed.) *Studies in Sussex Church History*, Sussex, Leopard's Head Press, 77–98.

Knox, R. B. (ed.) (1977) *Reformation Conformity and Dissent: Essays in Honour of Geoffrey Nuttall*, London.

Lake, P. (1978) 'Laurence Chaderton and the Cambridge moderate puritan tradition, 1570–1604', unpublished PhD thesis, University of Cambridge.

Lamont, W. M. (1969) *Godly Rule: Politics and Religion 1603–60*, London, Macmillan.

Lander, S. (1976) 'Church courts and the reformation in the diocese of Chichester, 1500–58', in R. O'Day and F. Heal (eds) *Continuity and Change*, Leicester, Leicester University Press, 215–37.

Laslett, T. P. R. (1965) *The World We Have Lost*, London, Methuen.

Lathbury, T. (ed.) (1852) Jeremy Collier, *An Ecclesiastical History of Great Britain*, 9 vols, London.

Latimer, H. See Corrie, G. E.

Lehmberg, S. E. (1970) *The Reformation Parliament 1529–1536*, Cambridge, Cambridge University Press.

Lingard, J. (1826 edn) *A History of England ... 1688*, Philadelphia.

Loades, D. M. (1970) *The Oxford Martyrs*, London, Batsford.

Lockyer, R. (1964) *Tudor and Stuart Britain*, London, Longman.

Luxton, I. (1977) 'The reformation and popular culture', in F. Heal and R. O'Day (eds) *Church and Society in England, Henry VIII to James I*, London, Macmillan, 57–77.

MacCulloch, D. N. J. (1977) 'Power, privilege and the county community: county politics in Elizabethan Suffolk', unpublished PhD thesis, University of Cambridge.

McGrath, P. (1967) *Papists and Puritans under Elizabeth I*, London, Blandford.

Mahew, G. J. (1983) 'The progress of the reformation in East Sussex, 1530–59: the evidence from wills', *Southern History*, 5, 38–67.

Maitland, S. R. (1849) *Essays on Subjects Connected with the Reformation in England*, London.

Maitland, S. R. (1906) *The Reformation in England*, London [a reprint of the above].

Manning, R. (1969) *Religion and Society in Elizabethan Sussex*, Leicester, Leicester University Press.

Marchant, R. A. (1960) *The Puritans and the Church Courts in the Diocese of York, 1560–1642*, Cambridge, Cambridge University Press.

Marchant, R. A. (1969) *The Church under the Law*, Cambridge, Cambridge University Press.

Milner, J. (1798–1801) *The History, Civil and Ecclesiastical, and Survey of the Antiquities of Winchester*, Winchester.

Milner, J. (1800, 4th edn 1810) *Letters to a Prebendary*, Baltimore edition.

Milner, J. (1825) *A Vindication of the End of Religious Controversy*, Philadelphia.

Monthly Review, 31, April 1800, 405.

Monthly Review, 32, May 1800, 24.

Morison, J. J. (1976) 'John Strype, historian of the English Reformation', unpublished PhD thesis, Syracuse University.

Mozley, J. F. (1937) *William Tyndale*, London, SPCK.

Mozley, J. F. (1940) *John Foxe and his Book*, London, SPCK.

Neale, J. E. (1949) 'A. F. Pollard', *English Historical Review*, 64, 198–205.

Neale, J. E. (1950) 'The Elizabethan Acts of Supremacy and Uniformity', *English Historical Review*, 65, 304–32.

Neale, J. E. (1952) 'Parliament and the Articles of Religion, 1571', *English Historical Review*, 67, 510–21.

Neale, J. E. (1957) *Elizabeth I and her Parliaments, 1584–1603*, 2 vols, London, Jonathan Cape.

Neale, J. E. (1966) *The Age of Catherine de Medici*, London, Cape.

Nevinson, C. (ed.) (1852) *Later Writings of John Hooper*, 2 vols, Cambridge, Parker Society. See Carr, S.

Nichols, J. G. (ed.) (1859) *Narratives of the Days of the Reformation*, London, Camden Society, 77.

Nicholson, G. D. (1977) 'The nature and functions of historical argument in the Henrician Reformation', unpublished PhD thesis, University of Cambridge.

Nicholson, W. (ed.) (1843) *Grindal's Remains*, Cambridge, Parker Society.

O'Day, R. (1972) 'Thomas Bentham: a case study in the problems of the early Elizabethan episcopate', *Journal of Ecclesiastical History*, 23, 137–59.

O'Day, R. (1973) 'The ecclesiastical patronage of the Lord Keeper, 1558–1642', *Transactions of the Royal Historical Society*, 23, 89–109.

O'Day, R. (1975a) 'The law of patronage in early modern England', *Journal of Ecclesiastical History*, 26, 247–60.

O'Day, R. (1975b) *Economy and Community: Economic and Social History of Pre-industrial England, 1500–1700*, London, A. & C. Black.

O'Day, R. (1975c) 'Cumulative debt: the approach of the bishops of Coventry and Lichfield to their economic problems, c. 1540–1640', *Midland History*, 3, 93–115.

O'Day, R. (1976a) 'Immanuel Bourne: a defence of the ministry', *Journal of Ecclesiastical History*, 27, 101–14.

O'Day, R. (1976b) 'The reformation of the ministry, 1558–1642', in R. O'Day and F. Heal (eds), *Continuity and Change*, Leicester, Leicester University Press, 55–75.

O'Day, R. (1976c) 'The role of the registrar in diocesan administration', in R. O'Day and F. Heal (eds), *Continuity and Change*, Leicester, Leicester University Press, 77–94.

O'Day, R. (1977) 'Ecclesiastical patronage. Who controlled the church?' in F. Heal and R. O'Day (eds) *Church and Society in England Henry VIII to James I*, London, Macmillan, 737–55.

O'Day, R. (1979) *The English Clergy*, Leicester, Leicester University Press.

O'Day, R. (1982) *Education and Society in Britain, 1500–1800*, London, Longman.

O'Day, R. and Berlatsky, J. (eds) (1979) *The Letter Book of Bishop Thomas Bentham, 1560–1561*, Camden Miscellany, 27, London, Royal Historical Society.

O'Day, R. and Heal, F. (eds) (1976) *Continuity and Change: Personnel and Administration of the Church in England, 1500–1642*, Leicester, Leicester University Press.

O'Day, R. and Heal, F. (1981) (eds) *Princes and Paupers in the English Church*, Leicester, Leicester University Press.

Original Letters relative to the English Reformation. See Robinson, H.

Outhwaite, R. B. (1971) 'Who bought crown lands: the pattern of purchases, 1589–1603', *Bulletin of the Institute of Historical Research*, 44, 18–33.

Oxley, J. (1965) *The Reformation in Essex to the Death of Mary*, Manchester, Manchester University Press.

Owen, D. (1970) 'The enforcement of the Reformation in the diocese of Ely', *Miscellanea Historiae Ecclesiasticae*, III, Colloque de Cambridge, 1968, Louvain.

Owen, H. G. (1959) 'Parochial curates in Elizabethan London', *Journal of Ecclesiastical History*, 10, 66–73.

Owen, H. G. (1960) 'The episcopal visitation: its limits and limitations in Elizabethan London', *Journal of Ecclesiastical History*, 11, 79–85.

Owen, H. G. (1966) 'A nursery of Elizabethan nonconformity, 1567–72', *Journal of Ecclesiastical History*, 17, 65–76.

Palliser, D. M. (1971) *The Reformation in York, 1534–1553*, York, Borthwick Paper, no. 40.

Palliser, D. M. (1977) 'Popular reactions to the reformation 1530–70', in F. Heal and R. O'Day (eds), *Church and Society in England Henry VIII to James I*, London, Macmillan, 35–56.

Palliser, D. (1979) *Tudor York*, Oxford, Oxford University Press.

Parker, M. See Strype, J.; Bruce, J.

Parker, T. M. (1950) *The English Reformation to 1558*, London, Oxford University Press.

Pearson, G. (ed.) (1844–6) *Myles Coverdale. Writings, Translations, Remains*, 2 vols, Cambridge, Parker Society.

Peters, R. (1963) *Oculus Episcopi: Administration in the Archdeaconry of St Albans, 1580–1625*, Manchester, Manchester University Press.

Pilkington, J. See under Schofield, J.

Pineas, R. (1962) 'John Bale's nondramatic works of religious controversy', *Studies in the Renaissance*, 9, 218–33.

Plowden, C. (1794) *Remarks on a book entitled Memoirs of Gregorio Panzani*, Liège.

Pocock, N. (ed.) (1865) Gilbert Burnet *History of the Reformation of the Church of England*, 7 vols, Oxford.

Pocock, N. (1870) *Records of the Reformation: the Divorce, 1527–33*, 2 vols, Oxford.

Pogson, R. H. (1974) 'Revival and reform in Mary Tudor's church: a question of money', *Journal of Ecclesiastical History*, 25, 249–65.

Pollard, A. F. (1902, 1905, 1951) *Henry VIII*, London, Longman; (1966) New York, Harper Torchbooks.

Pollard, A. F. (1904, 1926) *Thomas Cranmer and the English Reformation, 1489–1556*, London.

Pollard, A. (1911) *Records of the English Bible . . . 1525–1611*, Oxford.

Pollard, A. F. (1929, 1953) *Wolsey: Church and State in Sixteenth Century England*, London, Longman; (1966) New York, Harper Torchbooks.

Porter, H. C. (1958) *Reformation and Reaction in Tudor Cambridge*, Cambridge University Press.

Powell, K. G. (1971) 'The beginnings of Protestantism in Gloucestershire', *Transactions of the Bristol and Gloucester Archaeological Society*, 90, 141–57.

Powell, K. G. (1972) *The Marian Martyrs and the Reformation in Bristol*, Bristol, Historical Association, Local History Pamphlet no. 31.

Powicke, M. (1941) *The Reformation in England*, London, Oxford University Press; (1965 repr.) Oxford Paperbacks.

Preston, J. H. (1971) 'English ecclesiastical historians and the problems of bias, 1559–1742', *Journal of the History of Ideas*, 32, 203–20.

Price, F. D. (1939) 'Gloucester diocese under Bishop Hooper, 1551–3', *Bristol and Gloucester Archaeological Society Transactions for 1938*, 60, 51–151.

Prior, M. (1985) 'Reviled and crucified marriages: the position of Tudor bishops' wives', in M. Prior (ed.), *Women in English Society 1500–1800*, London, Methuen, 118–48.

Ridley, J. (1962) *Thomas Cranmer*, Oxford, Oxford University Press.

Robertson, J. C. (ed.) (1849) Peter Heylyn *Ecclesia Restaurata*, 2 vols, Cambridge, Ecclesiastical History Society.

Robinson, H. (ed.) (1842–5) *Zurich Letters*, 2 vols, Cambridge, Parker Society.

Robinson, H. (ed.) (1846–7) *Original Letters Relative to the English Reformation, 1531–58*, 2 vols, Cambridge, Parker Society.

Rowlands, M. B. (1985) 'Recusant women 1560–1640', in M. Prior (ed.), *Women in English Society 1500–1800*, London, Methuen, 149–80.

Rupp, E. G. (1947) *Studies in the Making of the English Protestant Tradition*, London, Cambridge University Press.

Sanders, N. (1877 edn) *The Rise and Growth of the Anglican Schism* [*1585*], ed. D. Lewis, London.

Scarisbrick, J. J. (1956) 'The pardon of the clergy', *Cambridge Historical Journal*, 12, 22–39.

Scarisbrick, J. J. (1960) 'Clerical taxation in England 1485–1547', *Journal of Ecclesiastical History*, 11, 41–54.

Scarisbrick, J. J. (1968) *Henry VIII*, London, Eyre & Spottiswoode.

Scarisbrick, J. J. (1984) *The Reformation and the English People*, Oxford, Blackwell.

Scholefield, J. (ed.) (1842) *James Pilkington, Works*, Cambridge, Parker Society.

Sheils, W. J. (1976) 'Some problems of government in a new diocese: the bishop and the puritans in the diocese of Peterborough, 1560–1630', in R. O'Day and F. Heal (eds), *Continuity and Change*, Leicester, Leicester University Press, 167–87.

Sheils, W. J. (1977a) 'Religion in provincial towns: innovation and tradition', in F. Heal and R. O'Day (eds), *Church and Society in England Henry VIII to James I*, London, Macmillan, 156–76.

Sheils, W. J. (1977b) (ed.) *Archbishop Grindal's Visitation, 1575: Comperta et Detecta Book*, York, Borthwick Texts and Calendars.

Sheils, W. J. (1979) *The Puritans in the Diocese of Peterborough 1558–1610*, Northampton, Northampton Record Society, 30, 51–66.

Sheppard, E. M. (1983) 'The Reformation and the citizens of Norwich', *Norfolk Archaeology*, 38, 44–58.

Shipps, K. W. (1971) 'Lay patronage of East Anglian puritan clerics in pre-revolutionary England', unpublished PhD thesis, Yale University.

Simon, J. (1966) *Education and Society in Tudor England*, Cambridge, Cambridge University Press.

Simon, J. (1970) *The Social Origins of English Education*, London, Routledge & Kegan Paul.

Smith, L. B. (1953) *Tudor Prelates and Politics*, London, Princeton University Press.

Smith, L. B. (1955) 'The reformation and the decay of medieval ideals', *Church History*, 24, 212–20.

Smith, L. B. (1966) 'Henry VIII and the Protestant triumph', *American Historical Review*, 71, 1237–64.

Sola Pinto, V. de and Rodway, A. E. (eds) (1965 edn) *The Common Muse. An Anthology of Popular British Ballad Poetry 15th–20th Century*, Harmondsworth, Penguin Books.

Spufford, M. (1971) 'The scribes of villagers' wills in the sixteenth and seventeenth centuries and their influence', *Local Population Studies*, 7, 29–43.

Spufford, M. (1974) *Contrasting Communities*, Cambridge, Cambridge University Press.

Stone, L. (1951) 'Thomas Cromwell's political programme', *Bulletin of the Institute of Historical Research*, 24, 1–18.

Strype, J. (1693) *Memorials of the Most Reverend Father in God, Thomas Cranmer*, London; (1840) Oxford, reprint.

Strype, J. (1701) *Historical Collections of the Life and Acts of John Aylmer . . .*, London; (1821) Oxford, reprint.

Strype, J. (1709–31) *Annals of the Reformation and Establishment of Religion* . . ., 4 vols, London: (1820–40) 4 vols, Oxford, reprint.

Strype, J. (1710) *The History of the Life and Acts of* . . . *Edmund Grindal*, London; (1821) Oxford, reprint.

Strype, J. (1711) *The Life and Acts of Matthew Parker* . . ., London; (1821) 3 vols, Oxford, reprint.

Strype, J. (1718) *The Life and Acts of John Whitgift, D. D.* . . ., London; (1822) 3 vols, Oxford, reprint.

Strype, J. (1721) *Ecclesiastical Memorials, Relating Chiefly to Religion, and the Reformation of It, and the Emergencies of the Church of England, under King Henry VIII, King Edward VI, and Queen Mary I*, London; (1822) Oxford, reprint.

Sykes, N. (1956) *Old Priest, New Presbyter*, Cambridge, Cambridge University Press.

Thomas, K. V. (1971) *Religion and the Decline of Magic*, London, Weidenfeld & Nicolson; Penguin University Books.

Thompson, W. D. J. Cargill (1980) *Studies in the Reformation. Luther to Hooker*, ed. C. W. Dugmore, London, Athlone.

Thomson, J. A. F. (1965) *The Later Lollards 1414–1520*, London, Oxford University Press.

Tittler, R. and Battley, S. L. (1984) 'The local community and the crown in 1553: the accession of Mary Tudor revisited', *Bulletin of the Institute of Historical Research*, 136, 131–9.

Todd, H. J. (1831) *Vindication of the Most Reverend Thomas Cranmer* . . ., London.

Took, P. M. (1979) 'Government and the printing trade, 1540–60', unpublished PhD thesis, University of London.

Trevelyan, G. M. (1926) *History of England*, London, Longman.

Turner, S. (1828) *The History of the Reign of Henry the Eighth comprising the Political History of the Commencement of the English Reformation*, 2 vols, London.

Turner, S. (1829) *The History of the Reigns of Edward the Sixth, Mary and Elizabeth*, 2 vols, London; (1835) (3rd edn), 2 vols, London.

Tyler, P. (1967) 'The status of the Elizabethan parochial clergy', in G. C. Cuming (ed.) *Studies in Church History*, 4, Leiden, 89–97.

Tyndale, W. See Walter, H.

Usher, R. G. (1905) *The Presbyterian Movement in the Reign of Queen Elizabeth as Illustrated by the Minute Book of the Dedham Classis, 1582–1589*, London, Camden Society.

Usher, R. G. (1913, repr. 1968) *The Rise and Fall of the High Commission*, Oxford, Oxford University Press.

Walter, H. (ed.) (1848) *William Tyndale. Doctrinal Treatises . . .*, Cambridge, Parker Society.

Walter, H. (ed.) (1849) *William Tyndale. Expositions . . .*, Cambridge, Parker Society.

Ward, B. (1911–12) *The Eve of Catholic Emancipation: Being the History of the English Catholics During the First Thirty Years of the Nineteenth Century*, London.

White, H. (1951) *Tudor Books of Private Devotion*, Madison, University of Wisconsin Press.

White, H. (1963) *Tudor Books of Saints and Martyrs*, Madison, University of Wisconsin Press.

Williams, P. (1979) *The Tudor Regime*, Oxford, Oxford University Press.

Wrightson, K. and Levine, D. (1979) *Poverty and Piety in an English Village: Terling, 1525–1700*, New York, Academic Press.

Wunderli, R. M. (1981) *London Church Courts and Society on the Eve of the Reformation*, Cambridge, Massachusetts, The Medieval Academy of America.

Youings, J. (1971) *The Dissolution of the Monasteries*, London, Allen & Unwin.

Zell, M. L. (1974a) 'Church and gentry in Reformation Kent, 1533–53', unpublished PhD thesis, University of California, Los Angeles.

Zell, M. L. (1974b) 'The personnel of the clergy in Kent, in the Reformation period', *English Historical Review*, 89, 513–33.

Zell, M. L. (1977) 'The use of religious preambles . . .', *Bulletin of the Institute of Historical Research*, 50, 246–9.

Zell, M. L. (1981) 'Economic problems of the parochial clergy in the sixteenth century', in R. O'Day and F. Heal (eds), *Princes and Paupers in the English Church 1500–1800*, Leicester, Leicester University Press, 19–43.

Zinberg, C. (1968) 'John Strype and the Sixteenth Century: portrait of an Anglican historian', unpublished PhD thesis, Chicago University.

Zurich Letters. See Robinson, H.

Name index

The author wishes to thank Dr G. K. Roberts for the use of her indexing program to compile the indexes. These are not exhaustive but list people and subjects that are discussed in the text.

Subject index